Ombudsman Papers:
American Experience and Proposals

INSTITUTE OF GOVERNMENTAL STUDIES
University of California, Berkeley

Ombudsman Papers: American Experience and Proposals

By STANLEY V. ANDERSON

Department of Political Science
University of California, Santa Barbara

With a Comparative Analysis of Ombudsman Offices
by KENT M. WEEKS

Department of Political Science
The College of Wooster, Wooster, Ohio

$3.75
1969

Library of Congress Catalog Card Number 71-626759

To Mary

CONTENTS

Chart

Tables

Appendices

FOREWORD

In part through the good offices of Professor Eric Bellquist, who made the introductions, Stanley Anderson and the Institute have been associated in a continuing investigation of the Ombudsman and related organizations since 1963. In that year the pioneer American Ombudsman proposals were first offered in the Connecticut Legislature and in the United States Congress. Since then, Professor Anderson has served as the Institute's Ombudsman consultant, and has published a number of studies in the field, including Canadian Ombudsman Proposals (Berkeley: Institute of Governmental Studies, University of California, 1966).

As the title of this book: Ombudsman Papers: American Experience and Proposals suggests, the emphasis of the study rests both on the author's text and on the documents he has gathered and selected for verbatim presentation in the extended appendices. Altogether, the collection is a valuable source of material on the legislative history of the Ombudsman and related proposals, as well as detailed accounts of the way the American Ombudsmen respond to and solve the problems encountered in their new and developing field.

Chapter One defines the essential characteristics of the Ombudsman institution, and illustrates its possible application in the international community. Chapter Two analyzes the various proposals for Ombudsmen at the federal level. The American Bar Association committee report on this subject is included in the appendix, as is the report of Congressman Henry Reuss on his experiment with an Ombudsman in his district.

Chapter Three traces the proposals for State Ombudsmen, focussing on the year 1967. All of the proposals in that year are cited in an appendix. In the belief that a working Ombudsman office is its own best spokesman, the appendices also contain portions of the annual report of a comparable Canadian office, the

Provincial Ombudsman in Alberta, and the annual reports of the California Commission on Judicial Qualifications, previously available only in mimeographed form.

Similarly, in conjunction with Chapter Four on proposals at the local level, appendices present reports on the Ombudsman offices in Nassau County and Buffalo, New York. The report of the New York City Bar Association is also appended.

Chapter Five discusses the need for campus Ombudsmen, and refers the reader to the appended report of the Ombudsman at Michigan State University.

Jointly with the American Assembly of Columbia University, and the Institute for Local Self Government, the Institute of Governmental Studies sponsored a citizens' Assembly on the Ombudsman in June 1968. The report of that Assembly is also appended.

The final appendix, a chart on civil Ombudsman offices, was prepared by Kent M. Weeks, Assistant Professor of Political Science, the College of Wooster, Wooster, Ohio. The comparison brings together 22 categories of information concerning Ombudsmen of six nations, three Canadian provinces, and one American state. Professor Weeks was able to update his information to make it current as of June 1969.

Finally, in the "Selected Readings," Professor Anderson has compiled virtually a comprehensive list of English language articles and books on the Ombudsman.

The wording of the collected papers and stylistic details of capitalization and punctuation follow those of the originals. Some deletions were necessary because of space limitations--these have been indicated. With the exception of the comparative chart, the cutoff date for research on this study was December 31, 1967. A few items have been added since then, as they became available, but the author has made no attempt at consistent inclusion of material following that date. One inserted note refers to Herman Doi, who became Hawaii's Ombudsman in April 1969. Mr. Doi therefore has the distinction of being the first American State Ombudsman.

The author asked me to extend our thanks to Sophie Frandsen for research assistance in Hawaii; to Evelyn Mercer for help in checking footnote and reading list references; to Hazel Karns and Edna Jorgensen for final typing and preparation; and to Harriet Nathan for editing above and beyond the call of duty.

                              Stanley Scott
                              Assistant Director

CHAPTER I

INTRODUCTION--GLOBAL OMBUDSMEN[1]

We appear to be on the threshold of an Ombudsman explosion. From its home in Scandinavia, the office has spread to and been implemented in New Zealand and, in truncated form, in Great Britain. On this continent, there are now Ombudsmen in the Canadian Provinces of Alberta and New Brunswick.[2] [Ed. note: a Public Protector was named in Quebec, May, 1969.] Proposals abound throughout the world, as well as at all levels of American government--local, federal, and state. In 1967, one-half of our state legislatures had Ombudsman bills in their hoppers, and one--Hawaii--adopted an Ombudsman Act. [Ed. note: Herman Doi was named to the post in April, 1969.] Ombudsmen have also been proposed for a variety of institutional settings: campuses, boards of education, corporations, religious orders, and the armed forces, including the United Nations peacekeeping forces.[3]

Among the proponents of "global Ombudsman"--a phrase coined by William I. Nichols, publisher of This Week Magazine--are Professor Frank Newman of the School of Law at Berkeley, who urges the creation of "Ombudsmen for worldwide human rights,"[4] and Professor John Carey of New York University School of Law, who recommends "impartial investigation, followed by negotiation, and where necessary, publication" as the most fruitful "method...for international protection of individuals."[5] To examine these global proposals, one must first present the essential characteristics of the Ombudsman's office, and then test their transferability to the rudimentary government of mankind.

Origins of the Ombudsman

The word "Ombudsman" had its origin in a primitive legal order. In the decentralized governments of the Germanic tribes, two punishments could be inflicted upon lawbreakers. First, when the folkmeet gathered to apply the customary law as recited by the lawmen, it could convict the culprit and declare him to be an outlaw. The individual so branded was fair game. Anyone who killed him was merely enforcing the judgment of the folkmeet. While it seems rather savage, the institution of outlawry represented progress because it provided a substitute for family feuds.

The second option for punishment represented further progress: as an alternative to outlawry, it provided for a fine to be paid by the family of the culprit to the family of the aggrieved person. In England, this fine was called the Wergild. A modicum of administrative delegation was necessary to insure that the Wergild helped prevent violence. Thus, for a member of the aggrieved family to collect the Wergild directly might have resulted in violence; for a member of the culprit's family to go to the aggrieved family might also have encouraged vendettas.

Consequently, a neutral person was appointed to collect the fine and carry it to its destination; he was the OM-BUDS-MAN--"Om" being "About;" "Bud" being the messenger collecting the "fine." Imagine a Viking with horned helmet marching up to the door of a medieval Nordic hut. The man of the house answers the call, and then shouts back to his family: "It's the man about the fine: the Ombudsman."

Several hundred years later the word "Ombudsman" had come to include any kind of agent. In the Basic Law of 1809--only our own Constitution is older and still in use--the Swedes provided for a Riksdagens Justitieombudsman, "Parliament's Agent of Justice." The post was a counterweight in the balance of power whereby King and Parliament both controlled administration, that is to say primarily the judges and police. Finland followed suit when it gained independence in 1919.

The modern embodiment of the Ombudsman is reflected more accurately in the Danish version as provided in the 1953 Constitution. The Ombudsman as we now know him is a constitutional officer appointed by Parliament to receive, investigate, and report on citizens' complaints of bureaucratic abuse.

The Swedish and Finnish offices have come to serve the same function, as have the newer offices in Norway (1962) and those already mentioned in the Commonwealth countries.[6] The same theme characterizes current proposals.

The Ombudsman's Function and Setting

The essential characteristics of the Ombudsman post require that the individual filling it be: (1) independent, (2) impartial, (3) expert in government, (4) universally accessible, and (5) empowered only to recommend and to publicize.

In judging maladministration, the Ombudsman gives voice to collective conscience, just as the medieval Folkmeets expressed their own Volksgeist, the spirit of the people.

The contributions of the Ombudsman are to (1) resolve grievances, (2) improve administration, and (3) aid legislative oversight of administration.

The modern office of Ombudsman presupposes: (1) a nation-state: territory and population, (2) a bureaucracy, and (3) a consensus of positive morality.[7]

The contrasts with the world community are striking: (1) the nations of the world are not a community, but are more like the collections of tribes of medieval times; (2) international administration is minuscule; and (3) there is little consensus of values, as we shall see.

Perhaps, then, the notion of a Global Ombudsman is utopian, an expression of "Ombudsmania." I think not. Comparisons of the potential utility of an Ombudsman in the domestic and international spheres can be meaningful only if it is remembered that the domestic contribution is only incremental. To quote my colleague William B. Gwyn in his article in Ombudsmen for American Government? the institution is "an unspectacular and relatively minor governmental reform."[8] Its function is to remedy marginal defects in a basically sound system.

Application of the notion in the primitive world community must be done with appropriate changes, keeping in mind modesty of purpose and recalling the requirement of independence, impartiality, expertise, accessibility, and persuasive criticism based on preexisting standards.

Establishing the Office and Finding the Man

First, an Ombudsman was defined as a constitutional officer appointed by Parliament. Global Ombudsmen might be included in the Charter of the United Nations. Because that document is very difficult to amend, however, it might be preferable to establish the office through multilateral treaties proposed by the U. N. General Assembly.

Next, comes the problem of choosing the right man. It was specified that an Ombudsman had to be independent, impartial, and expert. To be impartial, a man must be independent. He must, moreover, have a judicial temperament, so that his decisions are not prejudiced, and further, he must know the workings of government. Locating such men is only part of the search for impartial expertise faced by all governments everywhere.

The Global Ombudsman should not be an executive official, such as the U. N. Secretary General. If he were such an official, political considerations--reasons of state--growing out of his power and responsibility, might necessarily prevent him from speaking out on troublesome complaints. He could not be independent and impartial.

Another requisite of the Ombudsman is that he both be accessible and have access to information. This turns upon the willingness of the governments to make this situation possible.

Then, the reader will recall, it was stipulated that an Ombudsman should have no authority other than that of recommending and publicizing. Here is a characteristic that is well suited to the international community. Indeed, nations would be most reluctant to grant the power to review and reverse decisions.

Presuppositions for an Ombudsman office included the existence of a nation-state and a bureaucracy, but the Global Ombudsman would direct his scrutiny at the national bureaucracies. Likewise, his successes would lie in resolving complaints against administration in existing states and in improving the quality of their administration.

This leaves only one Ombudsman characteristic still to be applied to the international sphere: a consensus on morality. This is a qualitative difference that will have to be taken into account. How much world Volksgeist is there; how much shared positive morality; how much coincidence of conscience? Is there something universal in human nature that produces a common sense of justice? Only in a formal sense can we find a universal feeling of justice. All men feel that "equals ought to be treated equally." But when it comes to the substantive fleshing out of the formal statement, there are many different definitions of justice.

Different modes of distributing the material and nonmaterial goods of society include: the infantile, socialistic, communistic, and capitalistic--"all to me," "to each according to his contribution," "to each according to his need," "to each according to the accident of his circumstances at birth." Even the terms "need" and "contribution" are subject to endless dispute.

The Search for Justice

A look at procedural justice is more fruitful. Even though we cannot agree upon a single definition of substantive justice, we can argue that every man has a right to just treatment and to have his claims heard.

Since justice delayed is justice denied, his claim should be heard with reasonable promptness, and, because no man should be a judge in his own case, the claim should be heard by an impartial arbiter.

Might not the judgment of the arbiter, however, all too often be the Scottish verdict "Not Proven?" Might not the judge simply have to reply: "You have had your hearing, due process has been observed. I can only say that you have not established a standard that has been violated." The claim to procedural justice would thus not be sufficient when the problem is more than procedural.

In the final analysis, then, common strands of substantive justice must be found. There is an emerging shared sense of injustice when any human being suffers from ignorance, sickness, or hunger. It is unjust, many believe, that any one should live below a minimum standard of health and literacy. Those who assert these minimal claims do so under the banner of the "Revolution of Rising Expectations."

Worldwide, there is a stronger shared feeling that no one should be denied a claim to just treatment by virtue of race, religion, or sex. Further, just treatment requires that the claimant be allowed appropriate participation in the political process. A Global Ombudsman could criticize nations who discriminated in these ways.

This commitment to equality of treatment may provide sufficient common ground to permit the development of other standards. In this connection, let us consider another peculiar aspect of the Ombudsman office: the circular reaction whereby a working Ombudsman improves the conditions for his own performance.

His independence and impartiality are buttressed through exercise. His judgments carry increasing weight as his impartiality, independence, and expertise are recognized. Finally, and most importantly, his judgments alter the standards of morality. Over time, increment by increment, the decisions of the Ombudsman can clarify, refine, and humanize the ethos in which he operates.

In addition, there is a more direct way out of the problem posed by the absence of preexisting standards: to enact such standards authoritatively as law. In the international sphere, action must of course be accomplished by treaty.

International Ombudsmen, Present and Proposed

So far, this discussion has been relatively abstract, but it can be made more concrete. There are already some international Ombudsmen, and current proposals call for the establishment of more. The

discussion now turns to these examples of existing or
proposed grievance machinery. One existing agency is
the United Nations Trusteeship Council, which receives
petitions from those in tutelage. It deserves further
study. So far, it supports the assertion that receiving, investigating, and judging complaints is a subtle
but effective tool for redressing grievances and improving administration.9

The new proposals are more dramatic. For example,
there is the International Covenant and Optional Protocol on Civil and Political Rights approved unanimously
by the General Assembly of the United Nations in December 1966. As Professor Newman explained in the University of Chicago Law Review, the treaty contains an
"ombudsman clause."10 The protocol provides that individuals may submit written grievances to the Human
Rights Committee. The committee will then notify the
accused nation, receive communications from the state
and the individual, consider them, and report its findings publicly.

The complainant must first exhaust domestic remedies. One consequence of the treaty might be that signa-
tories would establish national Ombudsman offices as a
standard domestic remedy, thus providing a double protection against bureaucratic abuse, and helping to keep
the Global Ombudsman's caseload within manageable proportions.

The Human Rights Committee will be composed of 18
members, persons of "recognized competence," chosen by
secret ballot by the member nations from among their own
nationals. The committee is to act by simple majority
vote. The Secretary-General will provide staff and
facilities.

Clearly, this collegial Ombudsman meets all of the
tests as enumerated by Professor Walter Gellhorn to be
"readily accessible, professionally qualified, wholly
detached critics to inquire objectively into asserted

administrative shortcomings....advisors, not commanders ....[who] rely on recommendation, not on compulsion."[11]

A similar collegial Ombudsman is provided for in the International Convention on the Elimination of All Forms of Racial Discrimination, adopted unanimously by the General Assembly in December 1965.

The third in this triad of treaties, the 1966 Economic, Social, and Cultural Rights Covenant, however, contains no such provision.

It should be noted that there are several variations in the structure of the Ombudsman's office. In Israel the Comptroller-General acts as a bureaucratic Ombudsman, and the original office in Sweden has very recently been revamped to become a three-man collegial office. The Norwegian Military Ombudsman chairs a seven-man Defense Ombudsman Committee. Also, the Executive Secretary of the California Commission on Judicial Qualifications acts as an Ombudsman on behalf of the commission, investigating complaints of judicial misbehavior.

As far as the new treaties are concerned, the "Great Question," as Professor Newman puts it, is their ratification.[12] The Civil and Political Rights Covenant, for example, must be ratified by 35 nations, of which at least 10 must also ratify the Optional Protocol that contains the Ombudsman clause.

Another proposal for a Global Ombudsman has been made to the General Assembly of the United Nations by the Economic and Social Council. The council has recommended the appointment of a High Commissioner for Human Rights who "would have access to communications concerning human rights submitted by nationals of member states and would bring them to the attention of the governments concerned."[13]

In summary, this discussion has attempted to support the establishment of a Global Ombudsman on grounds of feasibility. To speak the conscience of mankind, we must first listen to small separate voices and their individual expressions of grievance. A Global Ombudsman could hear those voices and amplify their message.

NOTES

to Chapter I

1. This chapter is based on a lecture given at
the University of California, Santa Barbara, as part of
the Centennial Lecture Series, 1968, "Man in the Age of
Revolutionary Change." The series was sponsored by
University Extension and the Associated Students, UCSB,
in cooperation with the Center for the Study of Democratic Institutions.

2. See Donald C. Rowat, "The Spread of the Ombuds-
man Idea," in Stanley V. Anderson, ed., Ombudsmen for
American Government? (Englewood Cliffs, N.J.: Prentice-
Hall, Inc., 1968), pp. 7-36.

3. All but the last are discussed in Chapter V.
For the Ombudsman proposal for United Nations forces,
see Lincoln P. Bloomfield, International Military Forces
(Boston: Little, Brown, 1964), p. 96. In addition to
Inspectors-General, the services now have Super-Sergeants
and Super-Chiefs. See Bob Umphress, "He Solves Sailors'
Personal Problems," Oakland Tribune, February 22, 1968,
p. 4. All of these are administrative complaint officers,
as explained in Chapter IV, and not Ombudsmen. The
Ombudsmen in Denmark, Finland and Sweden consider com-
plaints from military personnel. There are separate
Military Ombudsmen in Norway and West Germany.

4. Frank C. Newman, "Ombudsmen and Human Rights:
the New U.N. Treaty Proposals," 34 University of Chicago
Law Review 4: 951-962 (1967). See p. 959.

5. John Carey, "Procedures for International Protection of Human Rights," 53 Iowa Law Review 2: 291-324
(1967). See p. 324.

6. See Walter Gellhorn, Ombudsmen and Others
(Cambridge, Mass.: Harvard University Press, 1966);

Donald C. Rowat, ed., The Ombudsman: Citizen's Defender
(London: George Allen & Unwin, Ltd., 1965); and Roy V.
Peel, ed., "The Ombudsman or Citizen's Defender: A
Modern Institution," Annals of the American Academy of
Political and Social Science, 377: 1-138 (May 1968).

7.   See William B. Gwyn, "Transferring the Ombudsman," in Ombudsmen for American Government? note 2
above, pp. 37-69. See pp. 45-46.

8.   Ibid., p. 67.

9.   See James N. Murray, Jr., The United Nations
Trusteeship System, in Illinois Studies in the Social
Sciences, 40 (University of Illinois Press, 1957),
Chapter VII, "Petitions," pp. 150-174, and Chapter VIII,
"Visiting Missions," pp. 175-197.

10.   Newman, note 4 above, p. 953. For earlier
developments, see Egon Schwelb, Human Rights and the
International Community: the Roots and Growth of the
Universal Declaration of Human Rights, 1948-1963
(Chicago: Quadrangle Books, [1964]). But see John M.
Raymond, "Don't Ratify the Human Rights Conventions,"
54 American Bar Association Journal 2: 141-143 (1968);
and Eberhard P. Deutsch, "International Covenants on
Human Rights and Our Constitutional Policy," 54 American
Bar Association Journal 3: 238-245 (1968).

11.   As quoted by Newman, note 4 above, p. 959,
from Gellhorn, Ombudsmen and Others, note 6 above, pp.
422, 436.

12.   Newman, p. 961. See also Newman, "Natural
Justice, Due Process and the New International Covenants
on Human Rights: Prospectus," Public Law 274-313 (Winter
1967). See also Issues Before the 21st General Assembly,
599 International Conciliation (New York: Carnegie
Endowment for International Peace, September 1966), pp.
91-119, together with the background papers for United
Nations seminars on human rights, cited in the bibliography.

13. <u>Issues Before the 22nd General Assembly</u>, 564 <u>International Conciliation</u>, p. 95 (September 1967).

CHAPTER II

FEDERAL PROPOSALS

Any proposal for the institution of Ombudsman at the national level in the United States must come to grips with the problem of scale. How does an official deal with the complex government of 200 million people on (and partly outside) a vast continent? While the answer should be a sober one, it should not be a counsel of despair that would simply assume that the job could not be done. In addition, of course, Ombudsmen need not do the job alone.[1]

Supporters as well as opponents of the Ombudsman idea have noted the special difficulties related to size of jurisdiction. The Final Report of the American Assembly, for example, recommends that "Ombudsman offices be established in American local and state governments." It goes on, however, to caution that "We do not recommend the establishment of a single office of Ombudsman for the entire federal government, but we do recommend that applications of the concept be undertaken at the federal level."[2]

With equal caution, the American Bar Association Recommendation suggests the forms that national Ombudsman trials should take (discussed below), and concludes that "establishment of a federal government-wide Ombudsman system...should await findings based upon the experimentation recommended." (See App. VII)

Reuss and the Congressional
Ombudsman Proposal

The authors of Ombudsman bills in the United States Congress are aware of the difficulties still to be overcome. Congressman Henry S. Reuss (D, Wisconsin) included

14

a very severe restriction in his pioneer 1963 proposal, H.R. 7593: that the Administrative Counsel (Ombudsman) would be authorized to receive complaints only from Members of Congress.[3] The reasons for this restriction were twofold. First, the author hoped that the filtering device would reassure legislators who might otherwise fear the loss of the vote-getting potential of constituent service--an objection that will be examined in the next chapter. Second, it was thought that the interposition of a layer of congressmen between complainants and counsel would help to keep the caseload within manageable limits.

Congressman Reuss has kept the same basic provisions in his subsequent reintroductions, H.R. 4273 (1965),[4] and H.R. 3388 (1967).[5] In the 1967 bill he changed the designation of the proposed official to "Congressional Ombudsman." Although Henry Reuss is a respected and influential member of Congress, and his mounting seniority, now 14 years, has given him the chairmanship of several subcommittees: International Exchange and Payments (of the Joint Economic Committee), International Finance (of Banking and Currency), and Research and Technical Programs (of Government Operations), none have jurisdiction over Ombudsman proposals.

On May 19, 1965, Congressman Reuss managed to have his proposal heard by the House Committee on Administration, Subcommittee on Accounts. The bill did not get out of committee. A week earlier, on May 11, the congressman testified before the Joint Committee on the Organization of Congress. In its Final Report, the committee stated:

> The joint committee received much
> testimony on Members' problems in
> dealing with that portion of con-
> stituent service involving case-
> work. A number of witnesses sug-
> gested that many of these cases
> could be delegated to an adminis-
> trative counsel or "ombudsman."

. . . . .

> The joint committee, after careful
> consideration, decided against recom-
> mending creation of such an office
> at this time. We believe that case-
> work is a proper function of the
> individual Member of Congress and
> should not be delegated to an
> administrative body.[6]

In his supplemental views, Congressman Ken Hechler (D, West Virginia) added a comment supporting the Reuss proposal.

> I agree with the majority of the
> joint committee that it would be
> an abdication of our responsi-
> bilities as Members of Congress
> if casework were turned over to
> an "ombudsman." Still, there are
> many problems involving complex
> interagency relationships, or
> tedious investigations, which
> could properly be handled by a
> central group on referral by
> Members. Such referrals can be
> optional rather than obligatory,
> and some Members will find that
> they can utilize this service
> more frequently and effectively
> than others. If this procedure
> can save a member of his staff
> some time, it will be a wise
> investment. Personally, I feel
> that the expertise built up by
> such a central group of experts--
> whether led by an "ombudsman" or
> otherwise--will provide many
> shortcuts, thus freeing Members
> and their staffs for more time
> to concentrate in legislative
> issues.[7]

The Joint Committee viewed the question as one of staffing--it considered the matter under the rubric "Office Staff and Allowances."[8] Since the committee considered the individual congressman to be the proper recipient of constituent complaints, it apparently did not examine the possibility of increased efficiency, efficacy, and information to be gained from centralization. Conversely, support for the idea of a Congressional Ombudsman was phrased mainly in terms of freeing the congressman and his staff for other, more important tasks, and emphasized every congressman's option of keeping casework in his own office, if he chose to do so.

Opposition to the Reuss Proposal

Under the chairmanship of Professor Kenneth Culp Davis, the Ombudsman Committee of the Administrative Law Section of the American Bar Association came out against the Reuss proposal for the following reasons:

> Not only should establishment
> of a government-wide ombudsman
> await the experimentation recom-
> mended, but so should establish-
> ment of a central federal office
> to assist congressmen in handling
> constituents' complaints. Con-
> gressmen now handle more than
> 200,000 complaints about adminis-
> tration annually, and the idea
> of creating an office to help
> them with their enormous burden
> is a natural one. A central
> office would obviously be better
> organized for handling the vast
> mass of complaints than are the
> staffs attached to the office
> of each congressman. But the

ombudsman system serves a slightly
different purpose. It is not
linked to service for constituents;
the criticism is provided by those
who are performing no other function. For this reason, the further development of a system which
primarily emphasizes service to
constituents should await the
development, through actual experience, of better understanding of
systems of criticism by independent Ombudsmen. The long-term
objection should be effective
criticism of administrators by
independent officers who have no
stake, direct or indirect, in any
particular results.[9]

When Chairman Davis circulated a draft report to
the members of his committee, the author replied as
follows:

May I go on record as dissenting
from point 4. My reason is that
I believe that a central office to
assist congressmen in handling
constituents' complaints would
further the stated goal of
"effective criticism of administrators by independent officers."
Once a complaint had been referred
to the central office of any of the
535 congressmen, the central office
would investigate and report on the
merits, impartially and with no
ulterior motives. This would
improve the quality of casework,
help correct bad administration,
and lessen the opportunity for
harmful meddling by individual
congressional offices. I share

>the view stated in point 4 that
>"a central office would obviously
>be better organized for handling
>the vast mass of complaints than
>are the staffs attached to the
>office of each congressman."
>
>Apart from the above, I subscribe
>enthusiastically to the Ombudsman
>Report.[10]

By focussing on abstract assumptions about the
proper location and basic propriety of casework, the
debate on the Reuss proposal has not shed light on the
actual complaint-handling function of Congress. Indeed,
there is a paucity of information on the treatment of
grievances by elected officials in general, and by legislators in particular.

At the federal level, we have the occasional memoirs
of members of Congress, Walter Gellhorn's investigation
of 10 congressional offices for his book When Americans
Complain,[11] and a bibliographical essay by Walter Kravitz
of the Legislative Reference Service.[12] At the state
level, Dean Mann has written a pathfinding booklet whose
limitations are expressed in its subtitle: The Citizen
and the Bureaucracy: Complaint-Handling Procedures of
Three California Legislators.[13] At the local level,
there is nothing. The literature on the rudimentary
centralization of casework in congressional committees
is equally scanty.[14]

Both to jar his proposal off dead center and to
add to the pool of information on casework, Congressman
Reuss appointed an experimental District Ombudsman in
his constituency (in Milwaukee) for four months in the
spring of 1967.[15] (See App. V) During that period,
the experimental Ombudsman dealt with 467 cases. He
analyzed the final results, and made a number of observations including the magnitude of problems, the question of delay, and the impact of press publicity. One
way, and perhaps the only practicable one, to generate
comprehensive information of this sort would be to

centralize the casework function of all members of Congress, so that it is performed by a centralized staff.

Long's Proposal: Administrative Ombudsman

Even if the Reuss Congressional Ombudsman proposal,
or something like it, were to be instituted, there would
still be need for a federal Ombudsman external to Congress.   The leadership with such independent or administrative Ombudsman proposals has been taken by Senator
Edward V. Long (D, Missouri), who is Chairman, and Benny
Kass, Assistant Counsel of the Subcommittee on Administrative Practice and Procedure.

In March, 1966, Senator Long invited the Swedish
Ombudsman, Judge Alfred Bexelius, to testify before his
subcommittee.[16]   And on March 7, 1967, Senator Long
introduced S. 1195 in the 90th Congress, first session,
"A Bill to Establish the Office of Administrative Ombudsman."[17]

Unlike Congressman Reuss's Congressional Ombudsman,
who would receive complaints only through congressmen,
the Administrative Ombudsman would receive them directly
from the public.   His jurisdiction, however, would have
been limited to the Social Security Administration,
Veterans Administration, Internal Revenue Service, and
Bureau of Prisons.   On February 6, 1968, Senator Long
offered an amendment to his bill, adding the Selective
Service System to the roster of agencies to be included
under the jurisdiction of the Administrative Ombudsman.
Testimony and agency comments were presented to Senator
Long's Subcommittee in January, 1968.[18]

The Treasury Department opposed the enactment of
S. 1195.   By ignoring the standard requirement that
regular administrative remedies be exhausted before the
Ombudsman takes up a case, the Internal Revenue Service
is able to argue that an Ombudsman might "jeopardize
the effectiveness of the administrative handling of

disputes," and "jeopardize the present settlement procedures" by tempting the taxpayer to ignore these opportunities, and to seek Ombudsmanic intervention.[19]
Clearly, this would not be the case, as an Ombudsman
would require taxpayers to take advantage of normal
procedures. Indeed, one of the Ombudsman's major concerns would be the adequacy and improvement of internal
administrative appeal mechanisms.

More gently, the Veterans Administration concluded
that "we cannot recommend favorable consideration of
S. 1195...."[20] Both in the prepared statement and in
the oral presentation, the VA made a good case for the
assertion that it already did more than an Ombudsman
would do, in that Contact Representatives respond to
complaints by "sitting down [with the complainant] and
going through the VA file with him and explaining the
requirements of the law...and, where indicated, assist-
ing him in obtaining the evidence which might result in
favorable action."[21] Clearly, however, the VA has
nothing to fear from the institution of an Ombudsman,
and even the most efficient and most client-oriented
agency will have marginal defects arising from human
and other error. It would be inexpensive and unob-
trusive to add a further external and nonauthoritative
check to the present internal and authoritative system.
Such additions might make the system even better, and
would act as fail-safe mechanisms to remedy inevitable
shortcomings.

Ombudsman for the Bureau of Prisons

Dr. Myrl E. Alexander, Director of the Bureau of
Prisons, stated that his "personal judgment of the
Ombudsman principle must be deferred," but he allowed
that "Any system or device which would help us manage
these highly volatile prisons and institutions and provide an outlet for, many times, these rather emotionally
disturbed persons, can be no serious problem to us."
Significantly, Dr. Alexander also commented, "In two

recent instances in the past year, I have had a dis-
interested person actually retained to go to an institution to check out complaints on which I did not
want to be in the position of conducting a self-
investigation."22

For a number of reasons, it appears that a separate Ombudsman for the Bureau of Prisons should be
established without delay. First, the director is
receptive, and twice recently has utilized ad hoc
Ombudsmen. Bureau support would not only facilitate
enactment of appropriate legislation, but would enhance
the potential success of the office. Second, society
owes a special duty to prison inmates to watch their
watchers, because inmates are involuntarily immersed in
a totally encompassing institutional environment that
is sometimes unfeeling if not harsh and hostile. Finally, the job is sufficiently distinct from more conventional Ombudsman positions to warrant setting it
apart. (To a lesser degree, the same can be said of
the need for military Ombudsmen.)

A prison Ombudsman should know prisons, and he
should probably begin proportionally more inquiries on
his own initiative, based in part on anonymous complaints
from prisoners or guards during informal on-site visits.
Although the impact of a prison Ombudsman would not be
revolutionary, he could have a substantial and continuing influence on prison life.

Experimentation and the
Administrative Conference of the U.S.

As indicated at the start of this chapter, the
theme of Ombudsman proposals at the federal level has
been experimentation, primarily to adapt the simple
idea of Ombudsman to the complexity of national administration. Carrying the experimental approach one step
further, on March 8, 1968, Senator Long added to his
previous efforts: S. 3123, a proposal "To establish a

two-year study of the Office of Administrative Ombudsman"
that would cover federal agencies and employees in the
State of Missouri.

Turning to a different phase of experimentation,
the Administrative Law Section of the American Bar
Association has been concerned with the newly created
Administrative Conference of the United States. The
section urged the chairman of the Administrative Conference to consider complaints about selected governmental activities "for the primary purpose of developing
understanding of the potentialities of an Ombudsman
system for the federal government." In addition, the
conference was urged to study existing Ombudsman analo-
gues and to encourage agency experimentation. (See
App. VII)

The Conference Chairman, Professor Jerre S.
Williams, does not seem initially disposed to take
this advice. In a discussion following his address
to the Western American Assembly on the Ombudsman (see
App. VI) on June 7, 1968, Professor Williams indicated
that he would consider complaints, but not with a view
to individual rectification. Rather, he would be concerned only with the prospective improvement of administration that individual complaints might inspire. The
point of the ABA Report is that the Ombudsman office
is, to use Mr. Williams' words, one of the "remedial
procedural recommendations for improvements which will
redound to the advantage not just to the complainant
but to all citizens involved in those regulatory programs."23

NOTES

to Chapter II

1. See Walter Gellhorn, When Americans Complain: Governmental Grievance Procedures (Cambridge, Mass.: Harvard University Press, 1966) and Kenneth Culp Davis, "Ombudsmen in America: Officers to Criticize Administrative Action," 109 University of Pennsylvania Law Review 8: 1057-1076 (1961).

2. Report of the Thirty-Second American Assembly, October 26-29, 1967, The Ombudsman, pp. 6-7, reprinted in: U.S. Senate Com. on the Judiciary, Subcom. on Administrative Practice and Procedure, 90th Cong., 2d sess., Administrative Ombudsman Hearing, January 16, 1968, pp. 19-21. See p. 21. Hereafter cited as Administrative Ombudsman Hearing.

3. Reprinted in Rowat, ed., The Ombudsman, note 6, Ch. I, pp. 305-309, and in Congressional Record, July 16, 1963, p. 12069. See also Congressional Record, February 11, 1963, pp. 2078-2084; Congressional Record-Appendix, March 13, 1963, p. A1367; March 14, 1963, pp. A1459-1460; March 19, 1963, p. A1564; March 21, 1963, pp. A1583-1584; April 2, 1963, p. A1952; April 10, 1963, pp. A2218-2219; see also Congressional Record, September 23, 1964, pp. 21839-21841, for the introduction of a companion bill, S. 3205, by Senator Claiborne Pell (D, Rhode Island). And see H. Reuss and Everard Munsey, "The United States," in Rowat, ed., The Ombudsman, pp. 194-200.

4. Reprinted in: U.S. Senate Com. on the Judiciary, Subcom. on Administrative Practice and Procedure, 89th Cong., 2d sess., Ombudsman Hearing, March 7, 1966, pp. 368-369; (hereafter cited as Ombudsman Hearing) and in Congressional Record, February 3, 1965, p. 1845 and September 13, 1966, pp. 21554-21555. See also Congressional Record-Appendix, March 15, 1965, pp. A1165-1166;

July 15, 1965, pp. A3802-3803; October 21, 1965, pp. 26905-26910; February 17, 1966, pp. A835-837; April 1, 1966, pp. A1903-1905. But see Congressional Record-Appendix, February 3, 1966, p. A518. See Congressional Record, February 3, 1965, p. 1873, for introduction of companion bill S. 984, by Senator Pell. Congressman Alphonzo E. Bell, Jr. (R, California), introduced an identical bill, H.R. 6265, on March 15, 1965.

5. Reprinted in: U.S. Senate Com. on the Judiciary, Subcom. on Administrative Practice and Procedure, 90th Cong., 1st sess., committee print, Ombudsman: 1967, November 1967, (hereafter referred to as Ombudsman: 1967) pp. 206-207, and in Congressional Record, January 23, 1967, p. H498. See also Congressional Record-Appendix, January 24, 1967, pp. A238-239; and the Record, November 6, 1967, pp. H14670-14672; and see the identical proposal of Congressman Bell, H.R. 5391, previously introduced in 1965, and reprinted in Ombudsman: 1967, pp. 212-213.

6. U.S. Senate, 89th Cong., 2d sess., Report No. 1414, July 28, 1966, p. 36. Somewhat ironically, the 1966 Western States Democratic Conference endorsed "efforts of the Joint Committee...to modernize congressional procedures...and to study such suggestions as have been advanced including the concept of Ombudsman to enable Senators and Members of Congress to help their constituents more effectively and at the same time more effectively carry out their legislative duties."

7. Joint Committee on the Organization of Congress, Final Report, p. 81.

8. See Congressional Record-Appendix, June 17, 1965, pp. A3191-3195, especially p. A3193, where three political scientists also reject the Reuss proposal on principle, while treating the issue primarily as one of congressional staffing.

9. See App. VII, Recommendation 4, p. 251, and explanation under the title "Congressional Casework," pp. 253-254.

10. Letter dated February 4, 1968.

11. Gellhorn, note 1 above. On page 63, Professor Gellhorn notes that the results of his investigation are "offered for lack of anything better. 'Hard statistics' concerning the quantity or kinds of casework do not exist." See also Charles L. Clapp, The Congressman (Washington: Brookings Institution, 1963), for composite analysis of congressmen's introspections on casework.

12. "Case Work by Members of Congress," Library of Congress LRS-GGR-105, May 4, 1965.

13. Berkeley: Institute of Governmental Studies, University of California, February 1968. On page 3, Professor Mann notes, "The information now available is relatively scant, fragmentary, and unsystematic."

14. See Dale Vinyard, "Congressional Committees on Small Business," Midwest Journal of Political Science, 10 (3): 364-377 (1966), and "Congressmen as Washington Agents for Constituents," Business and Government Review, 8 (5): 19-25 (1967).

15. See Congressional Record-Appendix, February 7, 1967, pp. A507-508.

16. See Ombudsman Hearing, March 7, 1966. This 383 page document contains a number of useful appendices. See also Mary Hornaday, "Ombudsman Invites Swedish Complaints," Christian Science Monitor, February 17, 1966, p. 5; Stephen Gerstel, "Ombudsman Interests U.S.," Oakland Tribune, March 6, 1966, p. 33; Robert L. Asher, "Mr. Fixit Fascinates Senators-City Fathers," Washington Post, March 8, 1966; and "Washington considers complaint department," Christian Science Monitor, March 9, 1966, p. 5. But see editorial, "Power of the Ballot," in the San Diego Union, April 5, 1966, p. b-2.

17. Reprinted in Congressional Record, March 7, 1967, pp. S3201-3203, and in Ombudsman: 1967,

pp. 183-186. Senator Long's proposal for a District of Columbia Ombudsman is cited in Ch. IV, note 7.

18. See <u>Administrative Ombudsman Hearing</u>, January 16, 1968. Another proposal coauthored by Senator Long and relating to the Internal Revenue Service relates to so-called "Small Tax Ombudsmen," but would actually establish a small claims court for tax disputes concerning amounts not over $2,500. See <u>Ombudsmen: 1967</u>, pp. 192-205, including S. 18 (1967), by Senator Warren G. Magnuson (D, Washington) and others. The proposed commissioners would actually hear and decide cases, thus functioning as judges. Calling them "Ombudsmen" ignores the advice given by Donald C. Rowat, "The Spread of the Ombudsman Idea," in Anderson, ed., <u>Ombudsmen for American Government?</u> Ch. 1 note 2 above, that the use of the term should be restricted to "grievance officers" (p. 35).

19. <u>Administrative Ombudsman Hearing</u>, pp. 58-59.

20. Ibid., p. 61.

21. Ibid., p. 31.

22. Ibid., pp. 47-48. The Social Security Administration did not participate in the hearing.

23. <u>Administrative Ombudsman Hearing</u>, testimony of Chairman Williams, page 8. He also said, "...I do not envisage the Administrative Conference or the Office of the Chairman handling individual complaints on a substantive basis--that is, to determine the correctness or incorrectness of a particular action on the merits. But I do see the use of citizens' complaints as a means of pinpointing troublesome areas that the Conference might wish to investigate." This role is similar to the one adopted by the California Commission on Judicial Qualifications, discussed in the next chapter.

CHAPTER III

STATE PROPOSALS

Nowhere is the growth of interest in the Ombudsman more striking than in American state legislatures. The initial 1963 Connecticut proposal[1] was roughly contemporaneous with the federal bill introduced by Congressman Reuss. Ombudsman bills appeared in the legislatures of six states in 1965 and 1966. By the end of 1966, Ombudsman bills had been introduced in 10 states. (See Chart I)

CHART I

Ombudsman Proposals in State
Legislatures, 1963-1966

	1963	1965	1966
Alaska			x
California		x	
Connecticut	x	x	
Illinois		x	
Massachusetts		x	x
Michigan			x
New Jersey			x
New York		x	x
Rhode Island			x
Utah		x	

In 1967, 215 authors sponsored 60 Ombudsman bills in 26 state legislatures. (See Table I) Another proposal, with four authors, was put forward in Puerto Rico. Of the states that had previously proposed Ombudsman bills, all but Utah joined in the 1967 groundswell.[2] (See App. I)

Political Parties and Sponsorship

Sponsorship has come from both parties. The numerical preponderance of Democratic authors is exaggerated by the fact that there were 77 from Pennsylvania and Hawaii alone. Still, Democrats have been more active in introducing Ombudsman legislation than Republicans. In 1967, 11 states had proposals exclusively from Democratic sources, as compared with four proposals received exclusively from Republican sources. On the other hand, 11 states had Ombudsman authors from both parties. The Ombudsman idea is not intrinsically partisan, and the spread of authorship reflects its basic compatibility with the philosophies of both Republicans and Democrats.

Two governors, both Republicans, sponsored Ombudsman legislation in 1967. Governor Spiro T. Agnew of Maryland--now Vice-President of the United States-- drafted a proposal introduced as H.B. 701 and S.B. 465 (see App. I), and Governor Tom McCall of Oregon included an Ombudsman plank in his inaugural address.[3] Republican Governor David F. Cargo of New Mexico expressed support for the Ombudsman idea while the Democratically authored bill was pending in that state, and Democratic Governor Kenneth M. Curtis expressed approval of the Republican-authored bill in Maine. Other governors have kept silent, and even those mentioned made no substantial effort to get the proposals enacted.

Most of the 60 bills died in committee in their houses of origin. Five of the 1967 proposals were adopted by a single house. Only the Hawaii bill was

TABLE I

Ombudsman Proposals in State Legislatures, 1967

	Number of bills authored by:				Number of authors			
	D[b]	R[c]	D & R jointly	Total	D	R	i[d]	Total
Alaska	1		1	2	7	4		11
California	2			2	5			5
Colorado	1	1		2	2	1		3
Connecticut	1	4		5	1	6		7
Florida	2			2	3			3
Hawaii	3			3	34			34
Illinois	1	1		2	1	3		4
Indiana	1	1	1	3	2	3		5
Iowa		2		2		10		10
Maine		1		1		1		1
Maryland	1	1	1	3	2	3		5
Massachusetts	2		1a	3	8	1	1	10
Michigan	2			2	2			2
Minnesota		4		4		13		13
Missouri	1			1	1			1
Nevada	1			1	1			1
New Hampshire		1		1		1		1
New Jersey	1	1		2	1	5		6
New Mexico	1			1	1			1
New York	2	2	1	5	6	3		9
Ohio	1	1		2	3	1		4
Oregon	1			1	6			6
Pennsylvania	2	2	1	5	43	14		57
Rhode Island	1			1	1			1
Washington	2			2	2			2
Wisconsin	2			2	13			13
Total	32	22	6	60	145	69	1	215

[a] Plus Independent [c] Republican(s)
[b] Democrat(s) [d] Independent

enacted. In California, A.B. 1020 passed the Assembly, but was defeated in committee in the Senate.[4] In Illinois, S.B. 973 passed the Senate, but was defeated in committee in the House. In Indiana, H.C.R. 30 passed the House on a voice vote (February 15, 1967), but died in the Senate. S.P. 439 passed the Senate unanimously in Maine (June 1, 1967), but an "indefinite postponement" was voted by the House, 107 to 21 (June 6, 1967). The Rhode Island bill, S.B. 182, "was approved by a 31-13 margin on a standing vote with one switch in each party"[5] (February 14, 1967), but died in the House Committee on Finance.

The votes in California, Illinois and Rhode Island show clear-cut partisan divisions. The Democrats voted with the bill's author, Speaker Jesse M. Unruh, in the California Assembly. The Republicans voted with the bill's author, Majority Leader W. Russell Arrington, in the Illinois Senate. (See Table II)

The vote in Maine, on the other hand (as in Hawaii, discussed below), did not follow partisan alignments. The subsequent defeats in sister houses were clearly nonpartisan: opposition came from both parties, whether in committee in California and Illinois, or on the floor in Maine.

TABLE II

Roll Call Votes on 1967 Ombudsman Proposals

		Aye	No	Not Voting	Total
California (A.B. 1020)	D	37	-	5	42
Assembly, May 31, 1967	R	5	32	1	38
	Total	42	32	6	80
Illinois (S.B. 973)	D	2	12	-	14
Senate, June 7, 1967	R	30	1	2	33
	Total	32	13	2	47

The chief rivalry would seem to be related to house rather than party, and, for either of these, the roles of proponent and opponent are interchangeable. As with authorship, support for and opposition to Ombudsman proposals cut across party lines, and reflect the fact that the Ombudsman concept is consistent with the tenets of either major party.

Drawbacks to Enactment

Of the 60 bills proposed, why was only Hawaii's proposal enacted? Any proposal for a new institution has the burden of proving its worth, and giving assurance that it is potentially more valuable than alternative uses to which limited public funds might be put. The most commonly expressed basis of skepticism concerning Ombudsman proposals is the contention that elected legislators are already doing the job. Shortly after the introduction of S.P. 439 in Maine, Representative Joseph A. D'Alfonso (D) took the floor to exclaim:

> ...that I, Representative D'Alfonso
> do not need at any time an Ombudsman
> to speak for me on any matter relat-
> ing to state or local government, and
> I would strongly suggest that there
> is not a single member present in the
> Hall of the House among the 151 who
> at any time would need an Ombuds-
> man;...members of the Legislature,
> the Governor's staff, all members
> of Commissions and so forth are
> ready, available and always will-
> ing to render their services to
> any public-spirited citizen who
> has a legitimate complaint to
> bring before anyone in state gov-
> ernment, local government or even
> national government.[6]

Later, when the proposal reached the floor, the author, Senator Horace Hildreth (R), responded as follows:

> ...One question that is often asked about the Ombudsman is: with 151 representatives and 34 senators, who needs him? Don't the legislators now do everything that he would do? I think the answer is they don't, and they can't. The Legislature meets only six months out of every two years. During that time most of us are tremendously busy on legislative matters. We all get complaints and problems from our constituents which we try to handle for them. Sometimes, if they are simple, we do a good, calm job, but how often do we merely go to the agencies that our constituent is complaining about and ask them to look into it? How often do we merely grab at a routine answer that is sufficient to keep our constituent from getting mad at us? How diligent are we if we think our constituent is a nut or voted against us at the last election? Even more important, how good a job do we do during the other eighteen months when we have gone back to Fort Kent or to Kittery to try and catch up on our business, particularly if we are not planning to run for office the next time?
>
> Even if the legislator could adequately handle all of the

complaints of his constituents, and
I think this is open to very serious
question, he cannot begin to compare with the Ombudsman in the role
of a constructive administrative
critic. The agency is merely going
to breathe a sigh of relief when
the legislators leave and go right
back to doing the things they have
been doing in the same old way.
Nothing is going to be learned or
improved from the legislator's
efforts.[7]

Developments in Hawaii

Hawaii has moved past this stage in the Ombudsman
debate. Early in 1967, three identical Ombudsman bills
were introduced in the Legislature of the State of
Hawaii, two in the House of Representatives and one in
the Senate. The authors were 34 Democrats, led by
freshman Senator Duke Kawasaki.[8] (See App. I)

Opening on a somewhat discouraging note, the House
bills were referred to seven different committees, a
clear case of deliberative obstructionism.[9] Consequently, it was Senate Bill 19 that made its way through
the Senate Committee on Federal-State-County Relations
and Government Efficiency, the Senate Committee on Judiciary, the Senate Committee on Ways and Means, and the
House Committee on Government Efficiency and Public
Employment.[10]

On the floor of the Senate, two amendments were
adopted. The first, offered by Senator William E.
Fernandes (D), limited the size of the Ombudsman's
office to a total of four persons. The second, offered
by Senator David C. McClung (D), reduced the Ombudsman
salary level from that of Chief Justice of the State
Supreme Court ($28,000 a year) to a flat $22,000 a year

(the same as the legislative auditor), and deleted the entire $87,000 appropriation for the office. With these concessions, the proposal was adopted by a vote of 23 to 1.[11]   (See Table III)

TABLE III

Roll Call Votes on 1967
Hawaiian Ombudsman Bill, S.B. 19

			Aye	No	Not Voting	Total
Senate:	April 21, 1967	D	14	1	-	15
		R	9	=	1	10
		Total	23	1	1	25
House:	April 28, 1967	D	35	4	-	39
		R	3	8	1	12
		Total	38	12	1	51

On the House side, the Fernandes amendment was deleted, and the bill passed 38 to 12, still with reduced salary and without appropriation. (See Table III) The Senate approved the House version on April 29, and sent the measure to the governor for his consideration.[12]

On June 14, 1967, the 45th day after the end of the legislative session, the Hawaiian Ombudsman Act of 1967 became law without the signature of Democratic Governor John A. Burns. Governor Burns did not veto the measure; he thought it was a matter within the exclusive prerogative of the Legislature.[13]

Section 3 of the Ombudsman Act provides that the Ombudsman be appointed for six years "by a majority

vote of each house in joint session." Senator Kawasaki
encouraged those interested to apply, and indicated that
applicants would be screened by the Senate Committee on
Government Efficiency, which he chairs, and by a committee of the House.[14]

There was considerable speculation that the out-
going president of the University of Hawaii, Thomas H.
Hamilton, might be a candidate for the position. After
talking with Senator Kawasaki, President Hamilton wrote
to him as follows in March 1968:

> Your consideration of me as a pos-
> sible Ombudsman for the State of
> Hawaii was a source of great satis-
> faction. I consider the position
> important, the experiment in state
> governmental innovation significant.
>
> However, in analyzing the total
> situation, I feel that I should not
> be a candidate.[15]

On Tuesday, March 26, 1968, Senator Kawasaki's
committee heard testimony from or on behalf of six of
the 14 remaining applicants.[16] Kawasaki pushed for the
appointment of Herman Doi, director of the Legislative
Reference Bureau, a lawyer and formerly an active Democrat.

But when the fourth state legislature adjourned at
1:40 a.m. on Saturday, March 30, 1968, the position was
not yet filled, although $103,000 was appropriated for
the office. Senate Minority Leader D. G. Anderson (R)
was willing to support Mr. Doi, but the Assistant
Majority Leader Fred W. Rohlfing (R), and Senator
Wadsworth Yee (R) threatened to filibuster, if necessary, against the appointment, until the rapidly ap-
proaching deadline for adjournment arrived.[17]

If the Republican sentiment of partisanship on this
candidate was widespread, it was probably just as well

that the appointment was not made at that time. (Mr. Doi's appointment at the 1969 session, after this essay was written, indicated that partisan sentiment was not widespread.) It would not do for an Ombudsman to be tagged as an apologist for one party or another. One reason that Speaker Jesse Unruh did not attempt to force his 1967 proposal through the California Senate was his belief that the office would suffer if legislative support for it were not virtually unanimous.

Lessons from the Hawaii Experience

Using hindsight, it would be easy to criticize the Hawaii legislators for failing to make an appointment. The scramble for appointment on the part of several candidates--not including President Hamilton or Mr. Doi-- was a bit unseemly. Perhaps the Ombudsman Act should be amended to provide for a nonpartisan blue-ribbon nominating commission, like the one included in Missouri H.B. 486 (1967), cited in App. I.

Even these changes will not remedy the underlying difficulty presented by the inadequacy of the Ombudsman's salary. Senator McClung's amendment was crippling even though his intention was to facilitate passage. Honolulu has the highest cost of living in the nation. Since University President Hamilton was stepping down from a basic salary of $32,500, legislators and journalists alike agreed that it was unrealistic to expect him to take the Ombudsman post at $22,000 a year. He eventually accepted the higher-paying directorship of the Hawaii Visitors Bureau.

As far as the other candidates are concerned, the lesson to be learned is that the prospective Ombudsman should not seek the job, but should be sought for it. For example, the government of the Province of Alberta, conducted a search by advertising in the newspapers across Canada, offering a salary of $20,000. They found the outgoing local Commissioner of the Royal

Canadian Mounted Police, George B. McClellan, and named him the first Provincial Ombudsman.

California's Commission on Judicial Qualifications

The California Commission on Judicial Qualifications, which has been in operation since August, 1961, is an Ombudsman-like institution, having most of the essential characteristics of an Ombudsman as described in the introductory chapter. It is independent, impartial, expert, accessible, and empowered only to recommend. It differs from the typical Ombudsman (1) in its limited purview, and (2) in the degree of confidentiality of its investigation and reporting. (Cases are reported in statistical analyses, but individual cases are not written up, even with identities hidden, as in some Ombudsmen reports.) The commission's annual reports (see App. IX) have received some attention, all favorable, but not enough to give it any real public visibility.[18] Perhaps it is sufficient that bench and bar are aware of the commission's work.

Through its Executive Secretary, Jack E. Frankel, and one stenographer, the nine-man commission of judges, lawyers, and laymen seeks to monitor the behavior of California's more than 1000 judges.[19] In addition, the commission submits an annual report to the governor. (Reports from 1961 through 1968 are reprinted in App. IX.) The Ombudsman-like procedure followed by the commission is spelled out in the 1964 report. Upon receiving a complaint that is not unfounded on its face, the executive director solicits a response from the judge in question, and then secures information from informed fellow judges and attorneys. Unlike the conventional Ombudsman, however, the commission seeks to correct habitual or recurring patterns of judicial misbehavior, rather than to respond to individual instances or acts.

Despite the differences indicated, however, this judicial Ombudsman is much like its administrative counterpart in general results; it operates to remove defects in a system that is basically sound. While perhaps undramatic, the overall impact of the commission has been both wholesome and pervasive.

The concept underlying the California commission is spreading to other states, and deservedly so. It has been acclaimed by the profession. (Some of the annual reports contain pertinent selections from law journals; see especially the 1964 report, the 1966 report, and the 1967 report.)[20] The American Judicature Society and the President's Crime Commission have endorsed it.

In view of the current widespread interest in the office of Ombudsman at all levels of American government, it is striking that the first official Ombudsman-like institution in the United States, the California Commission on Judicial Qualifications, was invented by the then Chief Justice, Phil S. Gibson, independently of the Scandinavian model. The success of the California Commission offers encouragement to those who urge its adoption in the more conventional form of Ombudsmen for the administrative bureaucracy.

NOTES

to Chapter III

1. See Ralph Nader, "Ombudsmen for State Governments," in Rowat, The Ombudsman (see note 6, Ch. I),
pp. 240-246.

2. In 1967 the Utah Legislature adopted H.B. 201,
"providing for the appointment of a Joint Investigating
Committee," reprinted in Ombudsmen: 1967, pp. 170-171.
Established over the veto of Democratic Governor Calvin
Rampton by a Republican-dominated Legislature, the committee lacked the objectivity and expertise of an Ombudsman. See Richard I. Aaron, "Utah Ombudsman," 1967 Utah
Law Review 1: 32-61. See esp. pp. 60-61. On October
31, 1967, the act was declared to be unconstitutional
by the District Court of Salt Lake County, citing a
number of sections of the Utah Constitution.

3. See Malcolm Bauer, "Oregon education gets
push," Christian Science Monitor, January 17, 1967,
p. 5. In Massachusetts, H.B. 672 was coauthored by the
Secretary of the Commonwealth, Kevin H. White (D).

4. See Jesse M. Unruh, "The Ombudsman in the
States," in Peel, The Ombudsman or Citizen's Defender
(see note 6, Ch. I), 111-121.

5. "Senate Approves Position of Official Watch-
dog," Newport Daily News, February 15, 1967. In New
Mexico, S.B. 10 was defeated in the Senate by a single
vote, 21-20 (March 7, 1967). The Puerto Rican proposal,
P. de la C. 784, passed the House by a vote of 46 to 1
(May 23, 1968), only to languish in the Senate.

6. State of Maine, Legislative Record: House,
January 31, 1967, p. 166.

7. State of Maine, Legislative Record: Senate,
June 1, 1967, pp. 2679-2680. The flavor and quality of

debate in Maine lead one to wish that more state legislatures would keep a record of what is said on the floor.

8. See "State Legislator Will Try for Official
Watch Dog," Honolulu Advertiser, January 10, 1967, page
B-1, and "Bill for Isle Ombudsman would aid average
citizen," Honolulu Star-Bulletin, January 10, 1967, p.
A-7. The Honolulu Advertiser endorsed the Ombudsman
idea in an editorial on December 3, 1966, and supported
the Kawasaki proposal in editorials on February 2, 1967,
and March 22, 1967. In November, 1965, the Legislative
Reference Bureau of the University of Hawaii published
an 85 page report on The Ombudsman, drawing together
selected primary and secondary materials.

9. See "Ombudsman legislation is dying," Honolulu
Star-Bulletin, March 18, 1968, p. B-14.

10. The committees reported favorably on S.B. 19
on March 30, April 17, April 21, and April 28, 1967,
respectively. The committee reports are reprinted in
Ombudsmen: 1967, pp. 50-53.

11. See "Ombudsman Bill Wins Senate Approval,
23-1," Honolulu Advertiser, April 22, 1967, p. A-7, and
"Senate okays ombudsman bill," Honolulu Star-Bulletin,
April 22, 1967, p. A-3. The amendments are reprinted
in Ombudsmen: 1967, pp. 49-50.

12. See "Ombudsman Bill Back to Senate," Honolulu
Star-Bulletin, April 29, 1967, p. A-9, and "Ombudsman
Bill Passed," Sunday Star-Bulletin and Advertiser,
April 30, 1967, p. A-1A.

13. See Douglas Boswell, "2 key bills may move
without Burns signing," Honolulu Star-Bulletin, June 9,
1967, p. 1; "Hawaii is first State to create an ombudsman," Star-Bulletin, June 14, 1967, p. C-9.

14. See "Ombudsman This Term, He Predicts,"
Honolulu Advertiser, February 9, 1968, p. A-10, and

"Ombudsman Deadline Set," Advertiser, March 20, 1968, p. A-8. The Advertiser again carried a series of editorials, this time urging the appointment of an Ombudsman: "An Ombudsman--Now," February 19, 1968; "Who for Ombudsman?" March 12, 1968; and, "The Citizen Interest," March 26, 1968.

15. Quoted in Larry McManus, "Hamilton Turns Down Bid for Ombudsman," Honolulu Advertiser, March 23, 1968. See also "Hamilton not candidate for ombudsman," Honolulu Star-Bulletin, March 23, 1968, p. A-3.

16. See "Ombudsman candidates boast varied array of talents," Honolulu Star-Bulletin, March 27, 1968, p. A-10. See also "Ombudsman job seen as challenge," Star-Bulletin, March 29, 1968, pp. 1, A-4.

17. See "Senate clock runs out on ombudsman," Honolulu Star-Bulletin, March 30, 1968, pp. 1-A2.

18. See Harlan Trott, "Weeding the Judges' Garden," Christian Science Monitor, January 27, 1965, p. c; "Judges: Remedy for Unfitness," Time Magazine, March 26, 1965, pp. 63-63A; "Inquiries Led 9 Judges to Step Down in State," Sacramento Bee, January 16, 1967, p. B2; "Judging Judges," San Francisco Examiner, January 20, 1967, editorial, p. 28; Gene Blake, "Unfit Judges Go Quietly Under California System," Los Angeles Times, January 23, 1967, editorial page; Alexander Bodi, "Nine Unknown Judges Bounced," Palo Alto Times, February 6, 1967.

19. See John E. Moore, "State Government and the Ombudsman," in Ombudsmen for American Government? (cited in Ch. I, note 2 above) pp. 70-100. See pp. 73-74, 75-76

20. See also "The Chandler Incident and Problems of Judicial Removal," 19 Stanford Law Review 2: 448-467; see p. 457 (1967), and Comment, "Courts--Judicial Responsibility: Statutory and Constitutional Problems Relating to Methods for Removal or Discipline of Judges," 21 Rutgers Law Review 1: 153-178 (1966); see esp. p. 177.

CHAPTER IV

LOCAL PROPOSALS AND PROGRAMS

The name "Ombudsman" is a catchy one, and as its familiarity increases, we should be on guard to prevent its improper use. An office of inquiry and information, for example, is not an Ombudsman. While such an office may have expertise and easy accessibility, it lacks independence and impartiality--or, at least, may appear to lack them.[1] Further, it is encumbered by the power of the chief executive to whom it is responsible, who may do more than merely recommend change in an administrative decision. An office of inquiry and information is an integral part of administration, not independent of it.

For example, in 1966 the complaint center of the Chicago Office of Inquiry and Information received

> an average of 2,100 calls a day
> from Chicagoans on a variety of
> matters including sanitation,
> electricity, street traffic,
> parking, rodents, and weeds....
>
> Complaints are passed on to the
> proper departments, with the aim
> of having each cause of complaint
> corrected within 24 hours or as
> soon thereafter as feasible.[2]

Obviously, an Ombudsman could not handle such a volume of business. He is not a first-line trouble-shooter; he is a troubleshooter _for_ troubleshooters. Exhaustion of available remedies is normally a prerequisite for the intervention of the Ombudsman. Offices of inquiry and information offer remedies that should be tried before the citizen turns to the Ombudsman. Indeed, a complaint bureau may be essential in a large jurisdiction, such as the City of Chicago, in order to provide the basic efficiency that is a precondition of effective Ombudsmanic operation.

Officers for Citizen's Assistance, Community Service

In San Diego, the Citizen's Assistance Officer has had to resist the designation of Ombudsman. In a San Diego _Evening Tribune_ article, "Haden is Tagged as Ombudsman," Tom Gable wrote,

> Just about everyone is calling Larry Haden an Ombudsman and he doesn't like it at all....
>
> Haden inadvertently got the label with his new position last week and he feels it is about time he cleared things up....
>
> Haden said the difference between his job as citizen's assistance officer and that of Ombudsman is one of power....
>
> "I am responsible to the city manager.... When necessary, we will take quick action to satisfy a citizen's complaint or, in turn, explain the necessity of the city's position...."[3]

In Savannah, Georgia, on the other hand, the comparable official is called a "Community Service Officer (Ombudsman)." Without quibbling over the label, both San Diego and Savannah are actually upgrading and systematizing casework within the city chief administrator's office. As pointed out in the December 27, 1967, memorandum to the mayor and aldermen from Savannah City Manager Picot B. Floyd, the community service officer has the following advantages:

It has reduced some of the routine
casework load of the City Manager....

It has effectively protected citizens from potential administrative
oversight and provides for more
responsive City government.

It has allowed more effective and
earlier diagnosis, and provides for
the elimination of root causes of
recurring difficulties between
citizens and the City.[4]

The memorandum also concludes that it is more
efficient to establish the new office than to increase
the size of staffs in city departments.

What has been done in local government on the
executive side in Savannah and San Diego is much like
what Congressman Henry Reuss would like to do at the
federal level for the national legislature--i.e., to
centralize and rationalize complaint-handling machinery.

Theoretically, of course, there is no reason why
an office of inquiry and complaint could not be made
independent of administration, and hence impartial.
(In effect, this is what has been done with the Commissioner of Accounts in Nassau County, discussed
below.) With independence and impartiality, the office,
or officer, would be an Ombudsman, but with additional
informational responsibilities. This was the addition
proposed at the state level in Massachusetts in H.B.
2677 (1967), in a bill "for establishing the Massachusetts information and referral agency of the office
of Ombudsman." Actual proposals for local Ombudsmen
have not attempted such a combination.

City Proposals

Ombudsman legislation has been considered in a number of American cities. The pioneer proposal was in Philadelphia, in 1962--one year before the introduction of comparable proposals at the state and federal levels.[5] The measure was bottled up in city council committee, and instead Philadelphia got a director of citizens' relations--along the general lines of the offices in San Diego and Savannah--appointed by the acting mayor in January, 1963.

The proposals in New York City, starting in 1965, have so far resulted only in supplementing the commissioner of investigations with the establishment of neighborhood city halls. Both the commissioner and the neighborhood city halls are offices of information and complaint. Republican Mayor John V. Lindsay would rather merge and expand his offices of complaint and inquiry than set up a separate New York City Ombudsman, as proposed by City Council President Frank D. O'Connor (D).[6] (Mr. O'Connor's 1967 bill is taken from the Report of the Committee on Administration of the Association of the Bar of the City of New York, reprinted in App. VIII.)

The Philadelphia and New York City proposals are described by William Angus and Milton Kaplan in the background papers for the Thirty-Second American Assembly, held at Arden House on October 26 to 29, 1967. The authors also trace the consideration of three other proposals for municipal Ombudsman which failed of enactment in 1967--in Kansas City, Missouri, in Oakland, California, and in Washington, D.C.[7] In his second term inauguration speech, Mayor Tom Currigan (D) said he would sponsor the creation of a city Ombudsman for Denver, Colorado.[8]

In Baltimore, Maryland, the Ombudsman proposal authored by Councilman Leon A. Rubenstein (D) was adopted on March 20, 1967, by a vote of 13 to 6, (2 absent). It was the first enactment of a local Ombudsman law in this country, and perhaps in the world.[9] On April 24, however, Mayor Theodore R. McKeldin (R) vetoed the ordinance. After sounding out his colleagues, Councilman Rubenstein concluded that he was two votes short of the 16 required to override the mayor's veto.[10]

Although it received considerable publicity, the Oakland proposal did not reach the stage of being introduced in the city council. Instead, the council, by a vote of 6 to 3, refused to consider the 32-page report of City Manager Jerome Keithley. The report was the result of 10 months of negotiations between the Police Department and the Oakland Economic Development Council.[11]

What the sponsor, Mayor John H. Reading (R) had in mind was only a modest proposal for a citizen grievance representative, along the lines of the city manager's adjuncts in San Diego, California, and Savannah, Georgia:

> The OEDC-Police Department report on the grievance representative proposal would put him under the city manager. The grievance officer would receive complaints from citizens about alleged municipal abuses, investigate them and report to the city manager.
>
> It would be up to the latter official to determine what disciplinary action to take when abuses are proven.[12]

The proposal added no new powers to those already held by the city manager. Moreover, it stated that "the Representative would undertake investigations only when specifically directed by the City Manager." From an abundance of caution, the proposal specified that the

48

"Citizen Grievance Representative would have no power to alter decisions of the Chief of Police."[13] Still, a majority of the council refused "to consider anything that smacked of a civilian police review board."[14]

Some Proposal Results

The Ombudsman proposals in Philadelphia and New York City, and the proposal for a civilian police review board, which was defeated by referendum in New York in November, 1966,[15] at least had the impact of fostering improvements in the internal administrative grievance mechanisms of those cities. The Oakland proposal was denied even this accomplishment. As Mayor Reading put it:

> Nothing in my experience during this past year as mayor of Oakland has obtained greater public reaction than the issues connected with police authority and citizen rights. Unfortunately, emotion-charged presentations regarding police and community problems tend to limit effective discussion and constructive solutions.[16]

A County Commissioner

New proposals keep emerging, most recently at the county level in Maui, Hawaii,[17] and King County, Washington.[18] The only functioning local government Ombudsman established by executive order is in Nassau County, Long Island, New York, in the person of Judge Samuel Greason, Commissioner of Accounts. The origins and operations of the Nassau Ombudsman have been described extensively by Kaplan and Angus.[19] (The

Annual Reports of the Commissioner of Accounts to the County Executive are shown in App. III.)

Judge Greason summarizes the history of his office as follows:

> In June of 1966, the County Executive of Nassau County, Eugene H. Nickerson, appointed me to the Office of Commissioner of Accounts of the County of Nassau. He also submitted a proposed ordinance or bill to the Board of Supervisors... setting up the Office of Public Protector....
>
> The Board...appointed a large committee to investigate the concept of Public Protector and this...committee designated two of its members as a sub-committee to go to Scandinavia and gather first-hand information on the concept of the Ombudsman.
>
> After spending three weeks in Scandinavia and in England, the sub-committee reported favorably on the concept of the Ombudsman with some minor disagreements as to the method of appointment and confirmation. Thereafter, a compromise bill was approved by both the County Executive and the Board of Supervisors and was submitted to the electorate at the November, 1967, election. The bill was defeated through the activities of the police, who were afraid that the concept of Public Protector would be the opening wedge to the appointment of a civilian review board, and further due to the

activities of one of the political
leaders who opposed the concept for
no expressed reason....

There is no Ombudsman or Public
Protector in Nassau County but,
as Commissioner of Accounts, I am
still handling all the complaints
that are made in connection with
any agency of the County, towns or
special district governments.[20]

In spite of this formal defect, the Nassau commissioner operates effectively as an Ombudsman. Indeed,
he argues that his power is enhanced by the lack of
statutory restraints:

Under the proposal on the ballot,
the ombudsman would not have been
allowed to investigate complaints
against the police, the district
attorney's office, judges and
elected officials.

"You know [said Greason] I have
more power now than if the proposal passed. The only thing I
could have done as Ombudsman is to
appeal to the press and public
opinion. Now with my present
post I can still investigate any
damned thing I please—any county
agency, including the police."[21]

Judge Greason has all of the attributes of an
Ombudsman except permanence. His independence rests
upon the self-restraint of the county executive:

Nickerson said that the major difference between [the previous Commissioner of Accounts']...role and
Greason's was that the latter was

told he was not required to report
to the county executive on any complaints or findings.[22]

"So far," Professors Angus and Kaplan conclude,
"the utility and worth of an Ombudsman at the local
level appears to be justified by the Nassau County
experience."[23] This experience also demonstrates that
the Ombudsman function can be combined with an audit
function. Further, it indicates that offices of complaint can be turned into Ombudsman offices simply by
making them independent of administration. Normally,
they already are accessible and can provide the requisite expertise. Independence brings impartiality, and
removes the decision-changing power that is implicit in
a chain of command from the chief executive. In any
case, Judge Greason has the prestige, pay, and investigatory power of his position as commissioner of accounts.

The Buffalo Citizens
Administrative Service

The Buffalo Ombudsmen, on the other hand, operate
with no elective or appointive base whatsoever, although
they have the support of the mayor. The Buffalo experiment, called the "Citizens Administrative Service," is
also described by Professors Angus and Kaplan, who were
its originators.[24] (See the Reports of the Citizens
Administrative Service in App. IV)

The Buffalo Ombudsmen are students in the School
of Law at the State University of New York, working
under faculty supervision with the assistance of a grant
from the federal Office of Economic Opportunity. (So
far, no private philanthropic organization has supported
an Ombudsman office.) With the exception of tax complaints, the Citizens Administrative Service (CAS) takes
up matters involving all levels of government--city,
county, state, and federal.

The most striking innovation of the Citizens Administrative Service is that it seeks out complaints. In addition to its central office CAS has neighborhood offices, staffed with nonstudent aides who are charged with "searching out complaints which the students will then investigate."[25] The neighborhood offices are open in the evenings. By reaching out into the community, the Buffalo project has created the first Ombudsman for the poor.

As we have seen, 1967 was the year of State Ombudsman proposals. The foregoing discussion further suggests that a similar upwelling of proposals at the local level seems imminent. A number of enactments should follow. If such a development does occur, experience with local Ombudsman proposals suggests only one major danger--that the categories of Ombudsman/Administrative Complaint Officer may not be kept distinct. As Donald Rowat suggests, if the concept is not limited to "politically independent grievance officers...many American Ombudsmen will end up in the vest pockets of chief executives."[26] In order to function as a true Ombudsman, the local officer must secure the political independence of his office.

NOTES

to Chapter IV

1. As a case in point, the Honolulu Office of Information and Complaint has been criticized for becoming "a public relations office for the Mayor." See "Ombudsman Function Was Planned for City," Honolulu Star-Bulletin, April 26, 1967, p. B-11.

2. "Chicago Ombudsman," Chicago Daily News, July 8, 1966, p. 24.

3. The Public Reception Officer in Albert Shire, Queensland, Australia, had the same problem, according to a letter dated July 24, 1968, from N. Gampe, Shire Clerk.

4. See Frank Walls, "Savannah's New Problem Solver...Georgia's First Ombudsman," Georgia Municipal Journal, February, 1968, pp. 17-18. For a description of the Bureau of Public Information and Complaint in Port Huron, Michigan, see Ombudsmen: 1967, pp. 243-246.

5. See the "Final Report of the Mayor's Ad Hoc Committee on Improvement in Municipal Standards and Practices," March, 1962, reprinted in Local Government Law Service Letter, 16 (3): 2-3 (1966), and in Ombudsmen: 1967, pp. 241-243. The earliest American proposal (that I have found) to study the need for an Ombudsman was introduced in the California Legislature on April 21, 1961 (A.B. 3121) by Assemblyman Charles W. Meyers (D). It was not enacted.

6. See Seth S. King, "Ombudsman Bill Filed by O'Connor," New York Times, May 12, 1967, p. 36. The Office of Economic Opportunity was "extremely interested" in supporting proposals like the O'Connor one. See Charles G. Bennett, "U.S. Officers to Aid Ombudsman Plan," New York Times, June 7, 1967, p. 40. Note also

that identifying the party affiliations of councilmen and mayors does not imply that all are elected on partisan tickets. Many municipal elections--including all of those held in California--are conducted on nonpartisan ballots.

7. W. Angus and M. Kaplan, "The Ombudsman and Local Government," in S. Anderson, ed., Ombudsmen for American Government? (note 2, Ch. 1) pp. 101-135. See pp. 103-111. The federal proposal, S. 626, introduced by Senator Edward V. Long, is reprinted in Ombudsmen: 1967, pp. 188-190; see also Congressional Record, January 24, 1967, pp. 1306-1308. The Kansas City bill was introduced in the Missouri General Assembly as H.B. 511, and is reprinted in Ombudsmen: 1967, pp. 93-97.

8. See John Morehead, "Meet Changes, Mayor Urges," The Denver Post, July 3, 1967, p. 4. Lieutenant-Governor Mark A. Hogan, the only Democrat in statewide executive office, is carrying out his campaign promise to use his office to receive complaints, pending the establishment of an Ombudsman for the state of Colorado.

9. See John E. Woodruff, "Ombudsman Is Voted for Baltimore," Baltimore Morning Sun, March 14, 1967, pp. C24, C6, for explanation of passage of the measure on second reading. All of the councilmen were Democrats.

10. See John E. Woodruff, "Ombudsman Bill vetoed by McKeldin," Baltimore Morning Sun, April 25, 1967, pp. C26, C15. The proposed ordinance (No. 1867, introduced on December 8, 1966) and the Report of the Committee on Ways and Means are reprinted in Ombudsmen: 1967, pp. 235-240; excerpts from the mayor's veto message are included on p. 234. The mayor found the proposal "disturbing," and thought that it "would promote interference, interruption, even confusion and delay...." The committee amendments took away jurisdiction over elected officials, made the mayor's appointment of the Ombudsman subject to council approval, and shortened the Ombudsman's term from six years to a nonrenewable four-year term.

11.   In April, 1966, the council had directed the
city manager to arrange meetings between the police and
the OEDC.   See "Council Slams Door on 'Ombudsman' Pro-
posal," Oakland Tribune, February 8, 1967, pp. 1, 5;
Bill Martin, "Mayor Renews Bid for 'Ombudsman,'" ibid.,
February 12, 1967, pp. 1, B; "Oakland Council Shuns
Ombudsman," ibid., March 2, 1967, p. 9; and, "Reading
Presses Campaign for Ombudsman in Oakland," ibid.,
March 4, 1967, pp. 1, 3.   The Tribune carried a wishy-
washy editorial, "An Ombudsman Here?" on March 8, 1967,
p. 24.   See also "Oakland Plan for Grievance Officer,"
San Francisco Examiner, March 4, 1967, p. 4.

12.   Bill Martin, "Grievance Officer for City?"
Oakland Tribune, February 5, 1967, p. 1 and cont'd.

13.   The Citizen Grievance Representative proposal
is Exhibit 3 in Mr. Keithley's report to the city council, dated February 3, 1967.

14.   "Council Slams Door on 'Ombudsman' Proposal,"
Oakland Tribune, note 11 above, p. 5.   For an appalling
example of incompetent journalism, see "No Police Review
Setup for Oakland," San Francisco Chronicle, February 8,
1967, p. 4; the proposal for a citizen grievance representative is treated as if it were solely one for a
police review board.

15.   See Angus and Kaplan, note 7 above, p. 105.

16.   Remarks to the Walter Perry Johnson Institute
of Law and Politics, Boalt Hall School of Law, University
of California, Berkeley, March 3, 1967, as reported in
"For the People: What the Ombudsman Idea Could Mean to
Oakland Citizens," Oakland Montclarion, March 22, 1967,
p. 6.   Mayor Reading also delivered an address on
"Citizen Grievance Procedure" to the American Society
for Public Administration, San Francisco, California,
on March 28, 1967.   And see Kimmis Hendrick, "Oakland
mayor talks about his job," Christian Science Monitor,
February 14, 1967, p. 3.

17.   Jack H. Stephens, "Maui May Have Nation's First 'Ombudsman' Soon," Honolulu Sunday Star-Bulletin & Advertiser, June 30, 1968, p. D-8.   Actually, the Maui County Charter scheduled to take effect on January 2, 1969, provides for a three-man Board of Appeals (Article VIII, Ch. 13) whose powers are merely recommendatory.

18.   See "Ombudsman Recommended," Municipal News, 59 (7): 25 (April 22, 1968) and "Ombudsman," ibid., 10 (10): 37 (June 10, 1968).   The February 26, 1968, Report of the Municipal League of Seattle and King County to the King County Freeholders on a Home Rule Charter contains a provision for an Ombudsman--"A department to handle inquiry and complaints...separate from the Public Information Department" (p. 11).   See also Brantley Holt, Jr., "The Complaining Citizen," A Report to the Municipal League's Subcommittee on Comparative County Government (mimeographed, 3 pp.; n.d.).

19.   "The Ombudsman and Local Government," note 7 above, pp. 111-119.

20.   Letter to the author dated July 12, 1968.   See also William Cahn, Ombudsman Report, submitted to the Nassau County Board of Supervisors (Mineola, New York: mimeographed, 1966; 28 pp.) and Joseph L. Marino, A Detailed Study on the Need for an Office of Public Protector (Ombudsman), submitted to The Special Advisory Committee Appointed by the Nassau County Board of Supervisors (n.p.: n.d.; 31 pp.).   Neither candidate for the office of county executive made a strong issue of the Ombudsman proposal, although the incumbent, Eugene Nickerson (D), had originated it.   His opponent, Sol Wachtler (R), recommended a "No" vote on all three reform proposals: the new state Constitution, Nassau County charter revision, and the public protector.

21.   Agis Salpukas, "'Ombudsman' on L. I. Finds Defeat Has Given Him More Power," New York Times, December 3, 1967, p. 159 (paragraphs in the newspaper item were in the reverse order of that presented above).

As public protector, Commissioner Greason would have earned $5,000 more a year than his present salary of $20,000. The $25,000 annual salary is the same as that of a District Court judge, a position Greason held from 1937 to 1958.

22. "Caso to Greason: Quit as Ombudsman," Newsday, November 14, 1967. The commissioner of accounts serves at the pleasure of the county executive. The public protector would have had a six-year term. The proposals for local law creating a Nassau County Public Protector and a Nassau County Office of Information and Complaints are reprinted in Ombudsmen: 1967, pp. 222-228.

23. "The Ombudsman and Local Government," note 7 above, p. 119.

24. Ibid., pp. 121-131. See also Milton Kaplan, "Ombudsmen for Urban America: The Buffalo Experiment," 17 Local Government Law Service Letter 9-10: 3-5 (1967).

25. Dick Klug, "Will Ombudsman Prove to be Average People's Man for All Complaints?" Magnificat, August 11, 1967, Second Section front page.

26. "The Spread of the Ombudsman Idea," in Ombudsmen for American Government, (note 2, Ch. I) p. 35. (Emphasis in original)

CHAPTER V

OMBUDSMAN-LIKE INSTITUTIONS

For Corporations, Consumers, and Others

"A powerful case can be made for ombudsman-like institutions in <u>all</u> businesses and professions dealing with people. Why don't you start making it?" an advisor remarked.[1] The case should be made, but first, it must be pointed out again that an Ombudsman is no substitute for adequate internal grievance machinery. Most proposals for corporate Ombudsmen, for example, have merely recommended the creation of a right-hand man for the president.[2] By the same token the Ombudsman cannot simply be either an advocate for the public[3] or an office of information and referral[4] as urged in proposals for consumers Ombudsmen.

As indicated in Chapter I, the standards for an Ombudsman require him to be independent, impartial, expert, accessible, informed, and empowered only to express an opinion. Only a few of the suggestions for extraordinary Ombudsmen have kept this definition in mind. One of these is the proposal in Britain for a hospital Ombudsman:

> The hospital service must have
> someone to keep a watch on it.
> Professor Brian Abel-Smith is
> now campaigning for a hospital
> commissioner, like the parliamen-
> tary one, who has been kept out
> of the medical world by the doctors.
> The hospital commissioner would be
> independent of any Ministry, with
> power to investigate complaints;
> he would have his own staff, and
> possibly regional officers....

[H]e should have the power to drop
in to hospitals, to check how they
are being run.[5]

Similarly, one proposal for a religious Ombudsman--
inspired by the New Mexico Ombudsman bill--specifies
that the "ecclesiastical 'ombudsman' would have no right
to take corrective action beyond investigating the matter and reporting to all parties concerned...on the
validity of the complaints."[6]

Only when the categories are kept clear can an
intelligent decision be made with respect to which
offices, if any, are needed, and in what order or combination. In the corporate context, for example, advocates for management (public relations and personnel
officers) and labor (trade union officials, including
shop stewards) can be readily identified. The same is
true for judges; collective bargaining agreements have
judicialized the resolution of disputes between company
and worker by providing for binding arbitration. Charac-
terizing executive troubleshooters as Ombudsmen, however, only serves to obscure the other areas in which
such an official might really function.

Questions and Possibilities

A genuine corporate Ombudsman would operate exter-
nally to investigate complaints from the general public,
the purchasing and consuming public, the shareholder
public, and from workers and subordinate management.
In this context, a number of questions present themselves. Do these various publics need spokesmen more
than they need Ombudsmen? Do they need both? Should
the mode of settlement of grievances be judicial (i.e.,
coercive), or Ombudsmanic (i.e., noncoercive), or both?

The same questions can be posed with regard to
medical services. Here, too, the public is sorely

handicapped by lack of information and expertise; a code of secrecy protects possible malfeasance. Access to information and the ability to use it take precedence over the Ombudsman question. As far as doctors and hospitals are concerned, perhaps a modification of the Ombudsman concept along the lines of the California Commission on Judicial Qualifications would be acceptable. Thus cautious and confidential inquiries could be used along with all of the other Ombudsman qualities and powers, except the power to publicize.[7]

The possibilities are almost unlimited. Since there is a Commission on Judicial Qualifications, why not one on medical qualifications, or on lawyers' qualifications? Why not a commission for dentists, veterinarians, or accountants? With a substantial proportion of lay members and an effective executive secretary, there could be an end to the prevalent systems of self-judging in many fields, a practice that often degenerates into nonjudging, except in flagrant cases. Lay members provide impartiality; professional and staff members provide expertise.

Consumer associations (such as automobile clubs) and trade associations (such as affiliations of car repair shops) could hire independent Ombudsmen to investigate and express opinions on complaints related to unnecessary or faulty work. At the present time, the consumer has neither the information nor the expertise to judge the need for repairs or the quality of performance.

Very little is known about grievance mechanisms in commerce, industry, and the professions. One way to study them would be to establish Ombudsmen, as suggested in the preceding paragraphs.

Campus Ombudsmen

At present, experience with Ombudsmen outside the traditional realms of government administration is limited to the brief operation of campus Ombudsmen at Michigan State University and at the State University of New York in Stony Brook. Before examining these offices, it might be helpful briefly to survey the range of Ombudsmen or similar officers on the college scene.

California

The University of California at Berkeley provides examples of the panoply of Ombudsman-related roles. First, the Associated Students provided for a Student Advocate in Section 5 of their Constitution. The first Student Advocate, Siegfried Schnuetgen, was active on a number of issues, such as room rental rates for campus clubs,[8] and the definition of a "student" in terms of eligibility to use campus facilities.[9] As the name indicates, the position is that of advocate; the level of advocacy seems to have been both issue-oriented and case-oriented--lobbying as well as lawyering.

On the other side, the campus administration designated Associate Dean of Students Roland J. Maples "as an [informal] 'Ombudsman,' hearing student complaints and trying to rectify them."[10] Recognition of the need for an administrative complaint officer seems to be nearly unanimous. Governor Ronald Reagan (R) urged:

> isolation of hard-core rebels by remedying legitimate student grievances, thus denying the rebels of temporary allies. Student-administration communication should be constantly reviewed.[11]

University President Charles J. Hitch stated that:

> The University administration must un-
> derstand that dictation and requirement
> without explanation and consultation
> are no longer possible.... A thought-
> ful administration must make many final
> decisions but with a substantially
> greater input of student advice, coun-
> sel and opinion.[12]

A similar position has been effective at San Jose State College.[13] The Trustees of the California State Colleges would like "to provide each of the 18 State College campuses with an 'ombudsman'--an administrative assistant to specialize in smoothing relationships between students and the college."[14]

Somewhat belatedly, Columbia University has appointed a "Director of Student Interests--a kind of Ombudsman for students."[15] None of these complaint officers is an Ombudsman, because each is part of administration.

There have been a number of proposals for inde-pendent campus Ombudsmen, including one being imple-mented at Berkeley. The Academic Senate has appointed Professor George Leitmann as "a committee of one [to] hear complaints from students."[16] Other proposals cur-rent in California are at the University of California at Los Angeles[17] and Stanford University.[18]

In 1967, campus Ombudsman proposals were considered at Valparaiso University in Indiana[19] and at Southern Illinois University (Carbondale).[20]

New York

In the State University of New York at Stony Brook, Long Island, President John S. Toll appointed three

Ombudsmen in March, 1967,

> to serve as the President's special
> representative[s] in investigating
> any suggestions or complaints that
> might be brought to [their] atten-
> tion by members of the faculty,
> staff, or student body of the
> University.[21]

In response to complaints and suggestions, the
Ombudsmen made a number of recommendations on matters
of policy affecting the new campus: traffic, parking,
mail, student advising, personnel, and relations with
contractors, as well as on the need for elected representatives of students and faculty in University coun-
cils. For the 1967-68 academic year, the number of
Ombudsmen was reduced to two, and the president urged
that normal channels be "given a fair chance to respond"
before resorting to extraordinary ones.[22]

The Stony Brook Ombudsmen have acted partly as
officers of information and referral, partly as Ombudsmen investigating grievances, and partly as idea men
for ameliorating the inconveniences caused by campus
construction. This last need may disappear when the
campus reaches maturity, leaving a permanent campus
Ombudsman to function in more traditional ways. To
institutionalize their role, the Ombudsmen should be
given more independence than they now derive from serving
at the pleasure of the University president.

Michigan

The origins and operation of the Michigan State
University Ombudsman, starting in the fall of 1967, were
explained by the holder of that office, Professor James D.
Rust. (See App. X) To this statement, the MSU Ombudsman added the following information:

> Yes, my position is a full time one
> though I try always to teach one or
> two courses during the school year.
> Last year 525 individual students,
> ranging from freshmen to graduate
> students, and representing every
> college on the campus, brought me
> 556 complaints, problems, and
> questions. I have not yet taken
> up anything on my own volition
> though there have been times when
> the thought has crossed my mind.
> For the most part, however, I have
> been too busy with current clients
> to take on any additional work.
> ...[M]y office consists of myself
> and my secretary. I have not yet
> acquired an assistant though if
> my case load should increase very
> much I would have to have some
> help.[23]

The MSU Ombudsman is appointed by President John A. Hannan and has no fixed term. The operation of his office, however, is made independent by the following circumstances: (1) careful consensus in the nomination process (see the description in App. X); (2) prestige, arising from tenure and reputation which were conditions of nomination; (3) sweeping investigatory power; and sole reliance on reasoned persuasion. (The last three are also characteristic of the Nassau County Ombudsman.) Independence is reinforced by success. The additional functions of information, counseling, and referral seem to fit in well with the Ombudsman job.

The operation of a campus Ombudsman office presupposes a reasonably efficient administration with its own channels of communication to students and faculty. When there is a likelihood of punishment such as loss of privileges, suspension, or expulsion, students may require due process in the form of notice of alleged infraction of preexisting rules, access to information, assistance of a qualified spokesman, and hearing by an impartial tribunal.[24] An Ombudsman is not (1) a substitute for the judicial process (where this is appropriate), although he can investigate complaints of unfair procedure, nor (2) a court of appeals to review the substance of the decisions of disciplinary tribunals.

Campus Ombudsmen are not major participants in the political process of University governance, although an Ombudsman may foster the consideration of major issues by weeding out minor irritants. Finally, a campus Ombudsman is not a superadministrator, second-guessing line officers. In deciding whether or not to criticize, the Ombudsman asks "Was this decision reasonable?" rather than "Is this how I would have done it?"

Administration in American universities needs responsible, external, impartial critics, like the Ombudsman at Michigan State. Keeping the limitations (as expressed in the preceding paragraphs) in mind, there is little to lose and much to gain through the effective campus Ombudsmen. They can help the student have his grievances corrected or resolved; aid the administration in doing a good job and getting credit for it; and help the public avoid unseemly controversy. The Ombudsman method of persuasion is eminently appropriate in places of learning.

NOTES

to Chapter V

1. Memorandum dated July 1, 1968, from Stanley Scott to the author. (Emphasis in original)

2. See Isidore Silver, "The Corporate Ombudsman," Harvard Business Review, 45 (3): 77-87 (1967). Silver argues that the Ombudsman "must be deemed to represent the ultimate decision-making authority in the corporation, and he can only do this if he is a member of the president's personal staff" (p. 81). Similarly, Ron S. Heinzel, "'Ombudsman' Seen as Corporate Healer," Los Angeles Times, May 12, 1968, Section 1, p. 10, quotes J. Paul Sticht's definition of the company Ombudsman as "almost a deputy president."

3. See Paul J. C. Friedlander, "An Ombudsman for Tourism," New York Times, November 14, 1965, pp. XXI, 18.

4. See Irving Baldinger, "For a Medical Ombudsman," letter to the editor of the New York Times, November 14, 1967, p. 46.

5. Ann Shearer, "The Case for an Ombudsman," Manchester Guardian Weekly, June 13, 1968, p. 13. Technically, this is a proposal for a governmental Ombudsman, but the need for patient protection is the same, whether the facility be public or private.

6. Msgr. Francis Tournier, "On Learning from the Legislature," in the column, "Archdiocesan Daybook," The Renewal, February 24, 1967, published by the Italian Evangelical Society, New York. See also Albert Broderick, "An Ombudsman for Religious," America, 115 (6) 446-448, 455 (1966), for a careful adaptation of three reforms (p. 448): hearings, advocates, and Ombudsmen, the last to be called "intervenors."

7. See Justin J. Stein, "Board of Medical Examiners--Recent Changes in Laws Relating to Practice in California." California Medicine, 109 (1): 53-58 (1968), and George Dusheck, "More People Complaining About Doctors," San Francisco Sunday Examiner & Chronicle, July 28, 1968, Section A, p. 3. As for American Indians, they probably need advocates before they need Reservation Ombudsmen. Such would seem to be the lesson of the experience of law students at the University of Montana, Missoula, under the Montana Defender Project.

8. See Arleigh Williams, "Williams Explains Room Rent Policy," The Daily Californian, June 27, 1967, p. 7; "Room Rent Explained," ibid., pp. 1, 7; "Rent Forces Groups Off Campus," The Daily Californian, June 30, 1967, p. 5; Herb Trubo, "Problems Hit Bearhrs on Return to Campus," Siegfried Schnuetgen, The Daily Californian, July 21, 1967, pp. 1, 8; "Administration, ASUC to Confer on Rent-a-Room," The Daily Californian, July 25, 1967, pp. 1, 12.

9. See Bob Quinn, "Heyns Defines Student Status," The Daily Californian, July 14, 1967, pp. 1, 8; "ASUC Group Registered After Non-Student Problem," The Daily Californian, August 4, 1967, p. 3.

10. Doug Samuelson, "Dean Listens," The Daily Californian, July 23, 1968, p. 2. Dean Maples is aware of the limitations of his role: "Ideally," he states, "the position would be completely free of any partisan commitment, which would mean having me outside the Dean's office.... Obviously, I can't have much effect as a mediator if the Dean of Students Office is a party to the dispute.... I'll just have to try to promote communication as best I can, without being an impartial mediator." See also "Administration Adds Special Counselor," The Daily Californian, July 12, 1968, p. 1.

11. "Reagan Outlines Six Proposals to Halt Campus Rebel Threat," The Daily Californian, July 23, 1968, pp. 1, 8.

12.   "Hitch Urges Graduates to Build Bridges of Compassion," University Bulletin, 17 (1): 7 (July 1, 1968). University employees at Berkeley are also urged to get their problems out into the open. See "Staff Personnel Can Use 'Listening Posts' for Airing Complaints," Campus Report, 1 (16): 1-2 (February 9, 1967).

13.   See "A Declaration of Rights at San Jose," San Francisco Chronicle, September 22, 1967, p. 1; "San Jose Plan Praised by Negroes," San Francisco Chronicle, September 23, 1967, p. 4; "Campus Minister Appointed 'Ombudsman' by Dr. Clark," San Jose State College Spartan Daily, October 2, 1967, p. 1; Daryl E. Lembke, "San Jose State Ombudsman to Fight Race Bias," Los Angeles Times, October 3, 1967, p. 3; "An Ombudsman at San Jose State," San Francisco Chronicle, October 3, 1967, p. 4; Ralph Craib, "Ombudsman Allays Campus Racial Strife," San Francisco Chronicle, November 20, 1967, p. 13.

14.   See James Benet, "College Ombudsman Funds Asked," San Francisco Chronicle, April 25, 1968, p. 10.

15.   See Sylvan Fox, "Columbia Names an Official to Be Ombudsman for the Students," New York Times, May 29, 1968, p. 24. Victor Rosenblum, new president at Reed College, "believes the severe student rioting [at Columbia University] last spring was the product of a lack of communication to the president's office," according to John Guernsey, "Ombudsman Post Seen As Campus Need," The Sunday Oregonian (Eugene), August 25, 1968, p. 28. Guernsey quotes President Rosenblum as stating that "I don't believe the severity of the student unrest was related to the president before the thing exploded and got out of hand." See also Ellen Kay Trimberger, "Why a Rebellion at Columbia Was Inevitable," Trans-action, 5 (5): 28-38 (September 1968): See p. 29; "The students...lacked effective channels within the university to express their discontent and to influence administration policy."

16. See the Report of the Committee on Student Affairs, Notice of Meeting of the Berkeley Division of the Academic Senate for June 5, 1967, pp. 33-34, and Minutes of the Berkeley Division, June 5, 1967, p. iii. See "Academic Senate Votes for Faculty Ombudsman," The Daily Californian, June 22, 1967, p. 2. The Associated Students Senate urged the creation of such an office in November, 1966. See Judy Zimring, "Senate Recommends Ombudsman Stand," The Daily Californian, November 14, 1966, p. 6: "At first it was considered that the Ombudsman would be under the jurisdiction of the administration. 'But,' [Student Body President Dan] McIntosh explained, 'he would tend to be divorced from the rest of the academic community. If he is responsible to the Academic Senate, his decisions would be legitimized.'" See also "Ombudsman Plan Uncertain," The Daily Californian, May 10, 1967, p. 1. But see Caleb Foote, Henry Mayer, and Associates, The Culture of the University: Governance and Education, Report of the Study Commission on University Governance (San Francisco: Jossey-Boss Inc., 1968) p. 108, which recommends the establishment of an information office, and argues that, if an Ombudsman is appointed, he should be given "much more power or prestige than that presently conferred on the Senate ombudsman...." Perhaps the Study Commission is primarily concerned with the fact that "complaints 'arising from the regulation of student political activity' were explicitly excluded from his [the Ombudsman's] jurisdiction." (p. 107)

17. See the Academic Senate, University of California, Los Angeles, Report of the Committee on Academic Innovation and Development, Call to Division Meeting of December 5, 1967, Recommendation No. 5, p. 12; and the Final Recommendations of the Committee on Participation in Campus Governance and Community (mimeographed: May 29, 1968), Recommendation No. 2, p. 6. See also "Ombudsman Proposed for UCLA," San Francisco Examiner, December 6, 1967, p. 12, and Elisabeth Jonsson, "UCLA Adopts Changes in Rules and Discipline Procedure," The Daily Californian, July 26, 1968, p. 1.

18. The Stanford Chapter of the American Association of University Professors has set up a four-man Ombudsman Board both to act on its own and to inspire the administration to replace the AAUP Ombudsman with a regular University Ombudsman. See "Stanford Gets Three Ombudsmen," San Francisco <u>Chronicle</u>, May 28, 1968, p. 9. Also discussed in letter dated July 11, 1968, from William A. Clebsch, President of the Stanford University AAUP Chapter, and letter dated July 24, 1968, from Sanford M. Dornbusch, President-elect of the AAUP Chapter.

19. See **D. C.** Mundinger, "The University Ombudsman" (Valparaiso University, n.d., 18 typewritten pages) for an excellent analysis of the need for the office.

20. Letter dated June 8, 1967, from Stephen L. Wasby, on behalf of the Faculty Council ad hoc committee to look into the possibility of an Ombudsman. Outside the United States, the Hall-Dennis report in Ontario, Canada, urges the establishment of an "educational Ombudsman..., mainly to hear student complaints." See Barrie Zwicker, "To Further Man's Search for Truth," <u>Christian Science Monitor</u>, June 29, 1968, p. 7.

In 1965, the students of Simon Fraser University in Vancouver, Canada elected one of their own number to attempt an Ombudsman's job. See S. Anderson, "Ombudsman Proposals: Stimulus to Inquiry," <u>Public Affairs Report</u>, 7 (6): December 1966, Bulletin of the Institute of Governmental Studies, University of California, Berkeley.

Howard J. Grossman suggests that precollege school administration may also need an external critic, in "Do School Districts Need an Ombudsman?" <u>American School Board Journal</u>, 155 (6): 6-7 (1967).

21. See <u>Announcement of Selection of Ombudsmen</u>, March 29, 1967, memorandum to "All Members of the University Community of the State University of New York at Stony Brook."

22. See <u>1966-67 Report of the Ombudsmen</u>, (memorandum) with President Toll's comments, pp. 2-5. One of
the original three Ombudsmen went on sabbatical leave.

23. Letter dated July 18, 1968. A few of the
Ombudsman's cases are described in "O-M-B-U-D-S-M-A-N!
The New College Hero," the Oakland Tribune's <u>Parade</u>
Magazine, March 17, 1968, pp. 10, 11, 13. Students are
asked to state their problems in writing. See also
"Academic Ombudsman Appointed," <u>School and Society</u>,
96 (2302): 62 (February 3, 1968).

24. See Chapter X: "Law in the Campus Community,"
in <u>The Culture of the University</u>, note 16 above, pp.
148-172, and Ch. XI: "Basic Regulations Governing
Enactment and Enforcement of Campus Rules," pp. 173-
203.

CHAPTER VI

CONCLUSION

This book is a plea for adapting the Ombudsman idea to American institutions, a plea based on the conviction that Ombudsmen are humanizers. The need for the human touch becomes greater as bureaucratization increases. Modern industrial society requires depersonalized government; without undercutting government by rule, Ombudsmen repair the injuries to and restore the dignity of the individual.

Society must deal with grievances, instead of ignoring them. Indeed, more must be done with grievances than merely resolving them. Complaints are opportunities for improving government, but to be effective, the information they contain must be fed back into the system. The government should assure that this feedback occurs through information and referral services, offices of complaint, and formal avenues of appeal. Ombudsmen are fail-safe devices that signal malfunctions in the primary mechanism and thus prevent disaster.

This is a plea to implement Ombudsman offices now, to test the idea by trying it. America's limited experience and the experience abroad are encouraging; further experimentation is neither expensive nor irreversible.

At the same time, unrealistic expectations must be avoided. It would be grossly overoptimistic, for example, to expect Ombudsmen to cure urban crises. Ombudsmen cannot cool the long hot summers of ghetto violence. They cannot create jobs, provide transportation, or build homes. But while basic social issues are more urgent and more important than the Ombudsman, the establishment of Ombudsman offices need not await the resolution of those larger issues. Neither should Ombudsman proposals, offered as panaceas, be allowed to delay fundamental reforms.

In years past, a man who had a grievance about the workings of a bureaucracy might begin to seek redress by asking "Who can help me?" or "Whom do I know?" If he were lucky enough to know someone, to have a friend or acquaintance in government, he might use influence to get a prompt and sympathetic hearing. Of course, most people lacked such protection, and today both the total numbers and the comparative proportions of persons unacquainted with governmental personnel are larger than ever before.

In addition to excluding much of the population, the informal, personal-acquaintance system had and still has at least two major drawbacks: (1) it provides essentially unequal protection under the law, and (2) it opens the door for chicanery, exploitation, and even corruption. Recent trends in American political thought have reflected the urgency of the need for equal protection for all--that is for fair, courteous, and equitable treatment and for equal access to the machinery of redress. No Ombudsman at any level of government can single-handedly furnish all the motive power necessary to implement these concepts. Nevertheless, an Ombudsman's energies would be effective in the sensitive areas where they are needed most. As the man whom everybody knows and everyone can talk to, the Ombudsman could help cultivate a sense of openness and fairness in the way government deals with people.

We have had a half-dozen years of deliberation since the first American proposals for Ombudsmen were made in 1963. Now we need a comparable period for implementation. Then, as success warrants, we will have time for expansion. The time to start is now.

APPENDIX I

State Ombudsman Bills—1967

STATE OMBUDSMAN BILLS-1967

Ombudsman bills introduced in state
legislatures for consideration during
the calendar year 1967, with authors'
names and political party affiliations.

Because copies of Ombudsman bills are readily
accessible elsewhere, none are reproduced here. In a
Committee Print of the United States Senate Committee
on the Judiciary, [Long] Subcommittee on Administrative
Practice and Procedure, Ombudsmen: 1967 (Washington,
D.C.: November 1967), Chairman Edward V. Long has compiled two score at the state level, in addition to federal proposals. Citations to Ombudsmen: 1967 are
included in the list that follows.

Richard Aaron has appended the 1965 proposals in
California (A.B. 2956), Connecticut (H.B. 3194), and
Illinois (H.B. 1772), and the 1966 proposals in Michigan
(H.B. 3887), New Jersey (A.B. 121), New York (A.B. 1134;
S.B. 428), and Rhode Island (S.B. 62) to his article,
"Utah Ombudsman," in 1967 Utah Law Review, 32-93; see
pp. 62-92 (March).

The 1965 Connecticut and Illinois bills are also
included in the report of the March 7, 1966, Ombudsman
Hearing of Senator Long's subcommittee, on pp. 369-78.
The 1963 Connecticut proposal--the first in any American
state--is reprinted in Donald C. Rowat, ed., The Ombudsman, pp. 310-21.

While no legislation was introduced in Arkansas,
Richard Arnold included a draft proposal in his article
"An Ombudsman for Arkansas," in 12 Arkansas Law Review
2:327-335; see 333-335 (1967). Bernard Frank provided

a careful annotation of the 1967 Pennsylvania Ombudsman proposals in a report printed in Ombudsmen: 1967, on pp. 147-62.

Many of these bills are eclectic, taken from the early Connecticut proposal, which in turn came from the pen of Ralph Nader. He drew heavily on the New Zealand Ombudsman Act, which was inspired by the Danish office. More recent bills reflect Professor Walter Gellhorn's influence.

Draftsmen are urged to examine the annotated model bill prepared by the Harvard Student Legislative Research Bureau, "A State Statute to Create the Office of Ombudsman," in Volume II of the Harvard Journal on Legislation, June 1965, pp. 213-38. It is reprinted in the report of the Ombudsman Hearing held by Senator Long's subcomitttee, March 7, 1966, pp. 336-61.

The best source is Walter Gellhorn's "Annotated Model Ombudsman Statute" in Stanley Anderson, ed., Ombudsmen for American Government? pp. 159-73, reprinted in Senator Long's subcommittee Administrative Ombudsman Hearing, January 16, 1968, on pp. 65-73.

Abbreviations

C	Conservative	H.F.	House File
D	Democrat	P. de la C.	Proyecto de la Cámara (House Bill)
I	Independent		
R	Republican	S.B.	Senate Bill
A.B.	Assembly Bill	S.F.	Senate File
H.B.	House Bill	S.P.	Senate Proposal

Alaska

H.B. 8   Ted Stevens (R), Jalmar M. Kerttula (D), Terry Miller (R), Charles J. Sassara (D),

Don Smith (R), Willie Hensley (D), Gene Guess
(D), M. M. Moore (R), Frank Getman (D), Mike
Bradner (D)

H.B. 52   (reprinted in Ombudsmen: 1967, pp. 11-14).
Jalmar M. Kerttula (D), Bill Ray (D), Gene
Guess (D)

California

A.B. 1020 (reprinted in Ombudsmen: 1967, pp. 15-19).
Jesse M. Unruh (D), Winfield A. Shoemaker (D),
March K. Fong (D), Harvey Johnson (D)

S.B. 370   Mervyn M. Dymally (D)

Colorado

H.B. 1223 (reprinted in Ombudsmen: 1967, pp. 27-31).
Thomas T. Grimshaw (R)

S.B. 192   (reprinted in Ombudsmen: 1967, pp. 22-27).
Anthony F. Vollack (D), cosponsored by Rep.
Thomas Bastien (D)

Connecticut

H.B. 3606 Francis J. Collins (R), John W. Boyd (R)

H.B. 4137 (reprinted in Ombudsmen: 1967, pp. 31-36).
Henry T. Becker (D)

S.B. 1365 Frederick Pope, Jr. (R)

S.B. 1427 (reprinted in Ombudsmen: 1967, pp. 38-40).
Lucy T. Hammer (R)

S.B. 1455 (reprinted in Ombudsmen: 1967, pp. 36-38).
George L. Gunther (R), John M. Lupton (R)

Florida

H.B. 328   (reprinted in Ombudsmen: 1967, pp. 42-44).
Talbot "Sandy" D'Alemberte (D), Tommy Stevens
(D)

S.B. 301   (Identical to H.B. 328). George L. Hollahan,
            Jr. (D)

Hawaii

H.B. 94   Manuel S. Henriques (D), George H. Toyofuku
           (D)

H.B. 109   George K. Noguchi (D), Elmer F. Cravalho (D),
           Robert C. Oshiro (D), Manuel S. Henriques (D),
           James H. Wakatsuki (D), Jack Katsumi Suwa (D),
           Momi L. Minn (D), T. C. Yim (D), Rudolph
           Pacarro (D), Francis A. Wong (D), Tony T.
           Kunimura (D), Pedro de la Cruz (D), Clarence
           Y. Akizaki (D), George H. Toyofuku (D),
           William M. Furtado (D), Ted T. Morioka (D),
           Tadao Beppu (D), Hiroshi Kato (D), Toshio
           Serizawa (D), Stuart Ho (D), Barney B. Menor
           (D)

S.B. 19   (reprinted with pertinent committee reports
           in Ombudsmen: 1967, pp. 47-53). Duke Kawasaki
           (D), William E. Fernandes (D), David McClung
           (D), John J. Hulten (D), Sakae Takahashi (D),
           Walter M. Heen (D), John C. Lanham (D), Larry
           N. Kuiryama (D), George R. Ariyoshi (D),
           Donald D. H. Ching (D), Vincent H. Yano (D),
           Nelson K. Doi (D), S. George Fukuoka (D))

Illinois

H.B. 26, H.B. 27 (appropriation). Harold A. Katz (D)

S.B. 57   reintroduced with amendments as S.B. 973
           S.B. 974 (appropriation) (reprinted in Ombuds-
           men: 1967, pp. 54-57). W. Russell Arrington
           (R), Joseph R. Peterson (R), Robert Coulson (R)

Indiana

H.B. 1234 and House Concurrent Resolution 30 (reprinted in Ombudsmen: 1967, pp. 58-63). Richard A. Boehning (R), William S. Latz (R)

S.B. 120 Marlin K. McDaniel (R), James M. Plaskett (D)

S.B. 123 Victor Green (D)

Iowa

H.F. 483 (companion to S.F. 455). Joan Lipsky (R), Elizabeth Orr Shaw (R), Nathan F. Sorg (R), Cecil Reed (R), James T. Klein (R), Maurice Van Nostrand (R)

S.F. 455 (companion to H.F. 483) (reprinted in Ombudsmen: 1967, pp. 67-70). James A. Potgeter (R), John M. Walsh (R), Roger W. Jepsen (R), Arthur A. Neu (R)

Maine

S.P. 439 (reprinted in Ombudsmen: 1967, pp. 72-75). Horace A. Hildreth, Jr. (R)

Maryland

H.B. 426 (reprinted in Ombudsmen: 1967, pp. 78-81). C. Lawrence Wiser (D)

H.B. 701 (companion to S.B. 465) (reprinted in Ombudsmen: 1967, pp. 76-78). Marvin Mandel (D), J. Glenn Beall (R)

S.B. 465 (companion to H.B. 701). Edward T. Hall (R), John J. Bishop, Jr. (R)

Massachusetts

H.B. 672 (reprinted in Ombudsmen: 1967, pp. 82-83), reintroduced as H.B. 2677. Kevin H. White (D, Secretary of the Commonwealth), James R. Nolen (D), Joel S. Greenberg (D)

H.B. 2299 (reprinted in <u>Ombudsmen: 1967</u>, p. 81).
Thomas W. McGee (D)

H.B. 3228 Chandler H. Stevens, Jr. (I), Jack H. Backman
(D), Richard E. Landry (D), John R. Buckley
(D), Michael S. Dukakis (D), Dave N. Vigneault
(D), John W. Sears (R)

Michigan

H.B. 2968 (identical to S.B. 730) (reprinted in <u>Ombudsmen: 1967</u>, p. 84). Thomas W. White (D)

S.B. 730 (identical to H.B. 2968). Sander M. Levin (D)

Minnesota

H.F. 1336 (companion to S.F. 1536). Howard R. Albertson
(C), Alfred E. France (C), Ernest A. Lindstrom
(C), John A. Yngve (C)

H.F. 1340 (companion to S.F. 1118) (reprinted in <u>Ombudsmen: 1967</u>, pp. 85-90). Howard R. Albertson
(C), Emery G. Barrette (C), William E. Frenzel
(C), Clinton J. Hall (C), Robert G. Renner (C)

S.F. 1118 (companion to H.F. 1340). John Tracy Anderson
(C), Mel Hansen (C)

S.F. 1536 (companion to H.F. 1336). Robert J. Brown
(C), Dean A. Nyquist (C), Robert V. Leiseth (C)

Missouri

H.B. 486 (reprinted in <u>Ombudsmen: 1967</u>, pp. 91-93).
Ken Growney (D)

Nevada

A.B. 244 (reprinted in <u>Ombudsmen: 1967</u>, pp. 98-100).
Norman Ty Hilbrecht (D)

New Hampshire

S.B. 215   (reprinted in Ombudsmen: 1967, pp. 101-03).
            Creeley S. Buchanan (R)

New Jersey

A.B. 440   (reprinted in Ombudsmen: 1967, pp. 261-64).
            Raymond H. Bateman (R), Joseph C. Woodcock
            (R), Barry T. Parker (R), William K. Dickey,
            Jr. (R), Albert S. Smith (R)

S.B. 41   (reprinted in Ombudsmen: 1967, pp. 264-69).
            John J. Giblin (D)

New Mexico

S.B. 10   (reprinted in Ombudsmen: 1967, pp. 104-07;
            and in Aaron, "Utah Ombudsman," 81-85, cited
            on p. 77 above). Edmundo R. Delgado (D)

New York

A.B. 87   (prefiled jointly with S.B. 9) (reprinted in
            Ombudsmen: 1967, pp. 114-15). S. William
            Green (R), Leonard E. Yoswein (D), Stanley
            Harwood (D), Benjamin Altman (D)

A.B. 1566   Edward A. Stevenson (D)

A.B. 3372   (reprinted in Ombudsmen: 1967, pp. 112-13),
            superseded by A.B. 4013 (introduced jointly
            with S.B. 2684) (reprinted with annotations
            but without bill number in Ombudsmen: 1967,
            pp. 117-23). Milton Jonas (R)

S.B. 9   (prefiled jointly with A.B. 87) (reprinted
            in Ombudsmen: 1967, pp. 114-15). Jack E.
            Bronston (D), Basil A. Paterson (D)

S.B. 2684   (introduced jointly with A.B. 4013) (reprinted
            with annotations but without bill number in
            Ombudsmen: 1967, pp. 117-23). John R. Dunne
            (R)

Ohio

S.B. 243   (reprinted in <u>Ombudsmen: 1967</u>, pp. 124-27).
Charles J. Carney (D), Calvin C. Johnson (D),
William B. Nye (D)

S.B. 387   John H. Weeks (R)

Oregon

S.B. 19   (reprinted, with pertinent committee report,
in <u>Ombudsmen: 1967</u>, pp. 129-31).   Ted Hallock
(D), Cornelius C. Bateson (D), Edward N.
Fadeley (D), Albert G. Flegel (D), Don S.
Willner (D), cosponsored by Rep. James A.
Redden (D)

Pennsylvania

H.B. 794   (identical to S.B. 558) (reprinted in <u>Ombuds-</u>
<u>men: 1967</u>, pp. 132-36).   Herbert Fineman (D),
William C. Rybak (D), James F. Prendergast (D)
John Pezak (D), Eugene Gelfand (D), Lester K.
Fryer (D), Freeman Hankins (D), Anita Palermo
Kelly (D), James J. A. Gallagher (D), Roland
Greenfield (D), Max Pievsky (D), Norman S.
Berson (D), Bernard M. Gross (D), James P.
Ritter (D), Gerald Kaufman (D), Ronald G. Lencl
(D), Reid L. Bennett (D), C. Doyle Steele (D),
Max H. Homer (D), John T. McMonagle (D), Curtis
J. Clay (D), Robert R. Gerhart, Jr. (D), Rober
C. Wise (D), Harry A. Englehart, Jr. (D),
Robert K. Hamilton (D), K. Leroy Irvis (D),
C. L. Schmitt (D), Joseph F. Bonetto (D),
Francis J. Rush (D)

H.B. 837   (reprinted in <u>Ombudsmen: 1967</u>, pp. 136-39).
Lee A. Donaldson, Jr. (R), Marion C.
Klingensmith (R), William N. Tuscano (R),
Kenneth S. Halverson (R), Charles Luger (R),
H. Sheldon Parker, Jr. (R), Alvin C. Bush (R)

S.B. 501 (reprinted in Ombudsmen: 1967, pp. 139-42).
          William B. Lentz (R), James E. Willard (R),
          Albert R. Pechan (R), T. Newell Wood (R)

S.B. 518 (reprinted in Ombudsmen: 1967, pp. 142-47).
          Stanley G. Stroup (R), John H. Ware, 3rd (R),
          Clarence D. Bell (R), John H. Devlin (D),
          Paul W. Mahady (D), William J. Lane (D),
          William G. Sesler (D), Joseph M. Gaydos (D),
          John F. Byrne (D), Louis G. Hill (D)

S.B. 558 (identical to H.B. 794). John H. Devlin (D),
          Benjamin R. Donolow (D), William J. Lane (D),
          Henry J. Cianfrani (D), Gus Yatron (D),
          Thomas P. McCreesh (D), Louis G. Hill (D),
          Stanley M. Noszka (D), Joseph M. Gaydos (D),
          Thomas J. Kalman (D), Jeanette F. Reibman (D)

Rhode Island

S.B. 182 (reprinted in Ombudsmen: 1967, pp. 163-67).
          Julius C. Michaelson (D)

Washington

H.B. 756 (companion to S.B. 29) (reprinted in Ombuds-
          men: 1967, pp. 173-76). Arlie U. DeJarnatt
          (D)

S.B. 29   (companion to H.B. 756). Wes C. Uhlman (D)

Wisconsin

A.B. 77   (reprinted in Ombudsmen: 1967, pp. 176-79).
          Edward Nager (D)

S.B. 102 (reprinted in Ombudsmen: 1967, pp. 180-81).
          Martin J. Schreiber (D), Henry Dorman (D),
          William C. Hansen (D), Norman Sussman (D),
          Joseph Lourigan (D), cosponsored by Assemblymen
          Edward F. Mertz (D), Richard E. Pabst (D),
          William A. Johnson (D), Lloyd A. Barbee (D),
          Manny S. Brown (D), John Radcliffe (D),
          Mark G. Lipscomb (D)

Puerto Rico

P. de la C. 784. Luis F. Camacho (D), Osvaldo Torres
          Gomez (D), Pedro Roberto Rodriquez Gonzalez
          (D), Jaime Baez Rosario (R)

APPENDIX II

Report of The Ombudsman
Province of Alberta

January 1–December 31, 1968

The province of Alberta, Canada, was the first to institute the office of Ombudsman, and the incumbent, George B. McClellan, was the first to serve a Canadian province in that capacity. Portions of his most recent report are included in this volume on "American experience" partly because of the relevance of his record to the future of American Ombudsmen, and partly because, in a continental sense, both Canada and the United States are truly American.

APPENDIX II

Contents

Province of Alberta

REPORT

of the

OMBUDSMAN

For the period January 1 - December 31, 1968

Presented to the Legislature
Pursuant to Section 26(1) of
The Ombudsman Act

Printed by Lee S. Wall,
Printer of the Queen's Most Excellent Majesty
Edmonton, Alberta
1969

THE OMBUDSMAN

Mr. Speaker:

I have the honour to submit my second report since assuming the Office of Ombudsman for the Province of Alberta. This report covers the period from January 1 to December 31, 1968, inclusive.

Cases Handled--1967

At the close of the calendar year 1967, I reported that of the complaints received during that year, 97 were either still under investigation, or awaiting investigation. One previously concluded case was reopened, making a total of 98. These cases have now been disposed of as follows:

Under Investigation	16
Workmen's Compensation Board	16
No Jurisdiction	14
Rectified	17
Abandoned	7
Declined	2
Not Justified	22
Withdrawn	4
TOTAL	98

There were 39 complaints where the investigation was completed, being the sum of those "Not Justified" and those "Rectified." This figure excludes those which are under "Investigation" or where I had "No Jurisdiction," or were "Abandoned," "Declined" or "Withdrawn" during the investigation. It will be seen that the complaints "Rectified" of those completed were approximately 45 per cent.

The single largest category of unfinished investigations in 1967, is that against the Workmen's Compensation Board. It will be remembered from last year's report, that all investigations of complaints against the Board were discontinued, due to a ruling of the Appeal Court of Alberta in a civil matter, that the Workmen's Compensation Board was not an Agency of the Government of the Province of Alberta.

The Legislature amended The Ombudsman Act to bring the Workmen's Compensation Board within the Ombudsman's jurisdiction. The amendment came into force on April 25, 1968.

Following this amendment, it became necessary to contact each complainant again, and give him the opportunity to reopen his complaint, and again submit the documentary evidence that had been returned to him.

Investigation of complaints against the Workmen's Compensation Board has been necessarily slower than in most other categories, and I shall comment on this point later in my General Comments.

. . . .

Cases Handled--1968

During the calendar year 1968, 535 complaints were received. The totals by months are as follows:

January	56
February	37
March	75
April	74
May	49
June	48
July	26
August	24
September	29

October	46
November	41
December	30
TOTAL	535

Of the total number of complaints received in 1968, it was found that in 186 of them, the Ombudsman had no jurisdiction, leaving 349 cases requiring investigation or further action....

Cases Investigated

Of the 349 cases in which the Ombudsman had jurisdiction, 58 were found to be "Not Justified," and the complainants were so advised. Again this year, a number of the complainants were not satisfied with this decision, as was to be expected.

Twenty-five cases were "Abandoned" by the complainant during investigation. This abandonment was usually in the form of letters being forwarded to the complainant asking for further information, and no reply being received. There were a small number where the complainants had moved, and these were usually transient cases, where mail was returned "Address Unknown."

Eleven cases were "Withdrawn" by the complainant before the investigation was completed. These included such cases as persons who found that they could get their complaint rectified without further action by the Ombudsman.

Eighty-two cases were "Declined" by the Ombudsman for any of the several reasons where a discretion or prohibition is included in The Ombudsman Act. Of these 82, the largest number of complaints declined was against the Workmen's Compensation Board.

This latter group were usually declined where preliminary investigation showed that there were further
avenues of appeal to the Board, open to the complainant
which he had not pursued. I was therefore required to
decline to continue such investigation by the Act.*
Frequently the complainant was unaware that such avenues
of appeal were open to him until advised by the Ombudsman.

Seven cases were discontinued for such reasons as
a transfer in the category of the complaint from one
Department to another, or where the Ombudsman, at his
discretion, may decide that there is some other adequate
remedy; or that having regard to all the circumstances
of the case, no further investigation is necessary.**

Four cases were disposed of by referring the complainant to a specific Department or other Agency.
These were usually cases where the complainant has made
an initial complaint to the Ombudsman, without first
having properly laid the complaint before the Department
or Agency concerned, or where the complainant has made
a request for information rather than making a genuine
complaint. In such cases he was advised to make his
initial request to the Department or Agency responsible.

There were five cases of sufficient importance to
be the subject of a file, where the writer sought the
help of the Ombudsman in such things as bringing a case
to Court, obtaining Legal Aid, appealing to a Federal
Government Department and so on. In such cases, the
complainant was referred to sources where he could
obtain the information he needed, or the information
was provided him by the Ombudsman's Office.

There were a considerable number of other requests
of this nature received throughout the year, which were
dealt with by telephone, or did not require a record.

---

*Section 12(1) (a)
**Section 14(1) (a) and (b)

There were 126 cases categorized as "Investigation." This category includes cases under actual investigation; cases where additional information is being sought to establish jurisdiction; and cases where the investigation has been completed, and the report and recommendation to the Minister and Department are under preparation, or awaiting a reply.

The total number of complaints which were concluded to a point where the Ombudsman arrived at an opinion, as provided for in the Act,*** is the sum total of the complaints "Rectified," and the complaints "Not Justified," namely 89. This figure leaves aside those cases which are still under investigation.

Of the 89 cases referred to, 31 were rectified, which is slightly better than one third. It is gratifying to note that to date, there is no concluded case, where the recommendation of the Ombudsman has not resulted in the complaint being rectified.

Summaries of a number of the cases appear at the end of this report.... Such summaries will illustrate the wide variety of complaints received. They also demonstrate the manner in which some Departments of Government are more complained against than others.

It would be a mistake to judge the performance of Departments or Agencies solely on the number of complaints registered against them. It is most likely that the functions and responsibilities of one Department, are such as to make it more the natural target of criticism from the public than many other Departments.

Departments in such fields as Welfare, Justice, Highways, Lands and Forests, Health; and Agencies such as the Workmen's Compensation Board, whose actions are most likely to affect the daily lives of the public, will be

***Section 20

more complained against than, for instance, the Provincial Library, against which I have had no complaint whatsoever.

In my last report, I warned against judging the statistics therein, as indicating a pattern, due to the fact that the report only covered four months of the operations of the Ombudsman's Office. I think now that it can be anticipated the trend will be somewhat along the lines I have just mentioned above.

There is nothing as yet to indicate any decrease in the volume of complaints being received. Except for the summer months when the nation-wide postal strike was on, the numbers have remained reasonably constant.

In the first months of my office, a large number of very old complaints were revived and brought to my attention, some of them dating back over thirty years. In the past year, however, the incoming complaints have become more current, and with the odd exception, I think the period of having to deal with very ancient complaints is over.

At the same time, however, there is a notable increase in the number of complaints received, which are of so complicated a nature as to require lengthy investigation. As will be seen from the statistics, there are some cases from 1967 which are not yet completed. In a number of these cases, there are voluminous files which must not only be read, but thoroughly studied. It has been necessary to obtain transcripts of evidence of cases long concluded, or "Enquiries" terminated some years ago. There are also a significant number of cases, where the files of two or more Departments must be examined and discussed with the officials of those Departments.

It follows that a number of these investigations will take weeks or even months to complete. The result is, that from time to time, a considerable backlog of complaints awaiting investigation will build up. None the less, the quality of investigation must never be sacrificed in favour of quantity.

The text of the Sections of The Ombudsman Act referred to throughout this report, is included....
[on pages 117 to 121.]

Organization and Work of the Office

At the conclusion of the calendar year 1967, when I commenced preparing my report for that year, my staff consisted of one Secretary. In January, 1968, a Stenographer was added to the staff. In March, 1968, the first Investigator was appointed. Until his arrival, I had been carrying out all investigations myself and was rapidly losing ground.

In May, I was most fortunate in the appointment of a Solicitor to the Office of the Ombudsman in the person of Mr. A. B. Weir. Mr. Weir's previous career had been, not only in private practice, but as Solicitor to several Departments of the Provincial Government. His knowledge of the operations of Government and the Provincial Statutes has been of great value, particularly when it is realized that this office is not an office of specialists. It must be prepared to deal with Provincial Statutes, Regulations and Policies as they affect any and every Department or Agency of the Government of Alberta.

In September, an additional Investigator and an additional Stenographer completed the authorized staff.

It will be seen, that for almost half a year, the staff was not large enough to cope with the volume of work.

The number of complaints still under investigation or awaiting investigation at the end of 1968, is still considerably higher than it should be. I shall watch this situation carefully in the coming year, for, as I stated in my last report, I regard prompt investigation of complaints a prime requirement of the Ombudsman's Office.

It will be noted that this report is considerably longer than the previous one for 1967.

As has been indicated to me, it is the desire of the Legislators that my report for the calendar year should be available for tabling in the Legislature during the next Session. This means the books are closed on December 31st. Preparation of the actual report is begun, so that it may be printed and then tabled in the Legislature during the next Session, which usually commences about mid-February.

The task was not too difficult last year, as the report covered only four months, but the 1968 report required approximately one month for printing alone, before which the statistics must be classified, the summaries written and edited, and the general remarks thought out and committed to paper.

I must confess that the preparation of this report strained our resources greatly, in view of the fact that there was approximately one month to prepare the report and have it in the hands of the printers. At the same time, we had to maintain the flow of daily work.

I therefore propose, if you agree, to terminate the working year in 1969 on the 31st October. Such termination date should give ample time for the preparation of the report and its printing, so that it could be tabled in the Legislature early in the next Session. Thereafter, the work year for the submission of the Ombudsman's report would be from November 1st to October 31st of the following year.

There is a requirement for a moderate increase in staff, which is provided for in the Estimates.

It may be two or more years before any useful average of the approximate annual number of complaints can be forecast. My Office must respond to the volume of complaints which are received. My Office should have some budgetary and staff flexibility, to deal with any sudden unpredictable increase of complaints. Such flexibility will be particularly essential during the first few formative years, until some flow of work patterns is established.

It is to be hoped that in a very few years, any increase in the volume of complaints, would reflect only the normal growth of population or new areas of Legislation.

Publicity

I have given approximately 25 public addresses on the functions and duties of the Ombudsman's Office, and I am committed for a considerable number of further talks throughout the Province in 1969.

I have given several short television interviews, and two of considerable length in Edmonton and Calgary. As time permits, I would hope to extend these talks to many other areas in the Province so that the citizens of this Province may have a better idea of the function of the Ombudsman. The complaints crossing my desk, which are completely outside my jurisdiction, indicate that there is need for such publicity.

Additionally, I attended a short Seminar of the Mid-America Assembly at the University of Saint Louis, Missouri. The subject of the Seminar was "Ombudsman for America." I was able to learn much of the problems, which must be overcome in the establishment of the Office of Ombudsman in such a highly populated country as the United States.

At the invitation of Dr. Frederick D. Lewis, Dean of the School of Law at the University of Miami, I was privileged to be the guest speaker at the School of Law Annual Alumni Breakfast during the University Homecoming Weekend. My subject was "The Work of the Ombudsman of the Province of Alberta." I had the pleasure of meeting members of the Judiciary, The University Faculty, and the State Legislature who were present.

I also lectured on the subject of the Ombudsman to a class on Government at the same University, and was privileged to sit in an afternoon discussion with members of the International Law Society of the Law School. As a result of this visit, I have been able to provide copies of The Ombudsman Act of Alberta, and my First Report, to a considerable number of interested officials who requested them.

I am receiving a fairly steady flow of requests for information concerning the work of the Ombudsman in this Province, from Universities in Canada and the United States. I have had some particular requests from Universities in the United States, where there are faculties teaching Canadian History, and the Organization and Operation of Canadian Government. I have also had requests for information and publications from legal authorities in Germany and Switzerland. There can be no doubt that interest in the role of the Ombudsman generally, is on the increase.

Legislation authorizing an Ombudsman for the Province of Quebec has been passed, although as this report is written, the position has not yet been filled. This appointment will be the third in Canada.

Acknowledgments

I have continued correspondence on matters of mutual interest with Dr. W. T. Ross Flemington, the

Ombudsman for New Brunswick. I have just recently received copies of his first report, a copy of which I have forwarded to you.

The Publicity Bureau of the Department of Industry and Tourism, has been most helpful in providing me with clippings of comment on the function of my own office, and the Ombudsman generally.

Research

The following short courses were attended by the Solicitor to the Ombudsman's Office and the Senior Investigator:

Aspects of Social Functioning: (Solicitor)
(Senior Investi-
gator)
Leadership and Supervision in (Senior Investi-
the Social Agency gator)

The modest reference library in the office is being added to, as books of particular interest become available.

As will be seen elsewhere in this report, both the Solicitor, Mr. Weir, and myself have done considerable study on the question of the detention of the person, particularly with regard to persons detained in mental hospitals, both in Alberta and elsewhere.

Legislation

The problem which was reported in my last report, whereby the Chief Justice of the Appeal Court of Alberta had held that the Workmen's Compensation Board was not an Agency of the Government, was resolved by amendment to The Ombudsman Act, passed at the last Session of the Legislature.* The amendment makes the Workmen's Compensation Board an Agency of the Government for the purposes of The Ombudsman Act.

Again this year, we have run into no serious problems in the interpretation of the existing Ombudsman Act. At the same time I would repeat what I said last year, that a number of the Sections have not as yet been thoroughly tested, and it may be that in another year, I would wish to recommend some minor amendments.

So far I have found that the present Act gives me ample scope to carry out my investigations, and as I have received full co-operation from Government Departments in most of my investigations, there has been a lack of conflicting views which might bring certain Sections of the Act under scrutiny as to their interpretation.

During the past year, my attention has been drawn on several occasions to The Administrative Procedures Act, being Chapter 1 of the Statutes of Alberta, 1966.

It is not unusual for complainants to suggest that they have had less than a fair hearing, or more often, that they have not been given sufficient reason for decisions which have been taken by an "authority" as defined in that Act.

It was, in endeavouring to ascertain what policy or statutory authority existed on these questions, that I reviewed The Administrative Procedures Act. I was particularly drawn to Sections 4, 5, 6, 7 and 8. Wider application of, and adherence to the particular Sections mentioned in the Act, by Boards, Tribunals and other authorities could, in my view, eliminate a considerable volume of the particular type of complaint referred to.

---

*Section 2(a)

In one instance, when I was informed that a certain Board did not have to give reasons for its decisions, I enquired further to ascertain to what particular "authorities" The Administrative Procedures Act applied. Section 3 of that Act reads as follows:

3. The Lieutenant-Governor in Council may, by order,
   (a) designate any authority as an authority to which this Act applies in whole or in part,
   (b) designate the statutory power of the authority in respect of which this Act applies in whole or in part, and
   (c) designate the provisions of this Act which are applicable to the authority in the exercise of that statutory power, and the extent to which they apply,

and this Act only applies to any authority to tthe extent ordered under this section.

It will be seen that the Act applies only to those "authorities" which have been particularly designated by the Lieutenant-Governor in Council. My further enquiries revealed that only one "authority" had been so designated, and that "authority" is a Board consisting of one member.

With respect, I submit that a more generous application of the provisions of this Act could have a beneficial effect in reducing the type of complaint I have referred to. It would also provide a yardstick, against which the validity of such complaints could be measured when they are received.

While perhaps not properly a matter of Legislation, I have had some cause for concern as to the manner in which Form PAO 5, Employee Performance Rating Form, is used.

This is a form which is used generally throughout the Public Service to report on the progress, ability, and performance generally of civil servants. The obvious intent of such a form is that it should be used to rate a civil servant for advancement, and as a guide to place him where his particular skills and abilities can be most useful to the overall operation of Government.

A large part of the report must be shown to the civil servant, to whom it refers, and it is required that his faults, if any, be discussed with him. He is then required to acknowledge by his signature, that he has seen the report, and to indicate whether he agrees with it or not.

In several cases, where I have received complaints that civil servants have been requested to resign, or have been discharged from the Public Service, I have asked to see the Employee Performance Rating Forms. I have been particularly interested in two such forms. These are the last one before the employee's severance from the Public Service, and another one which must be submitted immediately after his severance. He does not see the latter, nor is he required to sign it. Quite frankly, I have found these forms to be misleading at times. Employees have been asked to resign or have been discharged, in some cases abruptly. Frequently there is no reference whatsoever on the Performance Rating Form, that there was anything wrong with the employee's service.

In one instance, in answer to the question "In what parts of the job has the employee been most successful?" the answer included the very feature which had brought about the request for the resignation of that employee. Subsequent to the abrupt resignation of that employee, the final Performance Rating form was submitted. In answer to the same question, it referred the reader back to the previous comments.

In such cases, I usually find that the complaints against the employee have been made separately by letter or memorandum to his superiors by an immediate supervisor. Those remarks, however, are too often not included in the Employee Performance Rating Form.

I am, of course, well aware from my own past experience, why this difficulty arises. It is simply that immediate supervisors are most reluctant to write derogatory reports on an employee, which they must put before him for his agreement or otherwise. The practice too often is to submit an average or better Performance Rating Form, and then endeavour to unload the poor performer by separate correspondence.

Obviously one of two things must follow. Public Service employees are going to be moved into positions for which they are not qualified, or the officers of the Public Service Commission are going to place less dependence on the reliability of these reports. I suspect that the latter has already happened.

It is perhaps significant, that on one occasion when I asked a Public Servant in a supervisory capacity, how he explained the disparity between the report and the facts, he finally admitted quite honestly, that he would not have put in such a report had he known there was going to be an Ombudsman.

I have found it necessary to adopt the view that the Employee Performance Rating Form is an official Government form, authorized for use in the Public Service, and when I find that the items reported on such forms are less than accurate, I must bring such discrepancies to the attention of the Departmental head.

General Comments

The Statistics and Case Summaries for 1968 indicate that again this year, I have had to concern myself with the cases of persons detained in Alberta Mental Hospitals.

The Ombudsman's report for 1967 dealt with the case of a Penitentiary prisoner transferred to an Alberta Mental Hospital, who had been unable to enter an appeal against his detention as a mental patient or to obtain a review of his mental health, as provided for in the Alberta Mental Health Act. As a result of my investigation, the complainant was Certified under the provisions of the Alberta Mental Health Act, and advised of his right to a review. The Attorney General's Department instructed that the same procedure should apply in similar cases.

In 1968, the Ombudsman's Office dealt with a number of complaints from persons who were found "Not Guilty" of criminal charges by reason of Insanity, or Unfit to Stand Trial. These persons were subsequently detained in an Alberta Mental Hospital at the pleasure and Order of the Lieutenant-Governor of Alberta. The authority for such detention is found in the Criminal Code of Canada, a Federal Statute, enforced under the direction of the Attorney General of the Province.

Some of these persons had been detained for periods of over twenty years; in one case 27 years.

The complaints received were usually requests to be released from the Mental Hospital. However, investigation revealed that the review provisions of the Alberta Mental Health Act were not applied to such cases. The complainants had never had a review of their mental situation by any independent Committee or Commission established by law. My investigation also revealed that the complainants had almost all been charged with Murder.

My office did considerable research into the law applying to such cases. I found that a considerable number of legal opinions had been expressed, some of them a number of years ago, when concern for the treatment and civil rights of persons, such as these complainants, had not advanced to the more positive views generally recognized today. To illustrate; the former Alberta Mental Diseases Act was succeeded by the Alberta Mental Health Act on January 1st, 1965.

As a matter of policy, and in the absence of any Statutory requirement, the Department of the Attorney General has called "ad hoc" committees from time to time to make recommendation to the Lieutenant-Governor regarding the further detention or the release of persons in the position of these complainants. These committees usually consist of a Justice of the Supreme Court of Alberta, and two or more Psychiatrists. There is no Statutory requirement for the calling of such committees. It is purely a matter of policy.

It appeared to me that such committees were usually called, only where the release of the detainee was considered probable. None of the complainants who came to the Ombudsman had ever received a review from such a committee.

The person so detained, is detained at the pleasure of the Lieutenant-Governor, upon Ministerial recommendation. In some of the cases with which I have dealt, the Lieutenant-Governor, who issued the Order of detention, is no longer in office, or is deceased. That particular Lieutenant-Governor is therefore in no position to reconsider his original Order. I could find no evidence that the cases of the complainants with whom I dealt, had ever been placed before any succeeding Lieutenant-Governor by the Department of the Attorney General. So far as I have learned, no succeeding Lieutenant-Governor was ever made aware that the complainants were being detained in a Mental Hospital at his pleasure.

As there is no law requiring that the circumstances of such persons be reviewed, at regular intervals by the Lieutenant-Governor, the initiative for bringing such cases to the attention of His Honour, lies with the Department of the Attorney General. The initiative had not been taken in the cases I refer to.

People who have been found Not Guilty of any crime by Reason of Insanity, or Unfit to Stand Trial, have been detained in Mental Hospitals of this Province for periods of over 25 years.

There are approximately thirty persons of these categories still detained in Mental Hospitals of this Province, who have had no review by an independent tribunal, and whose cases, so far as I am aware, have not been brought again to the attention of the Lieutenant-Governor since their original detention.

This situation should not in any way be inferred as a criticism of the administrative or medical staff of the Hospitals. The advice which the Superintendents of the Mental Hospitals have received from the Attorney General's Department, is that they cannot release persons detained by Order of the Lieutenant-Governor, which advice they must, quite properly follow.

My further research into the laws on indeterminate detention, revealed that persons who have been convicted under the Criminal Code as Habitual Criminals, and who are sentenced, as provided for by law, to an indeterminate sentence, are protected by the Criminal Code. It provides that their detention must be reviewed once a year. No such provision is made for those who have been found Not Guilty by Reason of Insanity, or Unfit to Stand Trial.

I formed the opinion that the existing laws provide for the lawful detention of such persons. They do not provide any obligatory review, or any requirement that such detentions be referred to the Lieutenant-Governor at regular intervals thereafter.

However, in such matters, I must apply myself to the terms of The Ombudsman Act under which I operate. Section 20(1)(d) of that Act states as follows:

> This Section applies where, after
> making investigation under this Act,
> the Ombudsman is of the opinion that
> the decision, recommendation, act or
> omission that was the subject matter
> of the investigation was wrong.

The word "wrong" is not usually used in legal terminology to describe specific offences in various Statutes. They are usually referred to as being "unlawful" or "contrary to law." Indeed the same section which I have quoted, provides additionally for decisions, recommendations, acts or omissions that appear to have been "contrary to law." It would appear to me, therefore, that the words "was wrong" were intended to be viewed in a different context to the words "contrary to law."

I tried to view this whole situation through the eyes of a reasonable man, not necessarily versed in the intricacies of formal law. The Province of Alberta recently retained an authority on Corrections to survey and advise on the treatment of convicted criminals, and their rehabilitation in this Province.

I reflected on the manner in which he emphasized modern Correctional thinking. He placed great weight on rehabilitation, and was critical of the detention aspects of the system. I thought on the parallel modern approach to the treatment of those detained in Mental Hospitals, where they are now regarded as patients and not prisoners. I had personal knowledge of the constant changes in the laws, legal decisions, and the forward thinking concerned with the civil rights of the individual.

Against these yardsticks, I measured the situation whereby a person convicted of no crime, can be held in detention for periods of over twenty-five years, deprived of any lawful requirement that there ever be a review of the changes, which may have occurred in his mental health, his personality, or other conditions.

Realizing that many of these people are, and may remain psychotic, and may never be released, I faced the question of how can the public be sure that such is the case, in the absence of any independent regular Commission of review.

I must, of course, pay due regard to the law in arriving at an opinion. I am also obligated by the Act under which I work, to give full regard to its provisions, such as the Section I have quoted.

I could come to no other conclusion, but that the situation which I have described, "was wrong."

I have not been able to bring to conclusion as many investigations of complaints against the Workmen's Compensation Board as I would have liked, despite most helpful co-operation from the members of the Board, its officers and staff.

As noted elsewhere in this report, I had no jurisdiction to carry out such investigations, until the amendment to The Ombudsman Act came into force in April, 1968.

It was then necessary to make a thorough study of the whole structure and operations of the Board. These are varied and complex, involving several types of claims and varying procedures for dealing with them. The Chairman and Members of the Board spent some hours in briefing my Solicitor and me, and in answering our numerous questions.

Arrangements were made for Mr. Weir to have frequent meetings with the senior officers of the Board, while I met with the Board itself less frequently. Mr. Weir's project was to make a detailed study of procedures, and the various rights to review and appeal, provided for the workman by Statute, Regulation, or Board policy. I have had further meetings myself with the full Board.

I am satisfied that this period of study and orientation was absolutely essential, if I am to know just what measures can be taken to ensure that a complainant receives the benefit of all the medical opinions provided, and other reviews which the law provides.

It is true that the pre-study and research period, has made it necessary to hold in suspension a number of complaints, but any delay will be more than compensated for by the fact that these, and future complainants, will benefit from investigations stemming from knowledge and appreciation, of the Board's functions and responsibilities.

Our work now is increasingly directed to actual case files and this trend will continue.

Another factor has prevented complaints from being concluded. In the majority of the complaints received, enquiry has revealed that there were additional avenues of appeal available to the complainant, which he had not yet pursued. I had to decline to investigate further until he had done so.*

Most of the complainants were unaware that they had a right to a further review or appeal, and they had not been told by the Board of any further right of appeal.

I have discussed with the Board the desirability of informing an applicant, when he has been rejected, of his right of further appeal, if it exists. On occasion he was advised, but it was not mandatory to do so, and I believe that in the majority of cases, it was not done at all.

---

*Section 12(1)(a)

From our discussions, I have every reason to believe that such notification will be given in future, and that a policy instruction to this effect is being issued.

A right is provided for medical cases where the applicant may ask for a further examination under the Act.* However, the results of such an examination may not only increase the compensation paid to the applicant, but it may also leave the compensation unchanged, reduce it, or eliminate it entirely.

It has not been the practice of the Board to inform an applicant seeking such an examination, that he may lose, as well as gain, financially.

When my investigations require me to tell the complainant of his right to ask for a further investigation under the Act, I have adopted a policy of reminding him of all the consequences, and suggesting that he consult his Physician, and possibly a Solicitor, before making his decision.

Obviously, it would be most improper for me to advise him what to do in such cases. I can only tell him of the rights available to him, and decline further investigation until he has exhausted the further appeal procedure. The Ombudsman Act requires me to do this.**

I have discussed with the Board, my views that all applicants should be advised of the varying decisions which can be made as a result of such an examination, under the Section referred to.

The Board had not made a practice of so advising the applicant. The Board felt that such a letter from the Board, could be interpreted as an attempt to discourage the applicant. The matter is being reconsidered by the Board.

---

*Workmen's Compensation Act. Sec. 27.
**Section 12(1)(a)

The question of the commutation of very small monthly payments into a lump sum payment, when requested, has arisen, due to one or two complaints received. However, the Legislative Committee will be reviewing the Workmen's Compensation Act very shortly, and the question has been held over until that review is completed.

This year I carried out my first investigation "of my own motion" as provided for in the Act.* The Ombudsman initiates an investigation himself infrequently; but it is done where warranted, usually in a matter of some public concern.

This one resulted from an article carried in a weekend supplement magazine, "The Canadian." The article was very critical of detentions at the Alberta Mental Hospital at Oliver. It contained two particularly serious items alleging mistreatment of patients by the staff.

The Minister of Health denied the story to the Press.

The writer of the article, a woman, who had obtained admission to the Hospital as a voluntary patient under an assumed name, replied, according to the Press, that statements and names of her sources of information could be made available to a "responsible official."

Due to public concern, I announced that insofar as the allegations of inhumane treatment alone, were concerned, I proposed to commence an investigation. I did so, as summarized elsewhere in this report.

When my investigation concluded, the Legislature was not sitting. I forwarded my report to the Deputy Minister of Health for the information of the Minister.

---

*Section 11(2)

I had received a number of calls from relatives of patients in the particular hospital, and other similar hospitals in Alberta, who were concerned for the welfare of their relatives. Therefore, in order to allay public concern, I exercised the authority given to me by The Ombudsman Act.* I forwarded copies of my report to the news media for publication and transmission.

I have had to deal this year, with one case in which the complainant was emotionally disturbed, to a point where I felt, that if my findings were not entirely in his favour, he might take some strong measures against those he blamed for his problem.

I endeavoured to dissuade him from carrying out the threats he was making. These were plain to me, but obscure enough that I could take no action, except to persuade him.

My investigation did not support his complaint. However, I did not advise him at once for the reasons I have mentioned, and I kept in touch with him. I finally received from him, a very definite threat of a serious nature, against the persons and property of an elected representative and a senior public servant. I took discreet steps to arrange for him to be placed under medical advice. He was Certified and admitted to a mental hospital. I am advised that he has benefited greatly from the medical treatment received.

This has been a full year of experiment and development of the Ombudsman's Office. I have learned much, and have confirmed my consciousness of having much to learn. I have received very good co-operation from senior and subordinate Public Servants, representing many Departments and Agencies of the Government of this Province.

---

*Section 26(2)(b)

I have not had to exercise any of the enforcement powers provided by the Act to obtain any information or interviews I have required. There have been no cases yet which have necessitated a special report under Section 20, Subsections (4) and (5).

I have been fortunate in the efficiency and enthusiasm of my staff; the Solicitor, Mr. Alex B. Weir; the two Investigators, Mr. Ted N. Groenland and Mr. Thomas Janakas; my invaluable Secretary, Mrs. Lois Holland; and the two Stenographers, Miss Diana Gizowski and Miss Carinne Manns. Much has been required of them and they have responded cheerfully and well.

I shall be pleased to provide further information about any aspects of my work, as may be desired by the Legislature.

GEO. B. McCLELLAN,
Ombudsman.

February 1, 1969

THE OMBUDSMAN ACT 1967

Texts of Sections Referred to in
[Preceding] Summary

2. In this Act,

(a) "agency" means an agency of the Government of Alberta; and includes the Workmen's Compensation Board.

11. (1) It is the function and duty of the Ombudsman to investigate any decision or recommendation made,
including any recommendation made to a Minister, or any
act done or omitted, relating to a matter of administration and affecting any person or body of persons in
his or its personal capacity, in or by any department
or agency, or by any officer, employee or member thereof
in the exercise of any power or function conferred on
him by any enactment.

(2) The Ombudsman may make an investigation either
on a complaint made to him by any person or of his own
motion, and he may commence an investigation notwithstanding that the complaint may not on its face be
against a decision, recommendation, act or omission as
mentioned in subsection (1).

12. (1) Nothing in this Act authorizes the Ombudsman to investigate

(a) any decision, recommendation, act or omission in respect of which there is under
any Act a right of appeal or objection or
a right to apply for a review on the merits
of the case to any court or to any tribunal
constituted by or under any Act, until
after that right of appeal or objection or

application has been exercised in the particular case or until after the time prescribed for the exercise of that right has
expired, or

(b) any decision, recommendation, act or omission of any person acting as a solicitor
for the Crown or acting as counsel for the
Crown in relation to any proceedings.

(2) If any question arises as to whether the Ombudsman has jurisdiction to investigate any case or class
of cases under this Act, he may, if he thinks fit, apply
to the Supreme Court of Alberta for a declaratory order
determining the question.

14. (1) If in the course of the investigation of
any complaint it appears to the Ombudsman

(a) that under the law or existing administrative practice there is an adequate remedy,
other than the right to petition the Legislature, for the complainant, whether or not
he has availed himself of it, or

(b) that, having regard to all the circumstances of the case, any further investigation is unnecessary,
he may in his discretion refuse to investigate the
matter further.

(2) The Ombudsman may, in his discretion, refuse
to investigate or cease to investigate any complaint

(a) if it relates to any decision, recommendation, act or omission of which the complainant has had knowledge for more than
12 months before the complaint is received
by the Ombudsman, or

(b) if in his opinion,

(i) the subject matter of the complaint
is trivial, or

        (ii) the complaint is frivolous or vexatious or is not made in good faith, or

        (iii) the complainant has not a sufficient personal interest in the subject matter of the complaint.

(3) Where the Ombudsman decides not to investigate a complaint, he shall inform the complainant of his decision and he may, if he thinks fit, state his reason therefor.

20. (1) This section applies where, after making an investigation under this Act, the Ombudsman is of opinion that the decision, recommendation, act or omission that was the subject matter of the investigation

        (a) appears to have been contrary to law, or

        (b) was unreasonable, unjust, oppressive, improperly discriminatory or was in accordance with a rule of law or a provision of any Act or a practice that is or may be unreasonable, unjust, oppressive or improperly discriminatory, or

        (c) was based wholly or partly on a mistake of law or fact, or

        (d) was wrong.

(2) This section also applies where the Ombudsman is of opinion

        (a) that in the making of the decision or recommendation, or in the doing or omission of the act, a discretionary power has been exercised

            (i) for an improper purpose, or

            (ii) on irrelevant grounds, or

            (iii) on the taking into account of irrelevant considerations, or

        (b) that, in the case of a decision made in the exercise of a discretionary power, reasons should have been given for the decision.

(3) If, where this section applies, the Ombudsman is of opinion

        (a) that the matter should be referred to the appropriate authority for further consideration, or

        (b) that the omission should be rectified, or

        (c) that the decision should be cancelled or varied, or

        (d) that any practice on which the decision, recommendation, act or omission was based should be altered, or

        (e) that any law on which the decision, recommendation, act or omission was based should be reconsidered, or

        (f) that reasons should have been given for the decision, or

        (g) that any other steps should be taken, the Ombudsman shall report his opinion and his reasons therefor to the appropriate Minister and to the department or agency concerned, and may make such recommendations as he thinks fit and in that case he may request the department or agency to notify him within a specified time of the steps, if any, that it proposes to take to give effect to his recommendations.

(4) If within a reasonable time after the report is made no action is taken which seems to the Ombudsman to be adequate and appropriate, the Ombudsman, in his discretion, after considering the comments, if any, made by or on behalf of the department or agency affected, may send a copy of the report and recommendations to the Lieutenant-Governor in Council and may thereafter make such report to the Legislature on the matter as he thinks fit.

(5) The Ombudsman shall attach to every report sent or made under subsection (4) a copy of any comments made by or on behalf of the department or agency concerned.

(6) Notwithstanding anything in this section, the Ombudsman shall not, in any report made under this Act, make any comment that is adverse to any person unless the person has been given an opportunity to be heard.

26. (2) The Ombudsman may from time to time, in the public interest or in the interests of any person or department or agency publish reports relating

> (b) to any particular case investigated by him, whether or not the matters to be dealt with in any such report have been the subject of a report to the Legislature.

APPENDIX III

Annual Reports of the Commissioner of Accounts County of Nassau

July 1, 1966–June 30, 1967
July 1, 1967–December 31, 1967

Samuel B. Greason
Commissioner

APPENDIX III

Contents

125

COUNTY OF NASSAU

INTER-DEPARTMENTAL MEMO

To   :   County Executive Eugene H. Nickerson

From   :   Commissioner of Accounts Samuel Greason

Subject: Annual Report: July 1, 1966 - June 30, 1967

Submitted herewith is the annual report of my office as Commissioner of Accounts and 'defacto' Public Protector, for the period of July 1, 1966 to June 30, 1967.

To date my office has processed 470+ matters. For the first six months subsequent to my designation as the Commissioner of Accounts, slightly less than 30 matters per month were processed. In the last six months, the number of complaints and matters investigated have averaged in excess of 50 per month.

I am sure that as the residents of Nassau County become more familiar with the scope of the anticipated and projected aims of this office of Public Protector; viz., to protect the public and the individual citizen against inefficiency, maladministration, arrogance, abuse and other failures of government, and to encourage sound and fair administration in the public interest-- my duties and responsibilities and the number of matters handled by my office will continue to increase.

Matters received from the public have involved practically every department or agency of the County: the three towns, the two cities, Glen Cove and Long Beach; villages and certain special districts within the Towns.

Matters outside the jurisdiction of my office have
been referred to agencies under the jurisdiction of
Federal and State government and to the Better Business
Bureau and the Grievance Committee of the Nassau County
Bar Association. There were 48 complaints regarding
the courts. While I have no jurisdiction with respect
to matters concerning the courts within Nassau County,
I did spend considerable time and effort with those
persons in an attempt to maintain or restore their confidence in the Judiciary.

I have estimated that, excluding those matters
which are outside the jurisdiction of my office and all
complaints concerning the Welfare Department, approximately 20% of all such complaints are justified and my
office succeeded in obtaining remedial action. Almost
all Welfare complaints had some basis and justification.

I have made certain recommendations to you through
the office of the County Attorney, as to proposed amendments in the Nassau County Charter and the Administrative Code, when it appeared such amendments were necessary.

Not only have all County departments and agencies
been most cooperative, but the towns, villages and
cities, including elected officials, have also fully
cooperated.

It may be of interest that the operations of this
office, the first Public Protector in local government
in the United States, have been and are being studied
by leading universities and by city and state representatives, who contemplate proposed legislation creating an
office similar to that of the Nassau County Public Protector.

Representatives of the United States Health, Education and Welfare Department have made an evaluation of
the workings of my office in connection with complaints
affecting the Nassau County Welfare Department, with a

view towards determining the possibility of creating a
post of Public Protector.

I. PROPOSED AMENDMENTS TO THE NASSAU COUNTY CHARTER AND ADMINISTRATIVE CODE

Foreclosure of Tax Liens

In five cases processed by this office, the owner
of record of real property has stated that he has
received no Notice to Redeem and he received no actual
notice that the property would be foreclosed for failure
to pay tax liens.

Those persons who have failed to pay one of the
several taxes imposed in this County are, by and large,
those persons who have been accustomed to paying taxes
to the bank holding their mortgages, and who are semi-
literate.

In at least two instances to date, the Treasurer's
office has accepted affidavits which show, on the face,
that the claimed Notice given to the property owner was
mailed to an incorrect address.

Section 5-51.0 of the Nassau County Administrative
Code requires a person foreclosing his tax lien, to
state under oath, that a Notice to Redeem was mailed to
the property owner. On January 23, 1967, I advised the
County Attorney's office that, in my opinion, the Code
should be amended to:

a. Require adequate proof as to the mailing of
the Notice to Redeem and its receipt by the
tax delinquent. For example: a receipt from
the Post Office indicating that said Notice
was sent registered or certified mail.

b. That where there has been actual delivery of the Notice to Redeem, there be a requirement that the return receipt be affixed to and made part of the affidavit.

In at least one instance, it appears that the purchaser of the tax lien used a fictitious name and address. Under the law as it exists today, there is no responsibility on the County Treasurer to inquire into the nature of the interest in the property of a person who seeks to foreclose a tax lien, other than for the Treasurer to examine and satisfy himself that the individual has complied with all of the requirements of the Notice of Redemption.

The County Attorney's office has indicated to me that it would be advisable to amend the Code to require an affidavit showing the identity of the purchaser of the tax lien and his address, together with proof of actual service of the Notice to Redeem on the owner of record.

I have noted also, in examining certain files from the Treasurer's office, that the affidavits submitted by the small group, who seem to specialize in profiteering on such tax liens, from time to time include in one affidavit, multiple listings of individuals to whom they mailed the required Notice affecting many parcels of property. In my judgment, a separate affidavit should be required with respect to each parcel of property.

My office is now consulting with Mr. Portela, Mr. Edel and Deputy County Attorney Weil, and all three agree that in those instances where a defect appears on the Notice to Redeem, the Treasurer's office should have the power to revoke or cancel the tax deed. I understand that as far back as 1957, the last time this problem was brought to the attention of the Treasurer, the Treasurer's office attempted by persuasion, to induce the owner of the tax deed to sign a quit claim deed to the owner of record and/or agree to revocation of his tax deed, notably without success.

There is no power in the County to take any legal
action on its own to nullify the tax deed issued in
error by the Treasurer's office, but I have been informed
that in an Article 78 proceeding, commenced at the
expense of the owner of record, the Treasurer will
stipulate in court that his office issued the deed in
error.

Within the past few days, I have interviewed a
gentleman with little knowledge of English who finds
himself in the position of being asked to pay $2,000.00
in legal fees in a proceeding to cancel such a Treasurer's deed. This responsibility should be that of
the County and I can't help but conclude that defective
Notices to Redeem are very common.

II. NASSAU COUNTY PLANNING COMMISSION

A. Amendment of Section 1610, Subdivision 5 of
the County Government Law of Nassau County

In connection with my investigation of the circumstances surrounding the approval of the Planning Commission of the application of Lawrence Country Estates
as to the map of Riviera Shores, Section 3A, I made
specific recommendations to the Planning Commission and
the County Attorney as to amending Section 1610, Subdivision 5 of the County Government Law. The Planning
Commission had originally refused approval of the application after holding extensive hearings, which were
attended by taxpayer complainants of the Merrick and
Bellmore area. The applicant thereafter commenced an
Article 78 proceeding in Nassau County Supreme Court
and the proceeding was thereafter transferred to the
Appellate Division, which in the summer of 1966, unanimously affirmed the decision of the Planning Commission.
Thereafter, Lawrence Country Estates, Inc., submitted
an amended application to the Planning Commission, dif-
fering from the original in that the developer agreed
to execute covenants not to build on the seven (7)
northerly plots along Cedar Swamp Channel until sewers

132

were installed. The Planning Commission held hearings
on the application, but no notice, other than the public
notice, was given to aggrieved taxpayers, including
those who had previously testified against the application.

Upon investigation as to the failure to notify
adjacent taxpayers, I learned that the assessment or
tax rolls, in many instances, do not show the address
of the record owner, but rather the address of the bank
holding a mortgage on such property. I concluded that
while notices might be mailed to bank mortgagees, in
many instances the owner of record of the property
received either a late notice, or no notice at all. As
a result, they were unaware of the application. On
June 19, 1967, the County Attorney submitted to me a
copy of the proposed Local Law amending the County Government Law as to notification to adjoining landowners
of a hearing by the Planning Commission on the approval
of a plat.

B. Town of Hempstead, United States Army Engineers

The taxpayers who complained with respect to the
actions of the Planning Commission as outlined above,
also complained as to the Town of Hempstead and the
Army Corps of Engineers with respect to dredging in
Cedar Swamp Creek by the Fort Neck Dredging Company.

My investigation disclosed that the Town of Hempstead approved the dredging of the channel 100 feet
wide and 4 feet deep, by resolution adopted on March 29,
1966. The Town of Hempstead at that time did not consider that approval of the Department of Army Engineers
was required to do the dredging that was actually performed. The Corps of Engineers agreed with my recommendation that Lawrence Country Estates, Inc., be compelled to apply for Army approval of plans showing the
extent of the dredging together with a proposed bulk-
head. Public notice, as well as actual notice should

be sent to all interested parties concerning the application.

It was my conclusion that much of the difficulties and complaints surrounding the dredging stem from a misunderstanding as to the extent of jurisdiction of the Department of the Army over the navigable waters in the Town of Hempstead. The Army Engineers and the Town will, in the future, develop a mutual exchange of information whenever work is proposed to be undertaken in navigable waters within the limits of the Town. In the future, the Town Board of Hempstead, in approving work or structures in Town navigable waters, will require verification that the approval of all concerned government agencies is secured before a Town permit is issued for any dredging work. In my opinion, such a procedure will make it unlikely that a similar situation will occur again.

It is interesting to note that in connection with this investigation, it was necessary for me to satisfy myself that the approval by the Planning Commission of the application of Lawrence Estates did not add to the pollution difficulties in the waters of Cedar Swamp Creek. I received full cooperation from the Board of Health, who made a complete and detailed study of the pollution and, who also made available to me, all prior data as to testings conducted by that department. It was also necessary for my office to request reports from the New York State Department of Conservation, from the Town of Hempstead Conservation Department; to maintain liaison with Congressman Tenzer concerning proposed federal legislation on this subject, [with] the Nassau County Department of Public Works and the County Attorney's Office.

III.   [WELFARE MATTERS]

As you will note from the statistical data submitted to you in this annual report, complaints regarding

Welfare matters comprise basically 15% of the matters handled by this office.

Among the items which gave me the greatest personal satisfaction were the following:

[1] Nassau County Pulmonary Hospital--I had received a request for aid from a T.B. patient in the hospital who had absolutely no funds. He pointed out to me that he was compelled to wear hand-me-down clothes which did not fit him--that he found it necessary to borrow a newspaper--and, in fact, to borrow the ten cents it took for his initial call to my office. The Welfare Department at first ruled that, with respect to [the] Aid to Disabled category, public assistance to a person in this hospital was prohibited and that in the past, no assistance had been granted to any patient in such a facility. Subsequent discussion and negotiation resulted in a conclusion that since the hospital is at present time not confined to Tuberculosis treatment, the Welfare Department is now permitted by law to furnish financial assistance in the form of an allowance for clothing and personal incidentals.

[2] In connection with aid to dependent children, it was the custom of our County Welfare Department to require a deed or mortgage from a Welfare recipient after receiving Welfare for ninety (90) days. I had presented to me, certain cases of personal heartbreak wherein a parent preferred to deprive her family of absolute necessities, rather than to comply with this regulation. I have since been informed by the Welfare Department that this demand for a deed or mortgage will not be required in the future insofar as aid to dependent children is concerned.

[3] My office has been instrumental in alerting the Welfare Department to the personal problems of businessmen, such as druggists and nurses, to whom payment is due for services under Medicaid. While it is impossible to eliminate all delays, because of the

tremendous volume of claims, I have concluded that the
Welfare Department is taking steps necessary to curtail,
as much as possible, excessive delays in reimbursements.
Other claims for payment by dealers furnishing oil or
other necessities to Welfare recipients, have been
speeded up, eliminating credit crises to the oil
dealers.

[4] From time to time, I have had problems con-
front me that required working with both the County
Welfare Department and the Social Security Bureau in
Mineola. I found, on occasion, that elderly persons
were unwilling to take advantage of certain medical
insurance provisions under federal law because it would
mean a $3.00 a month deduction from their Welfare pay-
ments. Through my office and that of the Welfare
Department, we are succeeding in making known to these
individuals that the Welfare Department will reimburse
them for the $3.00 monthly payment required.

Another striking example was that dealing with two
children, approximately 10 and 12 years of age, who
were orphaned in July 1966. A young couple, with three
children of their own, had been feeding the two children
and generally looking after them, while their mother
was dying in New York City. All concerned, at that
time, were residents of the City. The mother died in
or about August 1966, at a time when the young couple
had just completed a purchase of a home in Nassau
County. The orphans had no relatives. The couple
assumed personal responsibility for the two children,
brought them to Nassau County, and in the period of
the next seven months, incurred heavy financial expense
because of the need to enlarge their home and the need
to acquire a larger automobile, since their Volkswagon,
while satisfactory for five, could not seat seven. In
March, 1967, they approached my office in desperation.
Their personal resources had been exhausted and their
application for Social Security Death Benefits for the
two orphaned children had been snarled in red tape and
they had not obtained Welfare assistance for Aid to

Needy Children. Due to the complete cooperation of the
Director of Social Security for Nassau and Suffolk
Counties, the application was expedited and Social
Security benefits were received by the children.

The Welfare Department had originally regarded the
two orphans as the responsibility of New York City, but
it did comply with my request to render emergency assistance financially from the standpoint of food and clothing, until payments due from Social Security were
received. We located two bank accounts, which the
deceased mother had kept for the two children, (Totten
Trusts), each in the amount of approximately $1,000.00.

It is my hope that the children can now be raised
with a normal home life, rather than be placed in an
orphanage, which seemed to be the only alternative when
this problem was first brought to the attention of my
office.

[5] In another case involving an orphan, I was
requested by the 11 year old boy's godmother to assist
in effecting his adoption. This Negro woman and the
boy had a relationship similar to that of a natural
mother and son. For over two years, the woman had been
receiving payments from the Welfare Department for the
boy's support and, during most of that period, she had
been requesting of Welfare permission to adopt the Welfare client. I referred this woman to a private attorney and, with the cooperation of the Welfare Department,
I have offered him the full assistance of my office to
effect this adoption.

[6] In the latter part of 1966, I met with a
delegation of twenty or more residents of Long Beach,
together with the President of the local NAACP and the
"Can-Do" representative. I found that five of the six
individual complaints concerning the Welfare Department
were justified and remedial steps were taken. I brought
to the attention of the Welfare Commissioner complaints
regarding arrogance and delay and also brought to the

attention of the City and school authorities of Long
Beach complaints with respect to housing and certain
personnel conditions within the school district. I
have since been advised that the minority groups in
Long Beach have confidence in my office and are now
convinced, while not entirely satisfied with the results,
that the City of Long Beach and the Long Beach School
District are attempting to resolve housing and school
complaints.

[7] In the course of my investigation of
Mr. Purcell's charges involving the Economic Opportunity
Council groups, I have had occasion to speak with representatives of the "Poverty Target Area," consisting of
ten districts within the County of Nassau. I am sub-
mitting a separate report to you on this investigation.
It is my belief that this investigation will correct an
impression that the workings of my office are not known
to those within the poverty area. Since the investigation has commenced, I have been asked by Poverty representatives of the Roosevelt area to bring to your attention, and that of Mr. Caso, Supervisor of the Town of
Hempstead, the need for a Community Center in the
Roosevelt area. I have assured the group that you and
Mr. Caso would give serious consideration to their
request. I have urged them to submit to me their proposals, which I will, in turn, submit to you and
Mr. Caso.

IV.   JUDICIAL REVIEW OF ACTIONS OF COUNTY ADMINISTRATIVE
      AGENCIES

In reviewing the determination of certain administrative bodies, it was brought to my attention that
under our present County Government Law, a review of
the determination must go directly to the Appellate
Division.

I have noted in several instances that taxpayers,
with what appear to be legitimate complaints as to

determination of administrative agencies, are hesitant
to challenge the validity of the actions in our courts
because of the legal expense involved. Any matter which
must be reviewed by the Appellate Division directly,
will justify an attorney in asking for a fee which is
out of the reach of the majority of taxpayers.

I recommended to the County Attorney that consideration be given to amending the County Government Law, in
order to confer upon Special Term of the Supreme Court,
the right to determine whether the evidence supports the
finding of the administrative agency. It was my thought
that the County Government Law might include a provision
similar to that of 267(7) of the Town law and 179(B) of
the Village law.

The County Attorney disagrees with me on the ground
that when a quasi judicial body makes a determination,
it should be reviewed by the Appellate Division in the
first instance.

I would respectfully call your attention to a
recent case, that of Hansen against Baer, published in
the New York Law Journal on May 25, 1967, page 19, in
which Mr. Justice Meyer pointed out that the Board of
Assessors did not make or set forth specific reasons in
the particular decision, despite the rule of law that
an administrative body must make findings of fact. The
learned court further pointed out that the taxpayer had
requested a variance, which the Board is permitted to
grant, and in its determination, the Board of Assessors
made no reference to the request for the variance. I
drew an inference from Mr. Justice Meyer's decision
that the determination of the Board of Assessors will
be reversed by the Appellate Division, or at least,
would have been reversed by him, had he the power to
act. If I am correct in my conclusion, it may well be
that another six months will go by before the complaining taxpayer has a decision on his application.

V. NASSAU COUNTY PROBATION DEPARTMENT

In many cases, particularly those in District Court criminal matters, a judge, in imposing sentence, will place a defendant on probation with the condition that he pay over to the victim of the crime, through the Probation Department, certain amounts of money.

It is the custom of the Probation Department to retain the moneys paid over by the defendant until payment in full is received, at which time, a check is transmitted to the victim of the crime. On some occasions, two years or more go by before the amount is paid in full.

I have had several instances during the past year wherein a dire need was proven by the victim for payments of moneys collected to date by the Probation Department. In each such instance, Mr. Milone, Director of the Nasau County Probation Department, has cooperated with me and forwarded to the victim of the crime the amounts of money collected to date.

VI. CHILDREN'S SHELTER

A touching complaint regarding the management of the Shelter was that of a Nassau County employee against the Director of the Shelter for what appeared to be an arbitrary refusal to admit this grandfather to visit his emotionally disturbed grandchild. Through the cooperation of the authorities of the Family Court, I was successful in resolving what appeared to be a personality conflict between the complainant and the Shelter Director.

VII.   COMPTROLLER--SPECIAL DISTRICTS

My office reviewed over fifty reports of examination by the State of New York, Department of Audit and Control, Division of Municipal Affairs. With respect to the review of the reports of special districts, I have noted that surplus funds in non-interest bearing accounts and unspent funds are accumulating to such an extent, that a suggestion had been made by the Auditor that taxes be reduced, or the budget be decreased. There are reports of what appear to be a failure to comply with the law concerning purchases and competitive bidding. One matter was referred to the District Attorney for possible prosecution.

The reports of the State Department of Audit and Control have been physically delivered to the Nassau County Comptroller. Under Section 402 of the County Government Law of Nassau County:

> The Comptroller shall.... 6--Examine
> and audit of his own motion or when
> directed to do so by resolution of
> the Board of Supervisors, the accounts
> and records of any Town or Special
> District and make reports from time
> to time when requested by the County
> Executive or Board of Supervisors
> on the financial condition of the
> County or any or all of its politi-
> cal subdivisions.

GENERAL COMMENTS

In approximately thirty-five of the investigations conducted by my office during the first year, it was necessary to get in touch with both a County agency and an agency of a town, village or city, in an attempt to resolve a particular complaint.

[1]   For example, on page[s 131-133]...of this report is set forth the details of my investigation with respect to the Planning Commission of Nassau County and the Town of Hempstead in connection with complaints made as to the Planning Commission's approval of a map of Riviera Shores in Bellmore, and the Town of Hempstead granting a dredging permit to the Fort Neck Dredging Company. In that case, not only was the Planning Commission involved, but also the County Department of Public Works and the County Board of Health, in addition to the New York Department of Conservation, the Town of Hempstead Conservation Department, the United States Army Engineers and the Nassau County Attorney's Office.

[2]   In a complaint concerning approval of plans by the Planning Commission of Nassau County and the Village of Bayville, it was necessary to review the records and obtain information not only from those particular agencies, but also the Town of Oyster Bay as well. It would appear that taxpayers' complaints concerning accumulation of water on their private property from the West Harbor development in Bayville, was resolved with the Nassau County Planning Commission adopting a resolution on May 4, 1967, requiring the developer to construct dry-wells to alleviate the flooding conditions north of this development.

[3]   Concerning the complaint of owners and operators of cranes: it was brought to my attention that the Police Department has for years been issuing summonses to owners and operators of cranes and overweight vehicles, citing them for violation of law for operation of such cranes to town highways without a permit from the particular town. The courts, thereafter, levied fines for a first violation of $100.00, increasing the penalty to $250.00 for each subsequent violation, and marked the driver's license to reflect

the particular violation. Investigation disclosed that there was no procedure set forth within any one of the three towns whereby the owner of such a crane or overweight vehicle could obtain the permit referred to in Section 385 of the Vehicle and Traffic Law of the State of New York, permitting use of town roads. With the cooperation of each of the Town Attorneys, a procedure has since been instituted whereby a town application permit system was instituted pursuant to Subdivision 17 of Section 385 of the Vehicle and Traffic Law.

[4] A delegation representing the South Village Green Defense Committee of the Village of Levittown complained with respect to the Nassau County Police Department and the Town of Hempstead concerning conditions at the South Village Green in Levittown.

Cooperation by the Nassau County Police Department and the Town of Hempstead resulted in a more intense enforcement of the law, cleaning of litter, boarding up of buildings, etc. While conditions at the South Village Green are not ideal at the present time, there has been a great deal of improvement. It is anticipated that the Town of Hempstead will sell a portion of the Town-owned land adjacent to the abandoned shopping center to a builder who plans to erect seventy-five units of garden apartments at that particular location.

[5] A complaint from a representative of an organization within the Town of North Hempstead concerned itself with the following agencies: Nassau County Board of Elections, Nassau County Planning Commission, Town of North Hempstead and the Town of Hempstead.

As to the complaint concerning the Planning Commission, the Town of Hempstead and the Town of North Hempstead, investigation disclosed that the taxpayer was justified in his criticism of the towns as to their failure to file certain zoning ordinances with the Nassau County Planning Commission as required by Section 1608 of the County Charter.

The complaint also dealt with the operation of a taxi business at 245-04 Pembroke Avenue, Little Neck, New York. This property is on the boundary line of New York City and that of the Town of North Hempstead. Investigation disclosed that both the radio and callbox used by the taxi company are within the boundaries of New York City. The Borough Superintendent of the Department of Buildings in Queens County informed me that the use of a telephone and short-wave radio are not in themselves a violation of the laws coming under the jurisdiction of the New York City Department of Buildings. The presence of a structural radio tower located on the roof, partly in Queens County, resulted in a violation being placed against the owner of the property by the City of New York.

While the parking and/or storage of commercial vehicles might result in action being taken by New York City under its zoning resolution, it appears that such parking is not in violation of the Town of North Hempstead parking ordinances. The Police Commissioner of Nassau County has been requested to investigate the charge that repairs of the cars are being undertaken at the Little Neck address and to advise this office whether or not the cars are being parked in violation of existing Town of Hempstead ordinances.

In a complaint from certain residents of the Village of Freeport, this office attempted to coordinate the actions of the Nassau County Attorney's Office, the Village of Freeport Attorney's Office, the Nassau County Department of Public Works and the Freeport Department of Public Works. That matter dealt with the Village of Freeport's desire to complete certain work in connection with a change of grade and improvement on South Main Street. The Nassau County Department of Public Works had indicated its willingness to undertake the work requested by the Village of Freeport, but in accord with practices established within the Nassau County Attorney's Office, waivers of payment and releases were required of the property owners involved. Unfortunately, to date, not all of the taxpayers have been agreeable to signing the required waivers.

The statistical breakdown herein reflects the number of complaints filed with my office concerning agencies of towns, cities and villages, as well as special districts. Each complaint was thoroughly investigated and to each complainant, the matter involved was most serious, including dredging and highway problems, complaints of harassment by building inspectors, selective enforcement of zoning laws, etc.

I have attempted to make this report as concise as is possible, but I can, if you wish, provide you with the details of the approximately 475 matters processed by my office during its first year in operation.

I feel that each complainant, or person with a problem, has been courteously received and listened to. In the great majority of cases, we have been able to solve the troubles.

Where it has been impossible, because of limitations on my powers, to fully investigate or obtain a solution of the problem, the complainant, in every case, has expressed keen satisfaction in having been given an opportunity to voice his problem, and having been listened to with understanding and sympathy.

Samuel Greason
Commissioner

STATISTICAL ANALYSIS OF CASES

NASSAU COUNTY DEPARTMENTS*

No. of Cases

Board of Assessors
A. Overassessments 3
B. Exemptions 4
C. Improper Notices 1
D. Miscellaneous 2 — 10

Civil Service Commission	9
Comptroller	2
County Attorney	17
County Clerk	7
County Executive	1
County Sealer	2
Board of Elections	1
Department of Franchise	1
Fire Marshal	3
Health Department	12
Meadowbrook Hospital	6
Human Rights Commission	4
Central Library	1
Office of Administrative Services	1
Office of Economic Opportunity	1
Planning Commission	8

*In a number of matters, more than one agency is involved, and/or more than one municipality.

No. of Cases

Police Department
A. Arrogance Complaints	1	
B. Brutality Complaints	2	
C. False Arrest	1	
D. Violation of Civil Rights	2	
E. Missing Persons	3	
F. Traffic Surveys	4	
G. Traffic Regulations	11	
H. Harassment by Neighbors	5	
I. Inadequate Protection	5	
J. Animal Nuisances	3	
K. Lack of Enforcement of Ordinances	8	
L. Miscellaneous	7	52

Probation Department	3
Department of Public Works	20
Board of Supervisors	2
Treasurer's Office	4

Welfare Department
A. Medicaid	15	
B. Commercial	4	
C. Recipients Eligibility	4	
D. Recipients Request for Funds	22	
E. Housing	14	
F. Personnel	4	
G. Adoptions	2	
H. Abandonment	4	69

Total Nassau County Cases	236

	No. of Cases	
TOWN GOVERNMENT		
TOWN OF HEMPSTEAD		
Animal Shelter	3	
Building Department	12	
Comptroller	2	
Conservation Department	1	
Highway Department	14	
Parks Department	4	
Public Works Department	8	
Receiver of Taxes	2	
Sanitation Department	2	
Town Attorney	7	
Board of Zoning Appeals	7	
Miscellaneous	_3_	
[Total Town of Hempstead Cases]		65
TOWN OF NORTH HEMPSTEAD		
Building Department	6	
Highway Department	3	
Town Board	7	
Public Works	1	
Town Attorney	5	
Board of Zoning Appeals	_5_	
[Total Town of North Hempstead Cases]		27

TOWN OF OYSTER BAY	No. of Cases	
Animal Shelter	1	
Building Department	7	
Civil Service	1	
Highway Department	6	
Town Board	8	
Town Attorney	7	
Board of Zoning Appeals	3	
[Total Town of Oyster Bay Cases]		33
VILLAGE GOVERNMENT		
Village Boards	5	
Urban Renewal	1	
Fire Departments	1	
Building Departments	11	
Police Departments	4	
Boards of Zoning Appeals	4	
[Total Village Government Cases]		26
CITY GOVERNMENT		
LONG BEACH		
Courts	3	
Building Department	3	
Police Department	2	
Health Department	1	
School System	1	
[Total Long Beach Cases]		10

SPECIAL DISTRICTS		No. of Cases	
Garbage Districts		3	
Water Districts		_2_	
[Total Special District Cases]			5
FIRE DISTRICTS		2	
SCHOOL DISTRICTS		12	
COURTS			
Appellate Division		1	
Judicial Conference		2	
Nassau Supreme, County and District			
A. Unsuccessful litigants	42		
B. Operation of Court	_3_	45	
Family Court		9	
Grand Jury		3	
Marshal		1	
District Attorney			
A. Complaints	12		
B. Referred by District Attorney	3		
C. Referred to District Attorney	_2_	_17_	
[Total Court Cases]			78

UNITED STATES GOVERNMENT	[No. of Cases] Referred by this Office
Administrator of Legal Services	1
U. S. Army Corps of Engineers	3
Office of Economic Opportunity	1
Law Services Committee	2

	No. of Cases Referred by this Office
Congressional Representatives	2
Post Office	2
Small Business Administration	1
Social Security	2
[Total United States Government Cases]	14
NEW YORK STATE GOVERNMENT	
Attorney General	5
Board of Regents	1
Governor	5
Insurance Department	4
Labor Board	1
Mental Health Board	1
Motor Vehicle Bureau	6
Assemblyman	1
Parole Board	2
Public Service Commission	3
Public Utilities	7
Department of State	1
Tax Commission	1
Waterfront Commission	1
[Total New York State Government Cases]	39

		No. of Cases Referred by this Office
NON-GOVERNMENTAL MATTERS		
Attorneys	7	
Nassau County Bar Association	13	
Better Business Bureau	8	
Judicial Inquiry	10	
Legal Aid Society	14	
Public Defender	2	
Utilities	3	
[Total Non-Governmental Matters]		57
[Total Non-County Cases		368]
[Total Cases		604]

COUNTY OF NASSAU

INTER-DEPARTMENTAL MEMO

To   :   County Executive Eugene H. Nickerson

From   :   Commissioner of Accounts Samuel Greason

Subject: Semi-Annual Report: July 1, 1967 -
           December 31, 1967

Submitted herewith is the semi-annual report of
the Commissioner of Accounts for the period July 1, 1967
through December 31, 1967.

For this six months, July 1, 1967 to December 31,
1967, my office has processed 360+ matters. In this
six months, the number of complaints received and processed have averaged approximately sixty per month.

The proposition submitted to the people in the
November 7, 1967 election to establish the office of
Public Protector was rejected by the voters, although
both major political parties had agreed on the compromise proposition to be submitted.

In addition to the vociferous opposition by the
Police Department, based on a total misunderstanding of
what the bill and proposition sought to accomplish, and
despite distribution of approximately a half-a-million
sample ballots in the Town of Hempstead by the Town
Committee of the Republican Party urging the defeat of
the proposed State Constitution, the proposed Nassau
County Charter and the proposed Public Protector bill,
it is believed the main reason for the defeat of the
proposition was that very few people in the County of
Nassau knew what the proposed Public Protector bill
sought to accomplish.

Despite the rejection of the Public Protector system by the voters in November of 1967, it is interesting to note that delegations from as far as Tokyo, Japan, have called at this office to learn how the office operated in its Public Protector aspect, and Public Protector agencies are being set up now in Hawaii and in many cities across the United States.

Notwithstanding the general lack of knowledge on the part of the public, the monthly average of cases brought to the attention of the Commissioner of Accounts' office has increased to approximately sixty per month.

Complaints and matters received from members of the public have involved most of the departments and agencies of the County and of the three towns. Other matters involving the two cities, the villages and certain special districts within the towns have been received and processed on the theory that, while the Office has no authority to investigate matters involving the cities and villages, the officials would prefer to know of complaints and strive to eradicate the causes. Many matters referred to my office involved agencies of the Federal and State governments and have been handled with those agencies. Matters have also been referred to the Better Business Bureau, though the establishment of the Office of Consumer Affairs in September of 1967 resulted in many referrals of complaints to that County agency. Complaints involving lawyers were referred either to the Judicial Inquiry or the Grievance Committee of the Nassau County Bar Association.

The establishment of an investigating group in the Social Services Department has enabled that Department to take care of many complaints that would otherwise have been referred to the Commissioner of Accounts.

All County departments and agencies, as well as the governmental agencies of the towns, have been fully cooperative.

The amendment suggested to the Nassau County
Charter, relative to the notices required in the foreclosure of tax liens has been passed and approved by
the Board of Supervisors and is now in full force and
effect. It is believed that the rights of the owners
in default in the payment of taxes will be much more
adequately protected and will lead to fewer foreclosures
of tax liens. In this connection, I wish to express the
appreciation of my office to the office of the County
Treasurer, the Board of Tax Assessors and the County
Attorney's Office for their full cooperation and assistance.

This office has handled several complaints involving
foreclosure of tax liens and has discovered failures on
the part of the purchasers of the tax liens to properly
comply with the law insofar as giving notice to redeem.
We were thus able to assist the attorney for the owner
whose property had been sold at a tax sale, in the speedy
redemption of the property on payment of the arrears in
taxes with interest.

The only complaint involving police brutality was
made within the past few days and involved a complaint
made by a citizen against a policeman in a village
police department. The facts in this case indicated
that the complainant was planning to visit his son in
the village, but was not quite sure of the location of
his home. When he got to the street where the son
lived, he spoke to two young children on the porch of
a house and was told his son lived further down the
street. Apparently, the father of the two children,
a police officer in the village police department,
ordered the complainant, who is suffering from emphysema,
onto the porch, interrogated him, maltreated him and
eventually dragged him down to the police station where
he further beat him up and maltreated him. The police
officer obtained some sort of statement from the complainant, which the complainant said he was not allowed
to read and does not know what the contents were. The
police officer then took the defendant home and told

him to forget the whole thing. He was not arrested and no charges were made against him. He was advised to see the police surgeon of the village, who gave him a thorough examination, took x-rays and informed him that he had a cracked rib. After treatment and x-rays in one hospital, he was then released and sent to Meadowbrook Hospital.

This complainant was advised that, as this is a village matter, the Commissioner of Accounts could not interfere and conduct any investigation. It was suggested to him that his attorney could submit the matter to the District Attorney and, in addition, could bring a civil suit for assault against both the village and the individual police officer.

A complaint was received involving the claim of inadequate police protection in the Malverne Oaks area of West Hempstead. There had apparently been several burglaries in the neighborhood. When the complaint was forwarded to the Police Department, we were informed that within a few days an arrest had been made in connection with the burglaries and additional police protection had been accorded.

We received a complaint from a homeowner alleging that he was being bothered with noises late at night by teenagers drinking in cars and throwing cans and bottles on his lawn. He also claimed that the teenagers were drinking in two alleged discotheques. The Police Department satisfactorily took care of this complaint regarding throwing of bottles and cans on the complainant's lawn, but were not able to do anything about the complaint with reference to teenagers frequenting places which should have cabaret licenses, inasmuch as these places were controlled by the village and not by the town or County.

A complaint was received regarding drag racing on one of the streets in Uniondale. The complaint was forwarded to the Police Department, which immediately augmented its regular police patrol and also patrolled with

an unmarked car. The complainants were appreciative of
the quick response of the Police Department to their
complaint.

Many cases have been interesting. One involved
the complaint of a citizen in the Town of Hempstead who
had complained that when his driveway apron was to be
repaved, he refused to have it repaved with asphalt and
insisted upon having cement concrete. The result was
that the complainant's driveway was left unpaved. The
complainant was straightened out as to his <u>rights</u> and
his <u>obligations</u>.

Another complaint involved the Board of Fire Underwriters, the Long Island Lighting Company and the
Building Department of one of the towns. In this case,
the complainant stated that a heating unit had been
installed with an electric heating system. The company
that installed the electric heating system had partici-
pated in advertising with the Long Island Lighting Company on the particular type of unit. While the New York
Board of Fire Underwriters inspected the unit and a
Certificate of Compliance was issued, the heating unit
itself apparently did not have the Underwriters' labora-
tory label. After negotiations extending over many
months, the heating boiler was replaced with an improved
boiler. In this particular matter we were dealing with
a public service corporation and not with a County or
town agency.

Another complaint involved the enforcement by the
town of zoning regulations against one gas and service
station and the ignoring of the violations of ordinances
by five other service stations. When this was brought
to the attention of the Town Department of Engineering,
a complete investigation disclosed that the allegations
of the complainant were correct and proceedings were
brought to correct the violations.

A complaint involved the dredging of certain areas.
The dredging operation permitted a portion of the fill
to overflow the dike and create sand bars in the creek

and also prohibited boats from entering and leaving a marina. After an inspection, the town had their dredge take out the sand bars and restore the conditions that made it possible for the marina to operate.

A complaint involving the title to the lands between high and low water in Long Island Sound, west of Stehli Beach, concerned the right of the public to free passage on land submerged at high tide and bordering on property owned by the Piping Rock Club. We brought the complainant and the president of the Piping Rock Club together, as well as the officials of the town and village, and the matter was settled to the satisfaction of all.

We have had several complaints with reference to the operations of the Motor Vehicle Bureau. These complaints involved a State agency over which we had no control. We have, nevertheless, forwarded the complaints to the proper officials in the agency and, with no exceptions, have received complete cooperation. One case involved the compulsory vision acuity test. A resident of one of the towns complained as to an eye test taken at one of the offices of the Motor Vehicle Bureau which resulted in the refusal to renew and reissue her license because of alleged poor vision. The complainant's own doctor tested her eyes and she was informed that her eyes were perfect, 20-20 vision. She also had to pay a fee of $15.00 to her doctor for the examination. It then appeared that the Motor Vehicle Bureau wanted the doctor to fill out a form which he did not have and [had] not heard of. The Motor Vehicle Bureau refused to send the form to the doctor directly, but sent them instead to the Association of Optometrists and to the Medical Associations of the County to be distributed to the optometrists and to the M.D.s. The outcome of the complaint disclosed that the eye testing machine was defective. It was replaced, and the furnishing of the necessary forms to doctors was made.

A case that involved a village, and over which we had no jurisdiction or control whatever, was brought to the attention of this office and involved the complaint that a certain homeowner in the village was boarding between twenty and forty alleged relatives. Through the efforts of this office, further investigations were made by the village officials, summonses were issued, a trial was had and the defendant was found guilty of using his home as a boardinghouse, the boarders not being relatives. They were dispossessed and the adjacent property owners were placated.

A case referred to this office by one of the local members of Congress involved a bankruptcy case in the Northern District of New York, where the complainant was a creditor and investor of a concern that had swindled the complainant and many other local residents out of substantial funds in a building project involving a shopping center. This office, of course, has no authority over the bankruptcy courts, in which the matter was pending, and could only write to the Trustee and the referee to get information for the creditor, which he apparently was unable to get himself. He undoubtedly is going to lose ninety percent of his investment.

A complaint made to this office concerned an inmate of Pilgrim State Hospital who claimed that he had been prevented from attending a hearing in the Supreme Court, at which time an application was being made in an Incompetency Proceeding to have a committee appointed for the inmate. The authorities at Pilgrim State Hospital stated that the complainant was a paranoiac and refused to permit him to attend the hearing. We were able to persuade a Justice of the Supreme Court handling the case to permit the complainant to appear in court and to present his own defense and opposition to the appointment of the committee.

A complaint was made to this office alleging coercion in the obtaining of contributions and pledges to

the United Fund drive. A full investigation was made.
I am convinced that the contributions were not mandatory and were not coerced.

A complaint made to this office involved the
alleged failure by a builder to sell a house to a Negro.
The complainant, the builder and owner of the property,
is of Slavic origin and was...able to understand and to
talk very little English. Due to the language barrier,
there was an apparent misunderstanding between the
builder and the person alleging refusal to sell to a
Negro. This office is convinced that the State Human
Rights Commission was misled in this proceeding. The
motion by the State Human Rights Commission under Section 297, subdivision 4, of the Executive Law, for an
injunction was heard by one of the judges of the Supreme
Court, and he allowed the preliminary injunction only on
the filing of a substantial bond, and on the condition
that if it was ultimately determined that there was no
basis for the injunction, the petitioner would be
required to respond in damages for any injury caused to
the builder by the injunction.

A case involving a woman whose husband had abandoned
both wife and child was brought to our attention. It
appeared that the Family Court had ordered the husband
to pay a fixed sum for the support of the wife and child.
The husband moved to New Jersey, where he took up with
another woman, and he failed to pay the required sum
appointed by the Family Court. The Family Court [of
New York] had obtained an order in the Family Court of
New Jersey. Through the Family Court, we were able to
see that pressure was applied on the husband in New
Jersey to keep abreast of the required payments. This
was strictly outside our jurisdiction, as we have no
power to do anything about the courts.

We have had several complainants who complain that
they could not obtain the services of doctors, as their
treatment involved the Medicaid program. The Medical
Association of Nassau County and the Medical Society do

not give the names of doctors who participate in the Medicaid program. This office was finally able to persuade the Welfare Application Center to obtain the services for a patient of a doctor registered with Medicaid. Incidentally, this doctor later told the complainant that he would send her to Meadowbrook Hospital where they could take care of her. This situation is one that needs prompt attention by the Medical Societies of Nassau County.

We have received complaints from workers in one of the County homes. One in particular involved the deduction of pay for an absence when a worker was compelled to go to a dentist for treatment. There seemed to be a lack of communication and understanding between the supervisor and the person who claimed that he had advised her of his compelled absence. After an investigation, the complainant's sick pay was paid to him.

We received a complaint from a resident of East Meadow complaining that the New York Telephone Company's sub-contractor had left a large pile of dirt on her property resulting from the moving of certain telephone lines as a result of a road widening. A ditch had also been dug along the line of the property and the sub-contractor's equipment, including tractors, was parked on her lawn. We got in touch with the Telephone Company, and they were most cooperative in having their sub-contractor restore the lawn to its original condition and remove all the equipment.

On Election Day, ...a complaint was received by this office and was immediately handled. The complaint was that a voter, who had registered two years ago and had voted for each of the past two years, had been refused permission to vote. It turned out that the Board of Elections had sent the usual card to the complainant at the wrong address and that the card had been returned to the Board of Elections marked "moved, no forwarding address." When this information was conveyed to the Board of Elections, that the complainant still

lived at his original address and that the error was
that of the Board of Elections, the complainant was permitted to vote forthwith.

> Samuel Greason
> Commissioner

STATISTICAL ANALYSIS OF CASES

The complaints hereinafter enumerated are complaints having to do with subjects which are within the jurisdiction and control of the following units of Government:

NASSAU COUNTY DEPARTMENTS		[No. of cases]
Assessors, Board of		3
Civil Service Commission		7
Commerce and Industry, Department of		1
Community College		4
Comptroller		7
Consumer Affairs, Office of		15
County Attorney		7
County Clerk		3
County Executive, Office of A. Referred from	51	
B. Referred to	6	57
Elections, Board of		3
Fire Marshal		1
Health, Department of		10
Hospitals		7
Human Rights, Commission on		4
Labor, Department of		1
Motor Vehicle Bureau		8
Office of Administrative Services		8
Patterson Home		2

		[No. of Cases]
Planning Commission		6
Police Department		
A. Animal Nuisances	1	
B. Arrogance	4	
C. Civil Rights	4	
D. Crime Report Procedure	1	
E. Harassment by Neighbors	1	
F. Inadequate Protection	3	
G. Ordinance Enforcement	1	
H. Traffic Regulations	5	
I. Traffic Surveys	2	
Complaints Referred to Police	5	27
Public Works, Department of		13
Sheriff		2
Social Services, Department of		
A. Adoptions	1	
B. Commercial	1	
C. Eligibility	3	
D. Housing	5	
E. Increased Benefits	5	
F. Medicaid	4	
G. Personnel	4	23
Treasurer		9
Vocational Education and Extension Board		1
Total Nassau County Cases		229

TOWN GOVERNMENT

TOWN OF HEMPSTEAD

Animal Shelter	2

	[No. of Cases]
Building Department	30

Public Works, Department of

A. Highways	8	
B. Sanitation	1	
C. Other	6	15

Receiver of Taxes	3
Town Attorney	4
Town Board	2
Town Clerk	2
Zoning Appeals, Board of	1
[Total Town of Hempstead Cases]	59

TOWN OF NORTH HEMPSTEAD

Building Department	2
Receiver of Taxes	1
Town Attorney	6
Town Clerk	1
Zoning and Appeals, Board of	2
[Total Town of North Hempstead Cases]	12

TOWN OF OYSTER BAY

Building Department	10
Public Works, Department of	2
Receiver of Taxes	1
Town Attorney	4
Zoning, Board of	1
[Total Town of Oyster Bay Cases]	18

	[No. of Cases]	
VILLAGE GOVERNMENT		
Building Departments	6	
Fire Departments	1	
Police Departments	3	
Public Works, Departments of	3	
Receivers of Taxes	1	
Village Attorneys	2	
Village Clerks	1	
Zoning Appeals, Boards of	2	
[Total Village Government Cases]		19
CITY GOVERNMENT		
LONG BEACH		
Building Department	3	
Courts	1	
Public Works, Department of	1	
Zoning	1	
[Total Long Beach Cases]		6
SPECIAL DISTRICTS		
Sanitary Districts	3	
Water Districts	2	
[Total Special Districts Cases]		5
FIRE DISTRICTS		1
LIBRARY DISTRICTS		1
SCHOOL DISTRICTS		1

[No. of Cases]

COURTS
    A. Appellate Division   2
    B. Nassau Supreme Court   4
    C. Nassau Family Court   7
    D. Nassau County Court   2
    E. Nassau District Court   14

Marshals   1

Public Administrator   1

Judicial Conference   _1_
                                            32

DISTRICT ATTORNEY
    A. Complaints   4
    B. Referred by District
           Attorney   7
    C. Referred to District
           Attorney   _3_
                                            14

UNITED STATES GOVERNMENT

Congressional Repre-
    sentatives   19

Law Services Committee   3

Social Security Adminis-
    tration   _2_

    [Total United States
    Government Cases]   24

NEW YORK STATE GOVERNMENT

Attorney General   3

Education Department   1

Human Rights Commission   1

Hospitals   1

Insurance Department   2

	[No. of Cases]	
Labor Department	7	
Liquor Authority	1	
Motor Vehicle Bureau	3	
Public Service Commission	4	
Public Works	1	
Retirement System	1	
Unemployment Insurance Office	1	
[Total New York State Government Cases]		26
NEW YORK CITY GOVERNMENT		
Commissioner of Investigations	2	
Police Department	1	
Social Services Department	1	
Traffic Court	1	
[Total New York City Government Cases]		5
SUFFOLK COUNTY GOVERNMENT		1
NON-GOVERNMENTAL MATTERS		
Attorneys	25	
Better Business Bureau	3	
Fire Underwriters, Board of	1	
Hospitals	1	
Judicial Inquiry	4	
Legal Aid Society	8	
Long Island Humane Society	1	
Long Island Railroad	1	
Nassau County Bar Association	3	

	[No. of Cases]	
Press	2	
Utilities	8	
[Total Non-governmental Matters]		57
[Total Non-county Cases		281]
Total Cases		510

This figure of 510 complaints contains many duplications of entries, which may affect one, two, three or more agencies and actually the total number of matters handled is 360+.

APPENDIX IV

Reports of the
Citizens Administrative Service
Buffalo, New York

February 29, 1968
May 31, 1968
September 4, 1968

John H. Hollands
Director

January 24, 1969

Lance Tibbles
Director

APPENDIX IV

Contents

CITIZENS ADMINISTRATIVE SERVICE
FIRST REPORT

Buffalo's Ombudsman Project, with the official name "Citizens Administrative Service," opened its doors on November 17, 1967. It is now possible to report on its first three months' operations.

The report which follows is divided into three parts: (1) Organization, (2) Statistics and (3) The Police Department.

(1) Organization

The Citizens Administrative Service started operations on November 17 with two full-time lawyers and a secretary at its main office in downtown Buffalo and eleven law students manning two neighborhood offices in the so-called inner city on a part-time rotating basis. Office hours at the main office were from 9:00 A.M. to 5:00 P.M. Monday through Friday, and at the neighborhood offices were from 4 P.M. to 10 P.M. Monday through Friday and from 2 P.M. to 5 P.M. on Saturday.

The establishment of the Service was well publicized in the press. The Service's press release, upon which these newspaper articles were largely based, read in part as follows:

> The Citizens Administrative Service
> is a pilot project to test the feasi-
> bility and desirability of having, in
> a representative American city, a type
> of consultative service which in cer-
> tain smaller countries is run on a
> nation-wide basis. In these smaller

173

> countries (Sweden, Denmark, Norway, Finland, New Zealand) the official in charge is commonly called an Ombudsman, a Swedish word which may be roughly translated as 'people's representative.'
>
> The Service will receive, investigate, and try to dispose of complaints concerning policies and practices of the city and county governments which are brought to its attention by Buffalo citizens affected. The Service has no authority to compel action on the part of either the governments or the citizens concerned, nor will it bring lawsuits or otherwise take action in the law courts. Its only weapon will be persuasion.
>
> Mayor Frank A. Sedita and Erie County Executive Edward A. Rath have assured the Service that their administrations will cooperate with it in every way possible.

From the outset the Service received courtesy and cooperation from the administrators of the various departments of the city and county. As complaints arose involving one or more departments or divisions, the Director and the Deputy Director made it their business to call on the head of each department or division involved to pay their respects and ask how future complaints in the particular department or division should be routed.

Opposition to the project was not lacking, however. It centered in the Common Council of Buffalo and was led by Councilman Raymond Lewandowski. Initially the objection made was that the project would "harass and undermine city officials and cause chaos in city government," that it was unnecessary, and that it could "easily be interpreted as a pilot program by the federal government to take over City Hall." It was proposed that the Council adopt a resolution asking the Office of Economic Opportunity to revoke its grant. On November 28 representatives of the Service appeared before the Legislation Committee and answered Mr. Lewandowski's arguments. The Legislation Committee reported the proposed resolution to the Council without recommendation.

In the debates before the full Council the ground of attack was shifted. It was claimed that the project was a "civilian review board" and therefore a threat to the Police Department. On January 9, after receiving an opinion from the Corporation Counsel, Mr. Anthony Manguso, that the ombudsman lacked the powers of a civilian review board, the Lewandowski resolution was defeated 9 to 6. The ground of attack then shifted again. It was claimed that the Service was "a substitute for a civilian review board." On this last ground, on February 20, after further debate but without giving the Service any chance to be heard, a new resolution to the same effect as the original Lewandowski resolution passed the Council by a vote of 11 to 4.

The contention that an ombudsman is a "substitute for a civilian review board" is discussed in Part (3) of this report. At this point all that need be said is that this ombudsman project is the subject of a contract between the Office of Economic Opportunity and the Research Foundation of the State University, and that the University has been advised by the OEO that it has no intention of denouncing the contract or revoking its grant. The project will therefore continue.

During the first half of February the Service decided to enlarge its neighborhood activities. It had started using two neighborhood offices, one at 1352 Jefferson Avenue and one at 240 High Street, these being offices established by the University's Office of Urban Affairs as education and information centers.

Beginning February 19 there have been added an office
at 44 Pine Street and one at 381 Niagara Street. Both
of these are in centers maintained by the Community
Action Organization. Each of the four offices has a
neighborhood aide who works with the law students previously referred to. Because of the added offices,
office hours at the two old offices have been changed
to 5:00 to 9:00 P.M. and Saturday hours have been elimi-
nated. Office hours at the two new offices are 7:00 to
10:00 P.M.

(2) Statistics

During the three months from November 17, 1967
through February 16, 1968 the Service docketed 120 complaints and inquiries, of which 79 have been closed and
41 are still active. These figures do not include complaints which are immediately rejected as being outside
the ombudsman's jurisdiction because they involved cases
already in court or were concerned with persons and matters beyond the city limits of Buffalo; but the figures
do include complaints which were rejected, withdrawn or
referred elsewhere after some study.

It is interesting to compare these figures with the
experience of the ombudsman in Nassau County, New York.
He received 175 complaints in the first six months and
300 in the second six months. Nassau County has a population of 1,300,000, roughly twice that of Buffalo.

The complaints and inquiries docketed may be broken
down by subject matter as follows:

Building permits	2
Civil Service	4
Condemnation	7
Demolition	3
Dumps	2
Garbage removal	7

177

Landlord and tenant   7
Licensing   5
Paving   5
Police   5
Public housing   2
Recreation   2
Schools   3
Snow removal   12
Social Service   6
Street lighting   2
Taxes, income   2
Taxes, real estate   4
Traffic   2
Trees   2
Water charges   2
Zoning   5
Miscellaneous   13

Total complaints handled   104

Complaints rejected   10
Complaints withdrawn   1
Complaints referred
  elsewhere   5

Total complaints not
  handled   16

Total complaints docketed   120

(3) The Police Department

Because of the publicity which this topic has
received, including incorrect representations of the
Service's policy, some discussion seems in order.

To date the ombudsman has been in touch with the
Police Department in only five cases. In three of these
there was no hint of any criticism of police; instead
their help was being solicited.

Of the remaining two cases, one involved a claim of alleged discourtesy by a traffic policeman that had occurred more than a year previously. This correspondence was simply forwarded to the Department as a courtesy, in case it wanted to answer these old allegations. No answer was made. The second case was a complaint that a telephone call reporting a burglary had not resulted in any action. The answer given to the ombudsman by the Department was that at some point between the citizen, the complaint desk, and the squad car the numerals in the street address had become transposed, so that the car went to the wrong place.

When the ombudsman is accused of being a "substitute for a civilian review board" cases such as these are obviously not meant. What is meant is a kind of case that the Service has not had yet--the case in which a policeman is accused of acts which, if they actually occurred, would call for disciplinary action on the part of the Department. It is to deal with this latter type of case that, in a few cities, civilian review boards have been set up to hear both sides of an accusation, to call and examine witnesses, and ultimately to make a decision which is binding on the Department. An ombudsman could not do this even if he wanted to.

The ombudsman not only lacks the powers of a civilian review board but he proceeds on a different theory altogether. Generally speaking, he is an independent intermediary between the citizen and the government, trying to reconcile the two. He deals most of the time with subordinates in the various departments or with their immediate supervisors, the people with whom the public has contact. But when an employee of a department is accused of misconduct a special case is presented. The ombudsman then deals with officials at or near the head of the department. He does not present to them the case for the accused employee; they can ordinarily get from within the department all the information and arguments which are available in justification of the employee's conduct. The ombudsman's

main job in this type of case is to present the information and arguments supporting the accusation. In doing
this he performs a valuable function because he makes
it possible for the officials in charge to reach their
decision on the basis of a fuller, more rounded picture
than they would have if they relied on departmental
sources alone.

This reasoning is neither more nor less applicable
to the Police Department and the Sheriff's Office than
it is to any other department of the city or county.

John H. Hollands
Director

Lance Tibbles
Deputy Director

February 29, 1968

CITIZENS ADMINISTRATIVE SERVICE
SECOND REPORT

Buffalo's Ombudsman Project, with the official name "Citizens Administrative Service," opened its doors on November 17, 1967. This report covers the first six months of the project, through May 16, 1968.

The report which follows is divided into three parts: (1) Operations and Statistics, (2) The Project as Part of the Poverty Program, and (3) Some Tentative Conclusions.

(1) Operations and Statistics

During the second three months of the project its organization and procedures remained substantially the same as those described in the First Report. There was a considerable increase in the volume of inquiries and complaints received. Valuable experience was obtained by those connected with the project. Public officials continued to be cooperative.

In the table given below the complaints and inquiries docketed during the first and second three-month periods are listed on a cumulative basis.

	11/17/67- 2/16/68	2/17/68- 5/16/68	Cumulative Totals
Abandoned cars	0	3	3
Building permits	2	0	2
Civil service	4	5	9
Condemnation	7	14	21
Demolition	3	46	49

Dogs	0	4	4
Dumps	2	0	2
Employment	0	5	5
Garbage removal	7	22	29
Landlord and tenant	7	20	27
Licensing	5	2	7
Paving	5	34	39
Police, traffic	1	18	19
Police, other	4	20	24
Probation	1	4	5
Public health	1	49	50
Public housing	2	59	61
Public works	1	15	16
Recreation	2	4	6
Schools	3	14	17
Snow removal	12	6	18
Social service	6	46	52
Street cleaning	0	4	4
Street lighting	2	16	18
Taxes, income	2	2	4
Taxes, real estate	4	4	8
Traffic engineering	2	6	8
Trees	2	7	9
Water charges	2	1	3
Zoning	5	2	7
Miscellaneous	10	12	22

Total complaints handled	104	444	548
Complaints rejected	10	3	13
Complaints withdrawn	1	1	2
Complaints referred elsewhere	5	6	11
Total complaints not handled	16	10	26
Total complaints docketed	120	454	574

In a few cases the differences between the first
and second columns in the above table are seasonal (snow
removal, street cleaning, recreation). The increase
relating to public housing is largely accounted for by
the fact that the two neighborhood offices set up in
February are located in or near public housing projects,
while the two original neighborhood offices are not
close to any public housing. Changes in other items,
so far as we can now tell, simply represent normal
growth.

(2) The Project as Part of
the Poverty Program

Historically, wherever the ombudsman has appeared,
his services have been equally available to the rich
and the poor, the high and the low. How can this tradi-
tion of equality be reconciled with the fact that the
Buffalo project is financed by the Office of Economic
Opportunity, the key agency in the federal Poverty
Program?

The OEO apparently thought that the privilege of
calling on the ombudsman, like the privilege of sleeping
under a bridge, is one that the poor are more likely to
exercise than the rich. It made clear its position on
this question by inserting two conditions in its grant,
as follows:

> The Grantee will insure that members
> of the poverty community are apprised
> of the existence of this program, and
> specifically that the neighborhood
> offices institute procedures designed
> to effect meaningful communication
> with indigent residents of the target
> areas....

> Priorities for actions undertaken
> by the Grantee shall be determined
> solely by their potential for
> impact on the total community of
> Buffalo without regard to the
> source of complaints or the rele-
> vance of the action to members of
> the poverty population....

In other words, the ombudsman is to act in the
interest of the whole community, not of any one group
or class; but he has an affirmative obligation to open
up and maintain channels of communication with the poor.
He must see to it that the poor know that his office
exists. He must make it easy for them to reach it. The
well-to-do are welcome at the office but they have to
find their own way there. Some have. For example,
although in most landlord-and-tenant situations the
ombudsman has been approached by the tenant, there have
been at least two cases in which the office was consulted by the landlord.

Digging channels of communication to the poor has
proved harder than was anticipated. The Service set up
neighborhood offices in four areas where there is marked
poverty and hired a neighborhood aide for each, but it
was only during the fourth month of the project that a
substantial volume of complaints began to come in from
this source. The explanation is partly distrust, which
only time and familiarity can overcome, and which has
not yet, and may never, be fully overcome. Equally
important, however, particularly among those who are by
temperament less distrustful, is lack of information.
The Service has received excellent publicity in the
press and, to some extent, on television and radio, but
the poor get most of their information by word of mouth.
It takes time and careful cultivation for a new organization to establish any sort of reputation in such a setting.

We estimate that at least three-fourths of the
complaints received by the Service to date have come

from the poor. The balance has not necessarily all come from the well-to-do, but it has come from those who are or think of themselves as middle class, whatever their present circumstances.

In a Northern industrial city today the subject of poverty is closely tied to that of race. To pretend otherwise is to be unrealistic. Much of the distrust to which we have alluded has its origin in the tension between Negroes and whites. It is our belief, based not on theory but on our observation over the past six months, that an ombudsman's office can reduce this tension to some extent. The degree to which this can be done should not be exaggerated. The ombudsman is no sure antidote for riots. The typical rioter (according to the report of the National Advisory Commission on Civil Disorders) is "a Negro, unmarried male between the ages of 15 and 24." Only a few of the ombudsman's complaints have come from this group.

Nevertheless a claim of some reduction in tensions is justified. The reason for this does not lie in the racial composition of the ombudsman's office, however important that may be in attracting business.* It arises instead from the nature of the work the office does. The man or woman who goes to the ombudsman has a problem with the government. The ombudsman is in effect the citizen's ambassador to City or County Hall. The fact that he is not a paid agent, not even a lawyer acting for a client, but is more of an independent intermediary, an intermediary who does not hesitate to present the government's side of the question to the citizen as well as the citizen's side to the government, strengthens rather than weakens the tie between him and the citizen.

---

*In Buffalo three of the neighborhood aides are black, as is the neighborhood coordinator and the secretary in the Main Office, but the Director, the Deputy Director and, by pure accident, all of the law students participating in the program are white.

They are working on a problem together, the citizen's problem, working voluntarily, with mutual respect and without sentimentality. It makes a bond--not invariably, not even in a large majority of cases, but quite often.

The ombudsman's central purpose is to further administrative justice, efficiency and civility. Help to the poor and some reduction in racial tensions may be only by-products, but they are worthy by-products.

(3) Some Tentative Conclusions

The Citizens Administrative Service is an experiment scheduled to run until mid-September, that is, for ten months altogether. Final conclusions should not be drawn until the experiment has run its full course. Yet after six months a number of points have become reasonably clear to the writers. A few of these are discussed below in question and answer form.

Question: Should the ombudsman appear before courts and legislative bodies?

Answer: Only in exceptional cases. In local government the courts and legislative bodies sometimes, though rarely, discharge administrative functions. In such cases the ombudsman, as a kind of administrative specialist, may properly appear before them. An example of a legislative body's administrative function is the power of the Common Council to grant individual zoning variances (as distinguished from its power to alter or recharacterize entire zones, which is legislative). An example of a court's administrative function is the power of the County Court to grant, revoke and suspend pistol permits.

But such cases are rare. In the great bulk of truly legislative and judicial functions we believe that the ombudsman ought not to intervene. We take this position although it is contrary to the Scandinavian practice. We take it for several reasons, but mainly because it makes it possible for the ombudsman to conserve his energies for the work he is best qualified to do. We have operated experimentally on this basis and have found that it has caused us no embarrassment but on the contrary has removed embarrassments.

There is one theoretic exception to this rule, however. Suppose the ombudsman receives a series of complaints which seem to be well founded but which, upon investigation, prove not to be the result of unjust administration but rather the consequence of the conscientious enforcement of an unjust law. In this situation the ombudsman should be able to appear before the proper legislative committee or other body and tell the legislators of the apparent flaws in the law. Again, if a public administrative question is presented in a lawsuit and the ombudsman has views on the subject gleaned from his experience, he should be able to appear before the court as an amicus curiae.

The exception, then, is that when the ombudsman has opinions arising out of experience gained in the regular course of his duties, he should be entitled to express those opinions to courts and legislatures for whatever weight they may have. In the Buffalo experiment no occasion has yet arisen for making use of this exception, but an established ombudsman with some years of experience behind him might be able to make some worthwhile contributions. This exception is, of course, a very narrow exception. The ordinary rule should be that the ombudsman does not go to court or appear or lobby before legislatures.

Question: Should a municipal ombudsman take complaints involving state or federal agencies?

Answer: Yes, when the matter is one that can be dealt with by a local office of the agency; otherwise no.

To begin with, there are cases in which the state or federal problems are only part of a situation which also involves the City or County. An example is the budget of a family that is simultaneously receiving aid from county welfare, from state vocational rehabilitation and from the United States Veterans Administration.

But there are many cases in which the state or federal question stands alone. If the agency concerned has a regional or district office in Buffalo which is competent to deal with the problem, we have felt justified in taking the complaint and, with one exception, have found no difficulty in fitting it in with our regular duties.

The exception is federal and state taxes. The ombudsman should not try to build up a tax practice. That field is too wide and too deep. In the current program a few cases involving delays in refund, tracing returns and the like have been taken, but all large or complicated cases have been declined. With this one exception, however, the concept that we support is that of an all-purpose local ombudsman.

Question: Should the ombudsman take complaints from the whole metropolitan area?

Answer: In Buffalo, yes. The answer might well be different in Philadelphia or San Francisco.

In the present program only complaints arising within the Buffalo city limits have been taken and, for an experiment starting from scratch we believe this restriction was wise. For an established ombudsman, however, the restriction appears artificial. The suburbs have their problems too. So does a city like Lackawanna.

Perhaps for a year or two questions outside of Buffalo involving only a town or village, and not the County, ought to be excluded until the ombudsman's office has partially digested the increase in its jurisdiction. In any event the ombudsman's refusal to become involved in legislative matters should be applied with the utmost strictness in the towns. But with these qualifications the extension of the service countywide makes sense administratively.

Probably it also makes sense financially. Some increase in personnel and office space would be needed if more than twice as many people were to be served, but they would not have to be doubled. The present project was funded at $123,182 and actual expenditures should be well within that figure. A countywide program should cost between $150,000 and $175,000 per year.

Question: Should an established ombudsman be an arm of the legislature?

Answer: Not an arm of the legislature but a separate office of executive nature, created and kept independent by legislative enactment.

The proper comparisons here are with the Inspector General of the Army and the United States Comptroller General, offices created by Congress to serve as a check on executive excesses. It is true that in the Scandinavian countries and New Zealand the ombudsman is sometimes spoken of as an arm of the legislature, but these are nations having a parliamentary form of government without the separation of powers that we find at almost all levels of American government.

It should be understood that the opinions expressed in the above answers are only those of the writers. Authoritative opinions regarding the Service will be expressed only by the evaluators who will review the experiment several months from now.

John H. Hollands
Director

Lance Tibbles
Deputy Director

May 31, 1968

CITIZENS ADMINISTRATIVE SERVICE
THIRD REPORT

Buffalo's Ombudsman Project, with the official name "Citizens Administrative Service," opened its doors on November 17, 1967. This report covers the third quarter of its operations, from May 17 through August 16, 1968.

The report which follows is divided into four parts: (1) Operations and Statistics, (2) Sample Cases, (3) The Ombudsman Movement--Some Comparisons, and (4) The Project's Future.

(1) Operations and Statistics

During the third three months of the project its organization and procedures remained substantially the same as those described in the First Report. The volume of inquiries and complaints handled levelled off to 302, as compared with 104 in the first and 430 in the second three months. The figure for all cases docketed during the nine months is 902, of which 671 have been closed and 231 are still active.

In [the following tally]...the complaints and inquiries docketed during the first, second and third three-month periods are listed on a cumulative basis.

	11/17/67-2/16/68	2/17/68-5/16/68	5/17/68-8/16/68	Cumulative Totals
Abandoned cars	0	3	8	11
Building permits	2	0	0	2
Civil service	4	5	1	10
Condemnation	7	14	0	21
Demolition	3	46	36	85
Dogs	0	4	2	6
Dumps	2	0	0	2
Employment	0	5	3	8
Garbage removal	7	22	7	36
Landlord and tenant	7	20	5	32
Licensing	5	2	2	9
Paving	5	34	20	59
Police, traffic	1	18	21	40
Police, other	4	20	13	37
Probation	1	4	1	6
Public health	1	49	25	75
Public housing	2	59	18	79
Recreation	2	4	18	24
Schools	3	14	7	24
Snow removal	12	6	1	19
Social service	6	46	44	96
Street cleaning	0	4	5	9
Street lighting	2	16	8	26

Taxes, income	2	2	1	5
Taxes, real estate	4	4	0	8
Traffic engineering	2	6	2	10
Trees	2	7	15	24
Urban renewal	0	0	11	11
Water charges	2	1	11	3
Zoning	5	2	0	8
Miscellaneous	10	12	1	8
Correction		(14)	14	36
Total complaints handled	104	430	302	836
Complaints rejected	10	3	31	44
Complaints withdrawn	1	1	0	2
Complaints referred elsewhere	5	6	9	20
Total complaints not handled	16	10	40	66
Total complaints docketed	120	440	342	902

(2) Sample Cases

Statistics tell a story but they seldom tell the whole story. In any enterprise there are qualitative as well as quantitative factors to be weighed. This is particularly true of an ombudsman's activities. To get the flavor of his work the individual complainant with his individual needs must be considered. For this reason this part of the Report is devoted to summaries of a number of cases that have come to the Service. These have been chosen partly for their intrinsic human interest and partly to illustrate the variety of activities in which the Service engages. Of course the names of the persons concerned have been altered.

* * * * *

Mrs. L's pastor on her behalf asked the Service's assistance in coping with Mrs. L's son, S. S, aged 25, was mentally retarded. He had a long record of school truancy, arrests and jail terms. Mrs. L had gone to every agency she could think of, public and private, seeking some answer to S's problems.

The Service ascertained that because of S's age he could not be brought into Family Court. The best procedure seemed to be a voluntary psychiatric examination at the county hospital, if that could be arranged, otherwise a similar but involuntary examination based on a Cit Court warrant. [Mrs.] L and her pastor were so advised.

The above events occurred during May. Nothing came of them because after his latest arrest S had disappeared. In July it was learned that he had been thrown in jail again, this time for harassment, obscene language and petty larceny. The Service gave the Public Defender's Office an account of S's history and the Public Defender then persuaded S to accept a voluntary commitment to the county hospital for psychological and

intelligence testing and commitment to an institution
if warranted.

* * * * *

A Negro organization asked the Graduate Students
Association of the University to check the tax assessment rate structure in Buffalo. It was rumored that in
Boston the property tax assessment rate was 75% for
Negroes, 60% for businesses and 35% for whites. The
organization wondered whether a similar situation pre-
vailed in Buffalo. The Association asked the Service
for advice.

The Service prepared a memorandum discussing the
basis and procedure of property taxation in Buffalo.
The memorandum explained such concepts as assessed
value, tax rate and tax equalization rate, showed how
all of these are constants except assessed value, and
made it clear that differences in valuation were due
solely to differences in estimated market value.

* * * * *

Mr. R gave the Service the following story. Five
years previously he had come to Buffalo from Puerto
Rico with his five children, leaving behind his pregnant
wife, who had been unfaithful to him. In February 1968
he received a phone call from some unidentified authority
in Puerto Rico ordering him to bring his wife and sixth
child to live with him. He did this. His wife was sick
on arrival. Later she recovered and left home, taking
the youngest child with her. After a search he found
that she had been committed to the county hospital under
the auspices of the Social Services Department and that
the child had been temporarily placed with a foster
mother. R persuaded the foster mother to return the

child to him. Meanwhile the Social Services Department was obtaining an apartment for the wife. R was convinced that social workers from the Social Services Department, VISTA and the Children's Aid Society were engaged in a conspiracy to deprive him of his children or force him to support his wife and youngest child in a separate establishment.

At this point the ombudsman persuaded R and the Social Services Department caseworker to meet in the ombudsman's office to explore all sides of the problem. At this meeting Mrs. Anna Ramos, a neighborhood aide of the ombudsman, acted as interpreter. After much talk the following understanding was reached. The Department would provde the wife with an apartment and support, this provision to include the youngest child if the wife through her own efforts got custody. R agreed to allow all children to visit the wife. The Department agreed not to interfere with whatever steps R might take seeking a divorce or the wife might take seeking custody. On one point disagreement remained firm: the Department wanted R to contribute to the wife's support, which he refused to do unless she would return to Puerto Rico and live with her own relatives. The ombudsman advised R to seek legal advice.

It may be noted that, without resolving all questions, the ombudsman was instrumental in straightening out a tangled situation so that the parties understood each other and knew the courses open to them.

* * * * *

A niece of Mrs. J came from Pennsylvania to live with her in Buffalo. Mrs. J went with her to a nearby high school to arrange for her registration and conferred there with the acting principal. Some question was raised about the niece's papers from the Pennsylvania school, after which the principal, as Mrs. J understood him, told her to go to the ninth floor of City Hall and ask for the plumbers' office. Believing she was being ridiculed Mrs. J went home and phoned the Board of Education, who told her they would advise the principal to admit her niece. Later, after the niece had been going to school, the principal one day called her "a tramp." Because of these two incidents, and gossip among the schoolgirls, Mrs. J concluded that the principal was "prejudiced against Negroes and Puerto Ricans." Mrs. J and her niece are Negro.

The Service wrote the office of the Superintendent of Schools and the principal was asked to explain the incidents. He stated that both incidents involved misunderstandings. In the first instance he had told Mrs. J to go to the Pupil Personnel Office of the Board of Education on the eighth floor of City Hall. In the second instance, seeing the niece disheveled after she had come out of gym class, he had said, "Comb your hair, you look like a tramp." He denied any race prejudice and recommended that Mrs. J join the P.T.A. His replies were reported to Mrs. J, who expressed herself satisfied with the outcome, saying in effect that whether the principal was lying or telling the truth he would be more careful next time.

* * * * *

Mr. M called on the Service with the following story. He had bought a residential property within the past year, consisting of a front house and a rear house on the same lot. He had obtained permits to repair both. The city inspectors told him that as long as he was making progress in repair there would be no problem. The front house had been partly burned before M's purchase. Later the rear house was largely burned. Subsequently, without telling him, the city tore down the rear house and graded the ground. Then the city sent him a bill for $621 as the cost of demolition. M was unwilling to pay this bill and threatened violence if it was insisted on. He also said he would not proceed with repair of the front house until the city paid him for having demolished the rear house.

The Service checked records in the Erie County Clerk's office and the office of the City Buildings Division. It appeared that M had bought the property in July 1967; that in the previous March the previous owners had been ordered to demolish the buildings or the city would demolish them and put a lien on the property to assure payment; that in September 1967 a registered letter was sent to M, for which he signed a receipt, ordering him to demolish the rear building at once and to make reasonable progress on the repair of the front building within 30 days or the city would demolish. In October 1967 the city accepted a bid by a wrecking firm to demolish the rear building for $621. Demolition was completed in January 1968 and in a meeting of the Common Council later that month this demolition was approved and the cost was assessed against the property.

The Service sent M a letter reciting these facts and concluding as follows:

> The rear building was apparently
> damaged several times by fire in
> the latter part of 1967. The
> Buffalo Building Code, Section 34,
> provides that any wooden or frame
> dwelling which is damaged by fire
> to an extent of more than one-half
> of its value, exclusive of the
> foundation, shall not be repaired
> or rebuilt, but must be taken down.
> The policy of the Buildings Divi-
> sion in these cases is to require
> that the building be completely
> torn down including the cellar
> and the foundation and the land

graded. The rear building was damaged in excess of one-half of its value. The rear building was completely demolished and the ground graded over.

The City is going to continue to demand that the front building be repaired or demolished and that you pay for the demolition of the rear building. This request appears to be in complete compliance with the Buffalo Building Code. I suggest that you talk personally to Mr. Richard Bilski of the Buildings Division-Demolition to find out what repairs must be made and how soon they must be made.

The County deed records indicate that you received a warranty deed. The Buildings Division records indicate that the previous owners had received an order to repair, demolish, or remove the buildings prior to the sale to you. The effect of this condition in view of the warranty deed should be discussed with your attorney.

* * * * *

Mrs. K sought the Service's assistance in getting larger quarters than the 3 bedroom apartment occupied by her family in a public housing project. Her family consisted of herself, her husband, sons aged 15, 10 and 7 and daughters aged 14, 5 and 1. Five years previously she had applied for a larger apartment without results.

The Service talked with the project manager and, knowing that in such cases the Municipal Housing

Authority was influenced by the age and sex as well as the number of children, pointed out the merits of Mrs. K's case. The Service also prepared and sent to Mrs. K for her signature a written request setting forth the facts and requesting transfer to a 4 or 5 bedroom apartment in the same or another project. A week later Mrs. K called the Service to say that she had submitted the written request but had had no reply yet. She was told to be patient.

Three months later Mrs. K called the Service from her new and larger apartment to complain about poor flooring and a rusty, corroded, dirty oven. She said that the manager had promised to correct the flooring and she knew it would take some time but that she wanted the stove replaced soon. The Service called the project manager, who said that he had already arranged for one of his staff to call on Mrs. K and show her how to clean the oven. The Service called Mrs. K and asked her to wait for the staff man and then, if still not satisfied, to phone again. At present writing, 20 days later, the Service has had no further call from Mrs. K.

* * * * *

Mrs. L came to the Service for help in obtaining Social Security disability benefits for her son who had been in a state mental hospital intermittently for several years. Mrs. L had first applied for these benefits in 1958. Mrs. L did not understand whether or not there had been a final determination made on the case. She thought that Social Security might be saying that her son was not disabled. She did not understand this because he had been in the state hospital most of the time.

The Service contacted the local office of the United States Social Security Administration. All that the Service wanted Social Security to do was to review the case and write Mrs. L a letter telling her the result and the reasons for the result. Finally, after a long conversation, it was agreed that Social Security would review the file and write the letter. The point at issue was whether Mrs. L's son's disability began prior to his eighteeenth birthday. If not, he was not eligible for disability benefits.

One month after that conversation Mrs. L received the letter from Social Security. She was informed that the application was rejected because Social Security had decided that the disability did not occur prior to her son's eighteenth birthday.

The Service then went to the state hospital where the son was a patient and talked to the doctors about the case. They were told what the issue was and asked if they would review their files and write a letter to Mrs. L setting out any information that they had indicating whether the disability began before the son's eighteenth birthday. The doctors agreed to do this and, after reviewing the files, wrote a letter to Mrs. L giving the case history and the opinions of the doctors. Mrs. L took this letter to the Social Security office and refiled an application for disability benefits for her son.

It may be noted that the Service was not so much interested in whether Mrs. L's son was eligible to receive benefits as it was in assuring that Mrs. L understood the reason for the rejection so that she could obtain all possible evidence to present to the Social Security office.

* * * * *

Legal papers were served on Mrs. J in connection with the Oak Street Redevelopment Project. The papers contained the names of all owners and tenants of land on her block. They also contained a list of criminal bonds, court judgments and bankruptcies pertaining to various owners. Mrs. J objected to having this sort of information about her neighbors "imposed upon her."

The Service referred Mrs. J's complaint to the Urban Renewal Department, which in turn referred it to the Law Department. It developed that information regarding these matters was legally necessary in petitions for condemnation, but was not necessary in a notice of determination and hearing served on property owners; however, it had been included in such notices by the Department typists as a matter of supposed convenience. The Corporation Counsel advised the Service that, "as far as humanly possible, hereafter the Notice of Determination and Hearings will not include the specifics as to ownership, liens, encumbrances, etc."

* * * * *

Mrs. G was separated from her husband and on welfare. She claimed that the Social Services Department was not giving her full benefit of the payments her husband was making to the Department. She also claimed that the Department had promised her a stove, a refrigerator and bunk beds and had sent her vouchers for these but refused to send her cash, which she preferred. After various discussions with the Department, the Service wrote her as follows:

> This office contacted the Adjustment
> Unit of the Social Services Department about your case. You receive
> a cash grant, except that the Welfare Department pays your rent and
> utilities by voucher. You have
> requested bunk beds and a cook
> stove. Your request has been
> approved, but the Department decided

to issue vouchers instead of cash
for these items because of the substantial amount of money involved and
other factors. The vouchers are good
at any store, and with them you need
not pay the sales tax, which would
have to be paid if you paid cash. In
purchases of this type, the Department sometimes issues cash and sometimes issues vouchers, depending on
the particular circumstances of each
case. It is a matter of discretion
with the Department.

The Adjustment Unit told this office
that you rejected the vouchers.
Apparently your refrigerator has
now been condemned and the Department has authorized a voucher for
purchase of a new refrigerator.
You have apparently stated that
you will not accept this voucher
either. Your case has been taken
to the District Supervisor in the
Social Services Department, who has
also decided that these items should
be paid by voucher.

You asked about the payments that
your husband makes to Welfare. There
is a Welfare Department procedure
when a wife is receiving payments
from her husband or ex-husband which
are less than the amount that she
would receive from Welfare. Welfare
pays the wife the entire amount of
welfare assistance. Welfare collects
the payments from the husband, which
are less than the amount paid to the
wife. Even if the husband misses
some payments, Welfare continues to
pay the wife her full assistance.

You have been assigned a new caseworker, a woman--Miss M. Her telephone number is 856-7500, extension
123. You may wish to review your
case with her.

As nearly as this office can determine, the decision by the Social
Services Department to require that
the bunk beds, the cook stove, and
the refrigerator be purchased by
voucher is a decision that is properly within the discretion of the
Welfare Department.

It may be noted that the vouchers referred to are
good only for purchase of the items described, but may
be used at any store. Formerly vouchers rather than
checks were given in all cases involving purchases of
furniture or equipment but recently the administrative
policy has been changed to use checks except where there
is a history of unreliability in handling cash. There
was such a history in this case.

* * * * *

Mr. D told the Service that the vacant lot next to
his business contained piles of wood and other rubbish.
He said that this presented a very unsightly condition
and was bad for his business. The Service referred the
complaint to the Erie County Health Department.

The Health Department inspected the lot and found
cause to believe that there was a violation of the Health
Code. A check by the Health Department revealed that the
lot was owned by the City of Buffalo. The health inspector said that the City had been notified of the condition
of the lot, that it was city owned, and that the case was
therefore out of his (the County's) hands.

The Service later checked with the Buffalo Director of Real Estate and found that he was not aware of the report of the Health Department. He checked his records and found that the lot was in fact owned by the City. He informed the Service that he would immediately ask the City Street Sanitation Department to clean the lot. The Service informed Mr. D of these developments.

Some time later Mr. D contacted the Service again and said that the lot was never cleaned to his satisfaction, that piles of wood and rubbish remained. By this time the Service had made an arrangement with the Buffalo Director of Real Estate that, whenever upon a complaint from our office, he asked the Street Sanitation Department to clean a lot, from that time on any complaining neighbors would call him directly instead of going through our office again. The Service made it clear to both parties that it would become active in the case again if either party was not satisfied with the results obtained.

This case illustrates the occasional red tape involved in communications between the city and the county and the role played by the Service in cutting it. The case also illustrates the sort of arrangement that the Service may make with a particular official to aid him in his handling of citizens' complaints.

* * * * *

(3)   The Ombudsman Movement--
Some Comparisons

[Editor's note: section deleted because of space limitations.]

(4) The Project's Future

The Buffalo project was funded by the United States Office of Economic Opportunity for the period from September 1, 1967 to October 31, 1968. It was unable to start operations until November 17, 1967. Its present funding therefore gives it an effective life of approximately eleven and a half months, of which nine months have passed.

In the writers' opinion these nine months have demonstrated that the project has value. What it has accomplished, both quantitatively and qualitatively, is shown by Parts (1) and (2) of this Report. But present accomplishments do not exhaust the possibilities. In a number of ways, some of which are discussed below, the operation is still evolving. The demonstration--and this is what the OEO calls a "demonstration project"-- is not yet complete.

The project is important not merely for Buffalo, but as a general scientific test of the adaptability of the ombudsman concept to local government. Buffalo is a large industrial city. The problems facing Buffalo are fairly representative of the problems facing most urban areas in the United States. The Buffalo experiment should provide some answer to the question: what role can an ombudsman play in the complexity of modern urban life in the United States? This experiment is one of the very few illustrations of the local ombudsman to be found anywhere in the world. It is the only one that employs neighborhood offices in the core areas. As Part (3) of this Report shows, the Buffalo experiment occupies a unique place in the worldwide spread of the ombudsman concept.

Accordingly the Service recently wrote the OEO requesting an extension of the project to August 31, 1969. If for budgetary or other reasons the OEO denies this request, an effort will be made to obtain private financing. If that is not forthcoming the Service's needs will be presented to the City and County.

Reference was made above to the continued evolution of the project. Two trends will serve as examples.

Certain city services cannot be well performed without some cooperation from the citizens. For example, streets cannot be well cleaned when cars are parked along the curbs. If temporary no-parking signs are posted a difficult policing problem is presented if the signs are generally ignored and an even worse problem if they are torn down. Neighborhood cooperation requires organization. Through its neighborhood aides the Service has recently been active, and it intends to become more active, in the organization and encouragement of block clubs which, it is hoped, will be able to increase the level of cooperation and coordination between city officials and the neighborhood residents. In this work the Service will of course cooperate with the Citizens Advisory Committee on Community Improvement.

Writers about the ombudsman often refer to his expertness in administrative matters. The writers sometimes seem to forget that expertness cannot be acquired overnight. The Buffalo ombudsmen have at all times been aware of the fact that the officials with whom they deal can usually be expected to know their own jobs better than the ombudsmen do. But even ombudsmen can learn with experience. Enough experience has now been gained by the Service to enable it to make administrative suggestions more often in the future than it has in the past.

To sum up: The project is an experiment, a unique experiment in an important field. The experiment has been of value to date, but it is still incomplete. Because there has been so little experience with local ombudsmen anywhere in the world and because Buffalo offers an excellent test of the concept in urban America, this experiment has national significance. If the experiment is extended through the summer of 1969, its strengths and weaknesses can be more thoroughly appraised.

John H. Hollands
Director

Lance Tibbles
Deputy Director

September 4, 1968

CITIZENS ADMINISTRATIVE SERVICE

FOURTH REPORT

Buffalo's Ombudsman Project, with the official name "Citizens Administrative Service," completed a year of operation on November 16, 1968. The project has been sponsored by the Faculty of Law and Jurisprudence of the State University of New York at Buffalo and is funded by the United States Office of Economic Opportunity. This report is concerned largely, though not entirely, with the fourth quarter of operations.

This report is divided into four parts: (1) Extension of the Project, (2) Operations and Statistics, (3) Police Cases, and (4) Administrative Suggestions.

(1)   Extension of the Project

The original OEO grant became effective August 14, 1967 and was to expire August 13, 1968. Because of the time required to recruit staff and start operations, this expiration date was soon changed to October 31, 1968.

During the Service's third quarter, as reported in its Third Report, the OEO was asked to extend the project from October 31, 1968 to August 31, 1969. The basis for this request was the fact that the project is a so-called "demonstration project"--that is, an experiment--and that in the Service's opinion more time was needed to round out the experiment. This request was never acted on by the OEO. Instead, recognizing the OEO's budgetary problems, the Service made an alternative request for an extension to May 31, 1969 without any further grant of funds. The alternative request was accompanied by a proposed budget of the then unexpended portion of the original grant of $123,182. The OEO approved the proposed budget with minor modifications and granted an extension to April 30, 1969.

(2) Operations and Statistics

A distinctive feature of the project has been its neighborhood offices in the inner city. During the fourth quarter, due to a variety of developments, its neighborhood offices on the east side were consolidated into a single office at 415 East Ferry Street (telephone 882-0434) and its west side office was moved to 425 Niagara Street (telephone 852-2544). The neighborhood offices are open from 1:00 to 7:00 p.m. Monday through Friday.

During its first year of operation, from November 17, 1967 to November 16, 1968, a total of 1,059 complaints and inquiries were filed with the Service. Of this total, 87 were rejected, withdrawn or referred elsewhere, leaving 972 actually handled. At the end of the year, 876 complaints had been closed and 183 were still active. A breakdown of the complaints by subject matter is given in Appendix A to this report.

As explained in earlier reports, the Service's refusal to accept complaints arising outside the city limits of Buffalo has not prevented its accepting complaints involving the County of Erie as well as the City and also, whenever there is in Buffalo a regional or district office of the agency concerned, complaints involving the State of New York or the United States Government. The comparative number of complaints received involving these various governments may be summarized as follows:

City of Buffalo   71%
Erie County   20%
New York State   6%
United States   3%

(3)   Police Cases

In December of 1967 and January and February of
1968 the project was attacked in the Buffalo Common
Council, first on the ground that it was a "civilian
review board" and therefore a threat to the Police
Department, then on the ground that it was "a substitute
for a civilian review board." In Part (3) of its First
Report the Service answered these charges and explained
its policy with respect to complaints regarding the
Police Department, particularly those involving accusations which, if true, would call for disciplinary action
on the part of the Department. It was stated that, in
handling charges of misconduct by a police officer, the
Service would deal with officials at or near the head
of the department. It would present the information and
arguments supporting the accusation of misconduct since
the case for the accused officer is ordinarily easily
accessible within the Department. It was thought that
by following this procedure the ombudsman would perform
a valuable function by making it possible for the
superior officers in the Department to analyze the case
on the basis of a fuller, more rounded picture than they
would have if they relied on departmental sources alone.
After one year of operation, experience has confirmed
most of these initial suppositions but has also shown
some unanticipated obstacles.

The table of complaints in Appendix A shows 52 complaints and inquiries relating to traffic and 43 relating
to other police functions. The traffic complaints
involved requests for stricter enforcement of speeding
and other traffic offenses in residential zones, near
schools, etc., removal of cars abandoned in the street,

repair of broken traffic control signs and signals and of broken street name signs, enforcement of parking provisions, and the like. These cases were taken up with the Traffic Division of the Department by correspondence on a routine basis.

The 43 complaints and inquiries relating to other police functions involved a variety of matters, including a substantial number of requests for additional protection and enforcement of various laws, including also some complaints alleging misconduct by police officers. It is the complaints in this last category, alleging misconduct, which have presented obstacles that were not anticipated at the beginning of the project.

With few exceptions, when a person alleges that a police officer has physically mistreated him, the complainant himself has been charged with disorderly conduct or some other crime and has been placed under arrest as part of the incident. The alleged misconduct may have occurred before, during or after the arrest was made, but almost invariably the complainant has been arrested and is facing criminal charges.

When such a complainant comes to the ombudsman and tells his story, the ombudsman must be concerned with the criminal charges. Because the conviction of either a felony or a misdemeanor will result in a fine or imprisonment, as well as a black mark on the record of the accused, the defense in the criminal action must be given priority. Before taking any action which might affect the criminal case, the ombudsman feels obliged to talk to the complainant's attorney. It has been the Service's experience that the attorney will ordinarily ask the ombudsman to refrain from acting until the criminal case has been completed.

The first action in the criminal case by the complainant's attorney will often be to ask the District Attorney either to drop the charges or to reduce the charges to a lesser crime, to which the defendant will plead guilty. The attorney may believe that the chances of having the charges dropped or reduced will be adversely affected if at the same time the ombudsman is filing an accusation of misconduct with the Police Department. In addition, both the defendant's attorney and the Police Department may be unwilling to have a third party interview witnesses and participants prior to the decision or settlement of the case.

Frequently when the prosecution agrees to dismiss the charges, the defendant is required to sign an agreement holding the governmental unit and the officers involved free from liability for any action that occurred during the arrest and incarceration of the defendant. At least one attorney believes that such an agreement, at least morally, requires him to ask that the ombudsman take no action on the allegation of misconduct by the police officer. If the criminal charges are not dropped, and if the defendant pleads not guilty, some time may elapse before the case comes to trial. After this passage of time it is difficult for the Service to make an effective investigation of the allegation of police misconduct.

The Service has no criticism of the manner in which the Police Department has dealt with those complaints which the Service has brought to its attention.

(4)   Administrative Suggestions

In its Third Report the Service made the following statement:

> Enough experience has now been
> gained by the Service to enable
> it to make administrative sug-
> gestions more often in the future
> than it has in the past.

Appendix B to this report describes in detail four different situations in which the ombudsman has urged administrative changes. These situations involved, respectively, the Erie County Social Services Department, the United States Social Security Administration, the Buffalo Municipal Housing Authority, and the Buffalo Corporation Counsel's Office. Each situation involved what can only be called the minutiae of administration. Yet it is in correcting small administrative errors that the ombudsman is most useful. Taken cumulatively over a period of time, the small corrections become worthwhile.

> Lance Tibbles
> Director

January 24, 1969

[CITIZENS ADMINISTRATIVE SERVICE REPORT]
APPENDIX A

Abandoned cars	12
Building permits	2
Civil service	13
Condemnation	21
Demolition	95
Dogs	6
Dumps	7
Employment	8
Garbage Removal	43
Landlord and tenant	32
Licensing	10
Paving	68
Police, traffic	52
Police, other	43
Probation	6
Public health	90
Public housing	91
Recreation	24
Schools	31
Snow removal	19
Social service	119
Street cleaning	9
Street lighting	31
Taxes, income	5
Taxes, real estate	9
Traffic engineering	15
Trees	26
Urban renewal	15
Water charges	4
Zoning	8
Miscellaneous	44
Total complaints handled	972
Complaints rejected	63
Complaints withdrawn	2
Complaints referred elsewhere	22
Total complaints not handled	87
Total complaints docketed	1,059

[CITIZENS ADMINISTRATIVE SERVICE REPORT]

APPENDIX B

I

The ombudsman has informed the Erie County Department of Social Services that, in investigating a series of complaints, we have noticed what appears to be a lack of sensitivity of some welfare caseworkers to the basic requirements of building, housing and health codes and of the New York State Rent Control Law. In most cases it is the duty of the landlord to make the repairs necessary to bring the premises into compliance with these code provisions. Because caseworkers often visit the family in the home, as well as approve the home before the client moves in, the caseworker is in an excellent position to observe possible violations and to ask for an inspection by the appropriate governmental agency. If there is a violation, the agency can require the landlord to make repairs. In addition, the Social Services Department may withhold rent in some cases until the landlord makes the required repairs. But this all depends upon the reporting by caseworkers of possible code violations.

The same is true with rent control. It is a simple matter for welfare caseworkers to check with the Local Rent Administration office to see if the building into which their client is moving is (1) covered by rent control, and if so, (2) whether the rent charged is in excess of the allowable maximum. If the Social Services Department authorizes payment of rent in excess of the maximum allowable under the rent control provisions, it is unnecessarily expending public funds.

The ombudsman has investigated cases where building, housing, and health code and rent control violations in apartments rented to welfare recipients went unreported by the welfare caseworker. A flagrant example of both code and rent control violations was discovered by the ombudsman in a West Side apartment building. Welfare recipients occupied several apartments in the building.

215

It was obvious to the casual observer from conditions in
the building and the rent being charged that there were
probable health code and rent control violations. The
ombudsman asked the Erie County Health Department to
inspect for health code violations. The ombudsman also
checked the rent being charged for the apartments and
found that it was about four times as high as the listed
maximum rent. The ombudsman then assisted the welfare
recipient-tenants in filing protests for rent control
violations. The Health Department ordered the building
owner, among other things, to (1) hire a licensed roach
exterminator to treat the entire building, (2) correct
an electrical space heater, (3) exterminate rats and
seal rat holes, and (4) repair electrical fixtures.
After the filing of the rent control protests, an answer
by the owner, and a hearing, rent control violations
were found and refunds ordered.

II

A woman came to the office who was confused about
her current status with various public agencies,
including the Erie County Social Services Department,
New York State Workmen's Compensation, and the United
States Social Security Administration. In investigating the matter for her, we discussed her case with
a clerk in the Social Security office. We found that
she had earlier filed for Social Security Disability
Benefits and had been denied. She had also filed for
reconsideration of this denial. The letter from Social
Security, which informed her of the denial, stated,
"...it has been determined that your condition was not
disabling within the meaning of the law.... If you
believe that this determination is not correct, you may
request that your case be re-examined.... If additional
evidence is available, you should submit it with your
request."

The Social Security clerk with whom we talked said
that no additional reasons for the denial would be given

to a claimant. She said that it is improper to tell the claimant the results of the medical evidence relied upon for the denial of a disability application. The clerk admitted that the claimant could submit additional medical evidence for reconsideration, but stated that she could not examine the medical evidence or be informed of the medical information relied upon in making the determination.

The ombudsman was not satisfied. A claimant, without knowing more precisely the reasons for the denial, can not make a rational judgment about a reconsideration. The mere statement that the claimant is not disabled within the meaning of the law does not give the claimant useful information upon which to exercise sound judgment. It is also difficult for the claimant to submit additional relevant evidence, when he or she does not know the specific grounds for denial.

The ombudsman checked the statutes and regulations relevant to procedures when an application for disability benefits is denied by Social Security. It appeared that the claimant may ask for a reconsideration of the initial determination within six months of notification of the results of the initial determination, and if dissatisfied, may make a written request for a formal hearing either after the initial determination or after the reconsideration. At the hearing the claimant can present evidence and can be represented by counsel.

However, this claimant had already filed for a reconsideration, the files had been sent to New York, the reconsideration was under way and it was too late for the claimant to present additional evidence. The ombudsman, however, thought the disclosure to a claimant of the medical information relied upon for the initial determination was important enough to merit further investigation.

The procedures set out in the Social Security regulations differed considerably from what the clerk had said. The ombudsman talked with a Social Security official who confirmed that the procedures used by the local Social Security office are those contained in the Social Security regulations, not the ones stated by the clerk. This illustrates a problem in a large agency where the supervisors cannot always look over the shoulder of every clerk. However, it is important that the clerks are selected, trained, and guided so that the risk of their misinforming the public is kept at a minimum. For it is the clerk and not the supervisor whose daily function is to deal with the public.

The Social Security regulations and the written procedures under them appear sound. Because of the increasing number of people who are applying for Social Security disability benefits, the importance of the question of release of medical information, and the need for a claimant to know what medical evidence was used against him, these practices and procedures are set out below for their informational value.

The regulations provide that medical information directly concerning a claimant or prospective claimant may be disclosed to the claimant or his authorized representative, if disclosure of such medical information is reasonably necessary to carry out the purpose of the Social Security disability provisions. The medical information may be furnished in summary form or in such detail as is determined by the Social Security Administration to be consistent with the proper and efficient administration of its programs. Medical information concerning a claimant or prospective claimant may be disclosed to the claimant's physician or to a medical institution where the claimant is a patient if (1) the claimant consents to the disclosure of the information, (2) the source of the information consents to the disclosure, and (3) the disclosure is for the purpose of the care or treatment of the claimant or prospective claimant.

The letter to the claimant informing him that his disability claim has been denied is usually quite brief.

If the claimant comes to the Social Security office, a summary of the determination, which is all that the office has, is discussed with him.

Social Security does not permit the claimant to examine the medical evidence itself. They believe that this refusal is consistent with accepted medical practice. The claimant may be supplied a summary of the medical findings, but only a summary, if he is dissatisfied with the action taken on his claim. However, the sources that have furnished the medical information about the claimant may be identified for the claimant. Moreover, it is probable that, if the claimant were to obtain the authorization of his doctor, there would be no objection to allowing the claimant to examine the report, since both doctor and patient have agreed that the claimant may see it.

If on reconsideration the initial determination denying disability benefits is upheld, a letter giving a more detailed explanation of the medical reasons for the decision is sent to the claimant.

III

One of the regulations of the Buffalo Municipal Housing Authority is that any person who owes a debt to the Authority is required to pay this debt before an application for public housing will be accepted. This regulation applies even though the debt has been discharged in bankruptcy. The ombudsman disagrees with this regulation and recommends that it be changed to eliminate the requirement that a debtor-applicant pay the discharged debt before becoming eligible for admission to public housing.

The purpose of public housing according to the New York Public Housing Law is to provide adequate, safe, and sanitary dwelling accommodations for low income persons. The purpose of the United States Bankruptcy Act

is to relieve the honest debtor from the weight of
oppressive indebtedness and permit him to start afresh
free from the obligations and responsibilities conse-
quent upon business misfortune. However, the debt is
not extinguished, although legal proceedings to collect
the debt are barred. There is no doubt that a private
landlord can exclude persons whose past debts to the
landlord have been discharged in bankruptcy. However,
the Housing Authority is not a private landlord.

The ombudsman recommends that each case be examined
on its merits to determine whether the applicant is
qualified for public housing. This examination could
include any evidence, including the existence of unpaid
past debts, indicating that the applicant does not have
the present ability and determination to meet future
rent payments. But reluctance of an applicant to pay a
debt discharged in bankruptcy does not disprove such
determination. Obtaining a discharge in bankruptcy may
be a more accurate guide to the good intentions of the
family than the paying of a particular debt. In bankruptcy proceeding all creditors are given equal access
to the debtor's assets, without favoritism or preference.
As for ability, while the family may not have an accumulation of extra funds sufficient to pay a past debt, they
may be able to afford low cost public housing on a month
to month basis.

To these arguments the Municipal Housing Authority
responds that it has an obligation to its tenants to
keep operating costs and rent as low as possible. The
Authority is operating at maximum governmental subsidy.
All added costs must be passed on to the tenants in the
form of increased rent. When a tenant, who will not pay
future rent, is allowed to enter public housing, it adds
to the operating costs and ultimately to the rent paid
by other tenants. The payment of a discharged debt is
a positive indication of both the family's willingness
to accept responsibility and their ability and determination to pay the rent in the future. In any event, the
number of such applicants who have a debt discharged in

bankruptcy is small and a compromise is usually worked out in each individual case.

It should be clearly understood that the ombudsman makes no contention that the Housing Authority is acting upon some ulterior motive of harassing low income families. There is not the least suggestion of bad faith by Housing Authority officials. The disagreement between the Housing Authority and the ombudsman is entirely one of administrative practice.

IV

The ombudsman has suggested that the City of Buffalo maintain, in the Supreme Court Library, the Law School Library of the State University of New York at Buffalo, and the Buffalo and Erie County Public Library, current up-to-date copies of the Buffalo Charter, the Buffalo general ordinances, and the Buffalo Police Department Rules and Procedures.

The lack of accessibility of current copies of these documents has been of concern to the ombudsman. Both attorneys and laymen have expressed disappointment with their inability to obtain access to them. Each of the three libraries presently contains outdated versions of the Buffalo Charter and Ordinances.

The importance of maintaining current ordinances accessible to the public in a city the size of Buffalo cannot be overstated. Ours is a system of written law. We are assured of uniform application of the law when its provisions are readily available for inspection. With individual conduct becoming increasingly regulated by municipal ordinances, the accessibility of local laws is now of more importance than it was in the past. Local laws should be readily available to both attorneys and laymen.

The Buffalo Police Department Rules and Procedures is a public document and each member of the Department is provided with a copy. Although the internal procedures may not be a vital concern to most people, there is some dissatisfaction with the lack of access to them. A copy is available at the Police Academy, but many people would hesitate to walk into the police station and ask to see it.

Upon the ombudsman's suggestion the Buffalo Corporation Counsel has directed that up-to-date copies of the Buffalo Charter and Ordinances and the Police Department Rules and Procedures be placed in the three libraries.

APPENDIX V

District Ombudsman Report

Henry S. Reuss
Congressman

DISTRICT OMBUDSMAN REPORT BY
CONGRESSMAN HENRY S. REUSS*

...for four months last spring, I experimented with my own private Ombudsman in Milwaukee. The Ombudsman selected was Mr. James Buckley, a live-wire in his early thirties who had been until January, 1967, clerk of the Wisconsin State Assembly. At that point, the control of the assembly changed parties, and Mr. Buckley was, as the saying goes, at liberty.

My experimental Ombudsman had no statutory authority. I made room for him during the experimental four months on my Congressional Clerk allowance at a salary of $708 a month.

The experimental Ombudsman was a far different affair from the statutory Washington-centered Ombudsman which is the subject of H.R.3388. Far from relieving me from case-work, he made more case-work. But Mr. Buckley established by the Experiment that a sensitive and energetic person may do a great deal to humanize government and to ease the administrative difficulties of the average citizen.

My Ombudsman used as his headquarters my own Congressional office in downtown Milwaukee. At times, he had the assistance of volunteer workers who pinch-hit for him. He held regular office hours--widely publicized in press, radio, and TV--each week in six post offices in my district, the north side of Milwaukee. At the appointed hour each week, he would set up a

---

*From an address by Congressman Reuss to the Thirty-Second American Assembly on the Ombudsman, Arden House, October 30, 1967. Printed in Congressional Record, November 6, 1967, pp. H14670-72. See pp. H14671-72.

table, some chairs, and an identifying poster in the post office lobby. While the post masters offered Mr. Buckley the use of their private offices, he figured that the marking "private" on the official door might scare some people away. In fact, situating himself in the public lobby did not seem to inhibit complaints in the least.

Of the six post offices, three were in the inner core of Milwaukee, with heavy concentrations of low-income Negroes; two were in lower-middle to middle-income areas; and one was in an upper-income area.

Particularly during the first four weeks, the volume of complaints was almost overwhelming. People stood in long lines at the post office to see the Ombudsman.

In the four months of the projects, 467 "cases" were received. About 60 percent were cases involving Federal agencies, the remainder cases involving state and local agencies or private matters. Mr. Buckley received all complaints, handling the Federal ones through my office, and doing what he could with state and local government, like the State Insurance Commission or the Industrial Commission. While of course he had no investigatory power over the agencies involved, he reports that in no case was this a handicap. He also reports that the Congressional imprimatur was an effective entree to officialdom at all levels.

The break down of the 467 cases received is instructive:

Social Security	114
Miscellaneous	61
Medicare	47
Veterans' Administration	35
Military	35
Local government	34
Suggestions for new or amended legislation	29

Legal matters	19
Immigration and Customs	18
Small business and patents	17
Taxes	14
State government	14
Job requests	14
Local government--welfare	11
No action taken	5
Total	467

What was the result of Mr. Buckley's action in the 467 cases? In 90 cases the complaint was justified and the constituent's grievances redressed; in 62 cases complaints had previously been made to governmental agencies, and the Ombudsman's work was to expedite; in 75 cases the complaint seemed reasonable, but a final result had not been obtained by the end of the experiment last June (many of these cases have since had a successful outcome); in 148 cases the complaint was finally determined to be unjustified (though in most of these cases the Ombudsman's efforts were appreciated and the constituent felt better); in 91 cases the subject matter was not a complaint but an expression of opinion or a request for information.

The Ombudsman reports that those using his services come from a wide variety of income groupings, and are by no means confined to the poor.

Sometimes the Ombudsman's solutions are simplicity itself. For example, Mr. Buckley had some complaints that in one federal office building in Milwaukee employees were forced to use toilet paper to dry their hands in the lavatory, because of a paper towel economy drive. With a little leg work, the Ombudsman was able to convince the various federal building managers that agencies with surplus paper towels--and there were some-- should share them at the week's end with the deficit areas. It turned out there are enough paper towels to go around.

Here are some observations Mr. Buckley made on the pattern of his 467 complaints:

1.   The biggest single citizen difficulty was with governmental delay in the completion of cases. Take case #165. He had been waiting 5 months to begin receiving his monthly social security benefits. He had exhausted all of his resources, and had to keep pleading with the manager of a hotel to forestall eviction. There was no question of eligibility. #165 was himself partially to blame for not getting the necessary age-proving documents a bit sooner from his native land. After all the initial processing was completed, however, he still had to wait, and after several months was in severe straits. The Ombudsman repeatedly called the local Social Security office, and was assured they were doing all they could, that they had placed an "Urgent" status on the case with the Chicago Payment Center of the Social Security Administration. Repeated calls to the local office and their repeated calls to Chicago availed nothing. Finally, my office in Washington interceded with the Chicago office. After a day, we were informed that the source of the problem had been traced, and #165 could expect his initial benefit payment in about 10 days. But 10 more days of this was too much. A second intervention got #165 his check in three days.

2.   Complaints related primarily to ordinary problems, and did not involve gross injustices. No great scandals were uncovered by the experiment, which stressed the meat and potatoes of everyday existence; the denial of a Veterans Administration disability claim; the unwillingness of the Small Business Administration to give a reason for refusal of a loan; coaxing the Social Security office to expedite the payment of a death benefit claim.

3.   A surprisingly small number of complaints belonged in the "nut" category[, d]espite the Ombudsman's fears that he might have to spend endless hours with people who had thought up new ways to send rockets to the moon, or a secret elixir for maintaining eternal

youth. Surprisingly few such ear-benders showed up, although a number of citizens found in the Ombudsman a new source of friendship and took the occasion to "visit" with him longer than a statement of the complaint would have required.

4. The possibility of press publicity can help get action.

One of the first cases received concerned a lady who paid over $40 a month on a utility bill, yet had no heat or hot water to show for this expense. The Ombudsman suggested to her in the presence of a reporter that the Public Service Commission might be interested in her problem. The day after this appeared in the local press, representatives of the utility volunteered their willingness to look into the problem and to handle it on a purely local basis. They investigated, found mechanical problems in the equipment, repaired the default, and went one step further by putting the customer on their monthly low-cost budget payment plan. They probably would have done this anyway, had they known of the problem, but there is little doubt that the press attention given the case, and uncertainty over possible future attention, was helpful in eliciting a response, and spurred by the hope that the case would not be passed on to a regulatory agency.

My Ombudsman experiment may lead to something more permanent. The Law School of Marquette University in Milwaukee is now applying, at my suggestion, for a grant from the Office of Economic Opportunity to enable it to sponsor at least two Ombudsmen to operate within Milwaukee. The OEO has already funded a somewhat similar grant to Buffalo, N.Y., through the State university. The idea of the Ombudsman has been approved by the county executive, which affords him, in my judgment, enough of an official status so that he can do most of the good that the admirers of the device envisage. If the problem that arises is a federal one, I foresee no difficulty in his handling it directly, or referring it to me in Washington.

All told, more will be heard from the Ombudsman in America. The United States has created many of its political institutions by borrowing and adapting. We took the name of the Senate from Rome, our Speaker from the British House of Commons, and our doctrine of the separation of powers from the French philosophers. We could do worse than to borrow and adapt the concept of the Swedish Ombudsman.

APPENDIX VI

Report of the Western American Assembly on the Ombudsman

Includes pages 25 through 33 of the report as published in 1968 by the Institute of Governmental Studies, University of California, Berkeley, and edited by Stanley Scott.

APPENDIX VI

Contents

(Note: pages 1 through 24 of the
original printed text were omitted because of space limitations.)

233

ASSEMBLY REPORT*

At the close of their discussions
the participants in the Western
American Assembly on the Ombudsman
reviewed and approved the following
statement, as a group. Although
there was general agreement on the
statement, it should not be assumed
that every participant necessarily
subscribed to all findings and
recommendations.

In depicting American life in the second half of
the Twentieth Century, future historians may well
describe our era as the "Administrative Age." Government is increasingly complex and its decisions more
and more affect the daily lives of people in ways
unknown to and unfelt by previous generations.

There is a dilemma in the relationships between
the citizen and the governmental agencies serving him.
On one hand, agencies have an obligation to individual
citizens to provide fairly and completely services due
them. But on the other hand, agencies are expected by
the collective citizenry to handle each problem with a
minimum of cost and time.

The First Amendment guarantee of the "right...to
petition the government for a redress of grievances"

*From Stanley Scott, ed., Western American Assembly
on the Ombudsman: Report (Berkeley: Institute of Governmental Studies, University of California, 1968) pp. 25-
33.

does not necessarily assure that the government will
listen and attempt to effect a remedy. To many the
right is one in name only, with inadequate safeguards
to make the guarantee a reality.

This Assembly has been devoted to the need for
making the voice of the citizen more effective in his
relations with all levels of his government. A consensus was reached on the following findings and recommendations.

Findings

1. As government has grown in size and complexity
many citizens believe that it has become increasingly
inaccessible and impersonal.

2. Grievances, real or imagined, against governmental agencies and policies are found among all citizens. Types of grievances, however, tend to be identified with certain segments of the citizenry. For
example, the grievances of different socioeconomic
groups will vary, as will those of different age groups.

3. Grievances and complaints are most prevalent
with regard to governmental agencies which have the
greatest public exposure and most frequent direct contact with citizens. The number of complaints, however,
is not an adequate index of their importance.

4. Policies, procedures, and personnel are the
source of most grievances. Other grievances may arise
because a given problem confronting a citizen is the
responsibility of more than one governmental agency or
level and there is inadequate coordination and communication among them.

5. It is important that procedures exist for effective questioning of governmental policies and actions

and that the citizens know of them. Such procedures will enhance citizens' confidence in their government.

6. Many devices already exist to provide citizen access to government at all levels. These devices may be public or private, formal or informal. Most are useful and many fulfill their assigned functions effectively, but they are not currently adequate for all needs.

a. All citizens do not enjoy equal access to existing mechanisms for redress of grievances. Voices do not speak with similar clarity nor do they fall on equally receptive ears.

b. Elected officials in responding to selected complaints often provide solutions for specific cases, but may not solve the underlying causes of the problem itself. The result is often to provide a special service for some constituents rather than to bring about equity among all citizens.

c. Where complaint mechanisms exist in administrative agencies, their operation may tend to reinforce current procedures and to condone employee actions rather than to meet the problems causing the grievances.

d. Judicial resolution of citizen grievances is an important but limited and costly remedy.

7. Access to and the openness of appropriate official records is vital to a citizen's right to know what his government is doing. Openness of records serves as a further safeguard against administrative abuse or the unfounded charges of such abuse.

8. Although decentralization of large governments, such as the establishment of "neighborhood city halls," may not always provide action on major problems,

such centers can be sources of citizen information.
They may also encourage citizens to register their
grievances at these centers. Such enhanced access
could lessen citizen alienation and feelings of futility
about relations with governments.

9. Existing mechanisms need to be strengthened
and new ones established to amplify the voice of the
citizen in the halls of government.

Recommendations

1. We recommend that the Ombudsman concept be
established in the American governmental system as an
appropriate institution to aid in promoting high standards of competence, efficiency and justice in the relations of government with its citizens.

   a. The Ombudsman should be an impartial and inde-
      pendent official of stature who (1) receives
      and investigates complaints from aggrieved
      citizens, (2) reports back to the inquirer,
      (3) initiates investigations on his own, (4)
      recommends remedial actions, where appropriate,
      and (5) makes periodic public reports.

   b. The remedial weapons of the Ombudsman are
      investigation, persuasion and publicity. He
      would not have power to reverse decisions. He
      should, however, be empowered to request and
      receive assistance and information deemed neces-
      sary for the discharge of his reponsibilities.
      He should also have the authority to subpoena
      records and witnesses.

   c. The Ombudsman should serve as a further remedy
      for citizen redress, rather than as a substi-
      tute for existing devices. He would consider
      complaints only after reasonable resort to other

239

appropriate remedies. While his office would
be one for redress rather than advocacy, his
reports and findings would provide significant
additional information and advice to enable
legislators and executives to make policy and
procedural improvements.

d. The essential characteristics of the Ombudsman,
in addition to those noted above, are a realistic concern for justice, a willingness to listen and communicate, and a desire to render
service. His services should be available
without charge.

2. We recommend that the concept of the Ombudsman
be introduced at the federal level and urge the adoption
of imaginative proposals to humanize the remoteness and
occasional harshness of this large bureaucracy. Because
of the vast size and diversity of federal operations, we
do not recommend the establishment of a single office of
Ombudsman. We note with approval the effort of the
Administrative Conference of the United States and the
United States Congress to improve federal administrative
procedures.

3. We recommend the establishment of an Ombudsman
at the state level to cover all branches and agencies
of state government, with the exception of the governor,
legislators, and judges, and to maintain informal contacts with local governments. Coverage of state agencies
and programs can be achieved through the selection of
appropriate assistants and aides rather than the creation of a multiplicity of Ombudsmen.

4. We recommend the establishment of devices to
review the judicial branch, consistent with our separation of powers, such as the California Commission on
Judicial Qualifications.

5. We recommend the widespread adoption of the
Ombudsman concept in local governments. American local

governments vary so greatly in size, population, legal structure and vitality that we do not recommend a uniform design for the local Ombudsman. At this point, experimentation with the office is needed to provide useful guides for assuring acceptance, visibility, accessibility, and effectiveness.

6. Because of the need for impartiality and administrative expertise, we recommend that the office at all levels be filled by appointment. The proper appointing authority may vary; appointment may be by the legislative body, the executive, a combination of both, or an appointive commission of broadly representative and bipartisan membership. In any event, the method of appointment should be adopted which will best assure public confidence in the independence, impartiality and status of the Ombudsman. His term of office should be sufficient in duration to overlap that of the appointing body or bodies.

7. We recommend that the Ombudsman be empowered to select his own subordinates and that these positions be exempt from the classified service of the jurisdiction. The staff should be small, but adequate to the need.

8. We recommend that the Ombudsman be removed only for cause. Removal provisions must be carefully written to guarantee his independence while in office.

9. In conclusion, we recommend the prompt enactment of state laws and local ordinances to establish an Ombudsman or the Ombudsman concept, to handle citizen complaints and to enhance the voice of the citizen in the affairs of his government.

ASSEMBLY SPONSORS AND OFFICIALS

Sponsoring Co-Chairmen: Eugene C. Lee, Director,
 Institute of Governmental Studies, University of
 California, Berkeley
 Randy H. Hamilton, Executive Director, Institute
 for Local Self Government, Hotel Claremont, Berkeley
 Clifford Nelson, President, The American Assembly,
 Columbia University

Assembly Director: George S. Blair, Claremont Graduate
 School, Claremont, California

Associate Directors: Stanley V. Anderson, Department of
 Political Science, University of California, Santa
 Barbara
 Stanley Scott, Assistant Director, Institute of
 Governmental Studies, University of California,
 Berkeley

Publicity Director: Murray Brown, Editor, Western City
 Magazine

Principal Speakers: Mark A. Hogan, Lieutenant Governor,
 Colorado
 Jerre Williams, Chairman, The Administrative Con-
 ference of the United States
 Frank Curran, Mayor, San Diego

Discussion Leaders: Edmundo R. Delgado, State Senator,
 New Mexico
 Robert M. Christofferson, City Manager, San Dimas,
 California
 Albert P. Beltrami, Chief Administrative Officer,
 Mendocino County, California

Rapporteurs: James S. Roberts, Department of Political
 Science, University of Nevada, Reno
 Lloyd Musolf, Director, Institute of Governmental
 Affairs, University of California, Davis
 Judy Kelsey, Administrative Analyst, Los Angeles
 Police Department

ASSEMBLY PARTICIPANTS

AARON, Richard I.
Professor of Law
University of Utah
Salt Lake City

ADAMS, Jack
Police Captain
Covina, California

ANDERSON, Stanley V.
Department of Political
 Science
University of California
Santa Barbara

BARRETT, Edward L., Jr.
Dean, Law School
University of California
Davis

BELLQUIST, Eric C.
Department of Political
 Science
University of California
Berkeley

BELTRAMI, Albert P.
Mendocino County
 Administrator
Ukiah, California

BENNETT, William M.
Commissioner
California Public Utilities
 Commission
San Francisco, California

BLAIR, George S.
Professor of Government
Claremont Graduate School
Claremont, California

BRADLEY, Thomas
City Councilman
Los Angeles, California

BRIEGER, Mrs. Carl
League of Women Voters
Berkeley, California

BROWN, Murray
Editor, WESTERN CITY
 Magazine
Los Angeles, California

BURROW, Mrs. Inez
Office of Administrative
 Procedure
Department of General
 Services
Sacramento, California

CAMPBELL, O. W.
Vice-Chancellor--
 Business & Finance
University of California
Berkeley

CHRISTOFFERSON, Robert M.
City Manager
San Dimas, California

COBB, Mrs. Helen
Deputy Mayor
San Diego, California

COLTON, Miss Helen
Executive Director
Family Forum
Los Angeles, California

CRAIN, Chester R.
Mayor
Compton, California

CURRAN, Frank
Mayor
San Diego, California

DAVOREN, Patrick
Deputy Sheriff
Los Angeles Co., California

DeBOLSKE, John J.
Executive Director
League of Arizona Cities
 and Towns
Phoenix, Arizona

DELGADO, Edmundo R.
State Senator
Santa Fe, New Mexico

DESKY, Robert
Deputy City Attorney
San Francisco, California

DODSON, David P.
Campus Minister
First Congregational Church
Berkeley, California

DOI, Herman S.
Legislative Reference
 Bureau
University of Hawaii
Honolulu, Hawaii

DUFFY, Mrs. Ward
League of Women Voters
San Francisco, California

FISK, Winston M.
Professor of Government
Claremont Men's College
Claremont, California

FRANKEL, Jack E.
Executive Secretary
Commission on Judicial
 Qualifications
San Francisco, California

FRANKUM, Ronald B.
Governor's Special
 Assistant for Local
 Government
Governor's Office
Sacramento, California

GARDNER, Howard
Associate Director
League of California
 Cities
Berkeley, California

GRAHAM, Mrs. Jean
Department of Political
 Science
University of Denver,
Colorado

GREENE, Sheldon
Attorney
California Rural Legal
 Assistance
Modesto, California

HADEN, Larry
Assistant City Manager
San Diego, California

HALCOMB, Lester H., Jr.
Executive Officer
Commission on California
 State Government Organi-
 zation & Economy
Sacramento, California

HAMILTON, Randy H.
Executive Director
Institute for Local Self
 Government
Berkeley, California

HANKEY, Richard O.
Professor of Government
California State College
Los Angeles, California

HILBRECHT, Norman Ty
Assemblyman
Las Vegas, Nevada

HOFFMAN, Hallock
Center for the Study of
 Democratic Institutions
Santa Barbara, California

HOGAN, Mark A.
Lieutenant Governor
State of Colorado
Denver, Colorado

HOLLANDS, John H.
Director
Citizens Administrative
 Service
Buffalo, New York

IVEY, Richard
Student, University of
 California
Berkeley, California

JIMENEZ, Ramon
California Department of
 Employment
Los Angeles, California

JONES, Burton E.
Board of Directors
Institute for Local Self
 Government
South Pasadena, California

JACKSON, Mrs. Espanola
President
Rights for Social Ser-
 vice Recipients, Incor-
 porated
San Francisco, California

KENT, T. J., Jr.
Department of City &
 Regional Planning
University of California
Berkeley

KELSEY, Miss Judy
Administrative Analyst
Police Department
Los Angeles, California

LEE, Eugene C.
Director
Institute of Governmental
 Studies
University of California
Berkeley

LOADER, Clifford F.
Mayor
Delano, California

LOEB, Robert L.
Attorney, Executive
 Director
Community Mediation
 Center
Los Angeles, California

LOWERY, Joseph M.
Attorney
Los Angeles, California

MANN, Mrs. James R.
League of Women Voters
Oakland, California

McDANIEL, Gerald R.
Department of Government
Sacramento State College
Sacramento, California

MICHAEL, Jay
University of California
  Office
Sacramento, California

MISNER, Arthur J.
Professor of Government
California State College
Los Angeles, California

MOORE, John E.
Department of Political
  Science
University of California
Santa Barbara, California

MUSOLF, Lloyd
Director
Institute of Governmental
  Affairs
University of California
Davis, California

NELSON, Clifford
President
The American Assembly
Columbia University
New York City, New York

PRICE, Mrs. John
Oakland Community Relations
  Project of the American
  Friends Service Committee
Oakland, California

ROBERTS, James S.
Department of Political
  Science
University of Nevada
Reno, Nevada

RUSCO, Elmer R.
Bureau of Governmental
  Research
University of Nevada
Reno, Nevada

SCHNUETGEN, Siegfried
Student Ombudsman
University of California
Berkeley, California

SCOTT, Stanley
Assistant Director
Institute of Governmental
  Studies
University of California
Berkeley, California

SHEA, Con F.
State Controller
Denver, Colorado

SMITH, Charles L.
Berkeley, California

STANLEY, Mrs. George E.
League of Women Voters
Santa Rosa, California

STEPP, George A., Jr.
Chief, Management
  Services Division
Department of Budget &
  Finance
Honolulu, Hawaii

WILLIAMS, Jerre
Chairman, The Adminis-
  trative Conference
  of the United States
Washington, D.C.

APPENDIX VII

American Bar Association
Section of Administrative Law
Recommendation No. 1

and

Report No. 1 of the
Section of Administrative Law
on the Establishment of an Ombudsman

with covering letter and list of Ombudsman
committee members

THE UNIVERSITY OF CHICAGO

The Law School

1111 East 60th Street
Chicago · Illinois 60637

May 29, 1968

To members of the Ombudsman Committee of the American
Bar Association:

The Council of the Administrative Law Section at
its February meeting approved the report of the Ombudsman Committee. Then, at its May meeting, the Council
adopted a recommendation to the House of Delegates,
supported by a report signed by the Chairman of the
Section.

For your information, a copy of the recommendation
and of the Section's report is enclosed.

Kenneth Culp Davis

KCD:mr

Enclosure

[Editor's note. The Recommendation regarding the
Ombudsman concept was approved by the ABA House of
Delegates at the 1969 Midyear Meeting. Both the
Recommendation and the Report are shown in their
final versions.]

AMERICAN BAR ASSOCIATION

SECTION OF ADMINISTRATIVE LAW

RECOMMENDATION NO. 1

BE IT RESOLVED, that the American Bar Association recommends:

1. That states and local governments of the United States should give consideration to the establishment of an ombudsman authorized to inquire into administrative action and to make public criticism.

2. That each statute or ordinance establishing an ombudsman should contain the following twelve essentials: (1) authority of the ombudsman to criticize all agencies, officials, and public employees except courts and their personnel, legislative bodies and their personnel, and the chief executive and his personal staff; (2) independence of the ombudsman from control by any other officer, except for his responsibility to the legislative body; (3) appointment by the executive with confirmation by a designated proportion of the legislative body, preferably more than a majority, such as two-thirds; (4) independence of the ombudsman through a long term, not less than five years, with freedom from removal except for cause, determined by more than a majority of the legislative body, such as two-thirds; (5) a high salary equivalent to that of a designated top officer; (6) freedom of the ombudsman to employ his own assistants and to delegate to them, without restraints of civil service and classification acts; (7) freedom of the ombudsman to investigate any act or failure to act by any agency, official, or public employee; (8) access of the ombudsman to all public records he finds relevant to an investigation; (9) authority to inquire into fairness, correctness of findings, motivation, adequacy of reasons, efficiency, and procedural propriety of any action or inaction by any agency, official, or public employee; (10) discretionary power to determine what

complaints to investigate and to determine what criticisms to make or to publicize; (11) opportunity for any agency, official, or public employee criticized by the ombudsman to have advance notice of the criticism and to publish with the criticism an answering statement; (12) immunity of the ombudsman and his staff from civil liability on account of official action.

3. That for the purpose of determining the workability of the ombudsman idea within the federal government, the Administrative Conference should (a) experiment by constituting itself an ombudsman for limited areas of federal activity, and (b) encourage and study experimentation by particular agencies with the ombudsman idea.

4. That establishment of a federal government-wide ombudsman system, whether or not designed to assist congressmen in handling constituents' complaints about administration, should await findings based upon the experimentation recommended.

BE IT FURTHER RESOLVED, that the Section of Administrative Law is authorized to present the views of the Association and to encourage the establishment of ombudsmen in accordance with the provisions of this Resolution, by all necessary and appropriate means.

REPORT NO. 1

REPORT OF THE SECTION OF ADMINISTRATIVE LAW
ON THE ESTABLISHMENT OF AN OMBUDSMAN

The ombudsman idea. The basic idea of an independent ombudsman charged solely with the responsibility
to investigate and to criticize administration has much
appeal. The mere existence of such an officer gives
administrators added incentives to avoid injustice and
to correct maladministration. An ombudsman's criticisms
may provide effective relief to aggrieved citizens when
other protections are inadequate, as they usually are
when administrative appeal and judicial review are either
unavailable or too expensive for the circumstances; yet
an ombudsman may withhold criticisms when he finds that
other remedies are adequate. The Administrative Law
Section believes that the ombudsman system can be readily
adapted to American state and local governments, in
absence of special local reasons to the contrary. At
the same time, an ombudsman system cannot be a substitute for competent administration, for conscientious
personnel, for adequate supervision of public employees
by superiors, for administrative appeals, or for judicial review of administrative action. What is proposed
for states and cities is an addition to such protections,
not a substitute for them.

The twelve essentials. The twelve essentials the
Section recommends for state or local legislation establishing an ombudsman are set forth in the basic resolution. These principles govern the scope of his duties,
limitations upon his powers, and the degree of independence necessary for him to carry out his responsibilities. All twelve of these essentials are contained
in a widely-circulated model bill prepared by Professor
Walter Gellhorn, draft number 3, June 12, 1967, which
the Section recommends as a general guide for drafting
legislation for states and cities.

The federal government. In the federal government, the Administrative Section believes that experimentation should be the first step. The Administrative Conference Act of 1964, 5 U.S.C. Sections 573-576, authorizes the Chairman of the Conference to "make inquiries into matters he considers important for Conference consideration, including matters proposed by individuals inside or outside the Federal Government." The Section recommends that the Chairman should choose particular governmental functions about which he and his staff will consider complaints from aggrieved parties, for the primary purpose of developing understanding of the potentialities of an ombudsman system for the federal government. It is also recommended that the Administrative Conference should study ombudsman systems already existing within federal agencies and should encourage experimentation with the idea by additional agencies.

The Section believes that experimentation on a limited basis is desirable before moving toward establishment of a government-wide system, because the size of the federal government may change the essential nature of the ombudsman idea. The system of the ombudsman in other countries has been most successful when a single individual of great prestige has won such public confidence that his opinions are highly respected. Although an organization may be capable of doing what an eminent personage can do, an ombudsman's office for the entire federal government might require from 2,000 to 4,000 employees, and such a large bureaucracy may be less effective in checking the bureaucracy than a prestigious individual assisted by a staff.

Congressional casework. Not only should establishment of a government-wide ombudsman await the experimentation recommended, but so should establishment of a central federal office to assist congressmen in handling constituents' complaints. Congressmen now handle more than 200,000 complaints about administration annually, and the idea of creating an office to help them with their enormous burden is a natural one. A central office would obviously be better organized for handling the vast mass of complaints than are the staffs attached to the office of each congressman. But the ombudsman system serves a slightly different purpose. It is not linked to service for constituents; the criticism is provided by those who are performing no other function. For this reason, the further development of a system which primarily emphasizes service to constituents should await the development, through actual experience, of better understanding of systems of criticism by independent ombudsmen. The long-term objective should be effective criticism of administrators by independent officers who have no stake, direct or indirect, in any particular results.

The ombudsman system has been in operation in several countries, primarily in Scandinavia. The recommendation here under consideration was first proposed by the Ombudsman Committee of the Administrative Law Section, and the Committee's Chairman, Professor Kenneth Culp Davis. The Section, through unanimous action of its Council, urges the Association to adopt this resolution. No funds need to be specifically appropriated to implement the resolution.

Respectfully submitted,

SECTION OF ADMINISTRATIVE LAW

Ben C. Fisher, Chairman

Ombudsman Committee Members

Professor Stanley V. Anderson
University of California
Santa Barbara, California 93106

Sidney J. Barban, Esq.
4604 Lawnpark Road
Baltimore, Maryland 21229

David Booth Beers, Esq.
Shea & Gardner
734 Fifteenth Street, N.W.
Washington, D.C. 20005

Sheldon I. Cohen, Esq.
Chapman, DiSalle and Friedman
Pennsylvania Building
Washington, D.C. 20004

Professor Maurice S. Culp
School of Law
Western Reserve University
Cleveland, Ohio 44106

Charles M. Dosh, Esq.
Wormwood, Wolvington,
    Renner and Dosh
810 Symes Building
Denver, Colorado 80202

Bernard Frank, Esq.
517 Hamilton Street
Allentown, Pennsylvania 18105

Professor Walter Gellhorn
School of Law
Columbia University
New York, New York 10027

Benny Kass, Esq.
New Senate Office Building
Room 3210
Washington, D.C. 20510

Benedict T. Mangano, Esq.
112 State Street
Albany, New York 12207

Malcolm S. Mason, Esq.
4740 Connecticut Avenue, N.W.
Washington, D.C. 20008

William J. Moore, Esq.
Carnation Company
Carnation Building
Los Angeles, California 90036

L. Manning Muntzing, Esq.
The Chesapeake and Potomac Telephone
  Company of West Virginia
816 Lee Street
Charleston, West Virginia 25301

Thurlow Smoot, Esq.
55 Public Square
Cleveland, Ohio 44113

David A. Swankin, Esq.
Executive Office of the President
Washington, D.C. 20500

Raymond J. Turner, Esq.
Dawson, Nagel, Sherman & Howard
1900 First National Bank Building
Denver, Colorado 80202

Stanley Wolder, Esq.
521 Fifth Avenue
New York, New York 10017

Professor Kenneth Culp Davis, Chairman
University of Chicago Law School
1111 East 60th Street
Chicago, Illinois 60637

APPENDIX VIII

A Report on, and
Draft of, Proposed Local Law for a
New York City Ombudsman
by the
Association of the Bar of the City of New York
Committee on Administrative Law

APPENDIX VIII

Contents

The Association of the Bar
Of the City of New York
42 West 44th Street

Committee on Administrative Law

A REPORT ON, AND DRAFT OF, PROPOSED

LOCAL LAW FOR A NEW YORK CITY OMBUDSMAN*

The Committee on Administrative Law of The Association of the Bar of the City of New York recommends
that an independent Office of Public Complaints be
established in New York City, to be headed by an Ombudsman. To this end the committee has drafted the accom-
panying bill.

The "policy" declaration in the bill states two
objectives applicable to city agencies and employees:
first, "...to investigate and ameliorate grievances
arising out of allegations of...maladministration,
unfairness, unreasonableness, arbitrariness, arrogance,
rudeness, oppressiveness, inefficiency, improper motivation, unwarranted delay, clear violations of laws or
regulations, or other abuse of authority..."; and second, on the Ombudsman's initiative "...to investigate,
study and make recommendations with regard to agency
acts, practices and procedures."

The fact that there are such "grievances" is not
necessarily due to deliberate acts on the part of city
agencies or employees. In fact, New York City is noted
for the comparatively high caliber of its administrative
personnel. Many of the causes stem from the size and

_____
     *Reprinted in Congressional Record, May 10, 1967,
pp. S6637-39.

proliferation of the bureaucracies, the skyrocketing of costs of governing well, insufficient personnel, the lack of means of informing people about available services and procedures, especially for the poor and even those of modest means, and the enormous pressures on urban life today resulting from inadequate housing, conflicts in community relations, dilapidated transportation and the like.

The proposed bill will not solve these problems. Its aim is quite limited. Primarily, it seeks to build a bridge of understanding between the people and the agencies of the city government. An office which is interested in hearing the citizen's complaints and which has the ear of the officials complained about will be able, as experience elsewhere has shown, to "ameliorate" the great majority of grievances. It will undoubtedly also be a brake on those members of the official family who, for reasons not related to their jobs, provide grounds for complaint. Moreover, it will provide expertise on modern administrative practices and procedures for the assistance of the agencies which have neither the funds nor the personnel to study them.

Background of the Committee's Proposal

The committee's consideration of the desirability and feasibility of an office of public complaints for New York City began more than two years ago. It studied the ombudsman system as it originated and developed in Sweden since 1809, as well as in Finland, Denmark, Norway, New Zealand and Great Britain. It also examined the work of the Office of Public Protection, established in Nassau County, New York, in 1966. (It learned that on March 21, 1967, the City Council of San Diego, California, established an "Office of Citizens Assistance Officer".)

In addition, the committee has followed developments in those countries, such as Canada, which are now actively considering similar proposals, as well as in this country. Here, on the federal level, two bills have been introduced in Congress, one by Congressman Reuss of Wisconsin, providing for an "Administrative Counsel of Congress" (H.R.3388, 90th Cong.), and the other, proposed by Senator Long of Missouri, to establish an Ombudsman for the District of Columbia (S.3783, 89th Cong.). Senator Long has also introduced a bill to establish "...the Office of Administrative Ombudsman to investigate administrative practices and procedures of selected agencies of the United States". (S.1195, 90th Cong.) In New York State, Senator Bronson and Assemblyman Green have introduced a bill to create a state Office of Public Redress (S.9-A, Intro.A.87, 1967).

Model ombudsman bills have been drafted by Professor Walter Gellhorn, of Columbia University, (also the author of "When Americans Complain" and "Ombudsman and Others: Citizens' Protectors in Nine Countries") and the Harvard Journal of Legislation (v.2, p.213, 1965), both of which have been of much help to this committee.

In New York City, Councilman Paul O'Dwyer, in 1965, introduced a bill in the City Council to create an "Office of Citizen Redress", which was reintroduced by Councilman J. Daniel Diggs in 1966. Also in 1966, Council President Frank O'Connor introduced a similar bill. Councilman Edward L. Sadowsky, in November, 1966, filed a bill calling for the creation of an office of "Administrative Review" as an arm of the City Council.

Not only has the Committee on Administrative Law carefully analyzed all of these measures, but also it consulted with various scholars and public officials conversant with the subject. In February, 1966, it co-sponsored a forum at The Association of the Bar of the City of New York, at which addresses were given by Hon. Alfred Bexelius, the Swedish Ombudsman, and Sir Guy Powles, the New Zealand Ombudsman. (Their addresses are published in vol. 21 of the Association's "Record", p.385.) At various committee meetings, it had the

benefit of helpful comments by representatives of Mayor
Lindsay and Council President O'Connor, and by Professor
Gellhorn, Vincent L. Broderick, Esq., former New York
City Commissioner of Police, Commissioner Arnold Fraiman
of the Department of Investigation, and Benny Kass, Esq.,
legal assistant to Senator Long of Missouri. (None of
these persons, however, is responsible for, or committed
to, the bill or any of its provisions.)

Highlights of the Bill

One of the most essential aspects of the proposed
bill could not be incorporated in mandatory legislative
language. That is the stature, dignity and respect
necessary for successful operation of the office. An
effort is made in the bill's policy statement to assure
that the head of the office would be "a person of distinguished accomplishments in the field of law or administration". And, after much debate, it was decided that
the use of the title "Ombudsman" would be helpful in
this respect, because of its historical identification
with these attributes in other countries.

As to the agencies and employees covered, it was
felt there should be a minimum of exemptions. The Mayor
and the City Council, being answerable to the people in
regular elections, need no such oversight. Their
"staffs", it was also felt, should be exempt. The courts
were exempt because they have an extensive administrative
apparatus overseeing their functions, and also because
some of them are not subject to local law. The Board of
Estimate is exempted only insofar as it acts as a board.
Thus, its individual members acting in other capacities
would be subject to the Ombudsman's jurisdiction.

The appointing and removal process was designed to
insulate the Ombudsman from politics as much as possible.
His term of five years would overlap that of the Mayor's,
and his appointment would be by the Mayor with the advice
and consent of two-thirds of the Council. Various other

267

devices were considered, such as a nominating panel of
reputable citizens, but close analysis showed them not
to be workable. The salary, "equal to that of a Justice
of the Supreme Court of the State of New York serving in
New York City", should be sufficient to attract a man of
the requisite stature.

The scope of the investigative powers of the Ombudsman would be broad. He could investigate any complaint
and make "such findings and recommendations he deems
appropriate". Agencies are required to furnish information requested by him and make their records available
to him. He could initiate an investigation himself.
After giving an agency an opportunity to reply to his
findings and recommendations, he could issue them to the
press. He would, of course, report to the Mayor and the
Council.

However, the Ombudsman's powers would not include
any sanctions. He could only investigate, make findings
and recommendations and report. More definitive action
would have to be taken by the Mayor, the Council, the
electorate, or the agencies themselves.

Although the Ombudsman would have the authority to
act "in his sole discretion", he would be required both
to inform the complainant of the reason he does not
investigate, and if he does, of his findings and recommendations. But, to insulate him from harassment, his
action would not be reviewable in any court.

Effect on the Department of Investigation

The establishment of a separate Office of Public
Complaints would make it unnecessary for the Department
of Investigation to retain its complaint bureau which
has the power to receive complaints from the public
under Section 804 of the Charter. Thus, the bill provides that this section be repealed.

The Department of Investigation, however, will continue to exercise its primary functions, namely to "make any investigation directed by the mayor or the council" (New York City Charter,Sec.803[1]) and to "make any study or investigation which in his (the Commissioner of Investigation) opinion may be in the best interests of the city". (id.,Sec.803 [2]).

Although there may remain some overlap in the respective investigative powers of the Department of Investigation and the Office of Public Complaints, it is the committee's expectation that in such instances the Commissioner of Investigation and the Ombudsman would coordinate their activities.

To the extent the abolition of the complaint bureau in the Department of Investigation reduces its work load, its appropriation for such purposes could be allocated to the Office of Public Complaints. The text of the proposed bill follows:

Proposed Local Law For A New York City Ombudsman

A **LOCAL LAW** to amend the charter of the city of New York in relation to creating the office of public complaints headed by the ombudsman.

Be it enacted by the Council as follows:

Section 1. The charter of the city of New York is hereby amended by adding thereto a new chapter 54 to read as follows:

§1170. **Policy.** It is hereby found to be in the public interest to establish an office of public complaints in New York City, headed by a person of distinguished accomplishments in the field of law or administration, whose main functions would be (a) to investigate and ameliorate grievances arising out of allegations of agency maladministration, unfairness, unreasonableness, arbitrariness, arrogance, rudeness, oppressiveness, inefficiency, improper motivation, unwarranted delay, clear violations of laws or regulations, or other abuse of authority, and (b) on its own initiative, to investigate, study and make recommendations with regard to agency acts, practices and procedure.

§1171. Office of public complaints; ombudsman. There shall be an office of public complaints, the head of which shall be the ombudsman.

§1172. Definitions. a. "Agency" means any department or other governmental unit (whether or not within or subject to control or review by any other agency), any official, or any employee of the city of New York, other than (1) the board of estimate only insofar as it acts as a board, (2) the council, its members and their staffs, (3) the courts, and (4) the mayor, the deputy mayors, their assistants and their staffs.

b. "Agency act" includes every action, omission, failure to act, decision, rule or regulation, interpretation, recommendation, policy, practice, or procedure of an agency.

§1173. Ombudsman; appointment; term of office; removal; vacancy; salary. The ombudsman shall be appointed by the mayor with the advice and consent of the council, provided two-thirds of the councilmen, present and voting, concur. He shall serve for a term of five years, and shall devote his full time to the duties of said office. He may be removed by the council by a vote of three-quarters of the councilmen present and voting upon their determining that he has become physically or mentally disabled for more than six months or has been guilty of malfeasance. If the office of ombudsman becomes vacant for any reason, the mayor shall forthwith appoint a new ombudsman in the same manner as stated above to serve for the unexpired portion of the term. The ombudsman shall receive compensation in an amount equal to that of a Justice of the Supreme Court of the State of New York serving in New York City.

§1174. Organization of office of public complaints. a. The ombudsman may select, appoint, and compensate as he may see fit (within the amount available by appropriation) such assistants and employees as he may deem necessary to discharge his responsibilities under this law; and such appointments, to the extent permissible under the law of the State of New York, shall not be subject to the requirements of the civil service law.

b.   The ombudsman shall designate one of his assistants to be deputy ombudsman who shall serve as acting ombudsman when there is a vacancy in the office of ombudsman.

c.   The ombudsman may delegate to members of his staff any of his authority or duties under this law except this power of delegation and the duty of formally making recommendations to agencies or reports to the mayor or the council; provided, however, that the ombudsman may delegate any of his authority or duties under this law to the deputy ombudsman when the ombudsman is unable to perform them on account of disability or absence.

§1175.   <u>Powers</u>.   The ombudsman shall have the following powers:

a.   He may investigate, on complaint or on his own motion, any agency act, and make such findings and recommendations he deems appropriate.

b.   He may prescribe the methods by which complaints are to be made, received, and acted upon; he may determine the scope and manner of investigations to be made; and, subject to the requirements of this law, he may determine the form, frequency, and distribution of his findings and recommendations.

c.   He may request and shall be given by each agency the assistance and information he deems necessary for the discharge of his responsibilities; he may inspect and examine any and all records and documents of all agencies to the extent not prohibited by state law; and he may enter and inspect any and all premises within any agency's control; provided that any information received by him which by law is confidential shall not be disclosed.

d. He may issue subpoenas, in accordance with the provisions of CPLR Sec. 2302, to compel any agency or any other person to appear, give sworn testimony, or produce documentary or other evidence the ombudsman deems relevant to a matter under his inquiry. A person thus required to provide information shall be paid the same fees and travel allowances as witnesses in the courts of this state, and shall also be entitled to have counsel while being questioned.

e. He may, on his own initiative, undertake, participate in, and cooperate with general studies or inquiries of agency functions, practices and procedures, whether or not related to any particular complaint or agency act, and may make any findings or recommendations he deems appropriate.

f. He may do all things reasonably necessary or appropriate to the exercise of the foregoing powers.

§1176. Basis for action. The ombudsman may receive a complaint from any person concerning an agency act. He shall investigate the matters complained of unless, in his sole discretion, he determines that:

a. the complainant has available to him an adequate remedy which he could reasonably be expected to use;

b. the complaint pertains to a matter outside the ombudsman's jurisdiction;

c. the complainant does not have a direct interest in the subject matter of the complaint;

d. the complaint is trivial, frivolous, vexatious, or not made in good faith;

    e.   the complaint has been too long delayed;

    f.   the ombudsman's resources are insufficient for adequate investigation;

    g.   the matter is otherwise inappropriate for investigation.

Where the ombudsman decides not to investigate a complaint, he shall so notify the complainant, stating his reasons therefor.

§1177. <u>Findings and recommendations; notification of complainant and agency; publication.</u>

    a.   After completing the processing of a complaint the ombudsman shall, where possible, notify complainant of his findings and recommendations.

    b.   If, after investigation, but prior to publication of any findings, recommendations or report, the ombudsman finds that any agency should (1) consider the matter further, (2) modify, amend or cancel an agency act, (3) explain more fully the agency act in question, (4) take any other action, he shall notify the agency of such findings together with his recommendations. The ombudsman may request the agency to inform him, within a specified reasonable time, of any action taken by the agency on his recommendations.

    c.   After notification to the agency as above provided, and after the agency has had a reasonable opportunity to answer, the ombudsman may, if he deems the matter of sufficient importance, transmit his findings and recommendations to the mayor and the council or any of its committees. He may also make such findings and recommendations available to the press and the public. When publishing a finding or recommendation adverse to an agency he shall, unless excused by the agency or person affected, include any statement the agency may have made to him by way of explanation.

§1178. <u>Annual reports</u>. In addition to whatever reports he may make from time to time, the ombudsman shall on or about February 15 of each year report to the mayor and to the council concerning the exercise of his functions during the preceding calendar year.

§1179. <u>Disciplinary action against public personnel</u>. If the ombudsman has reason to believe that any public officer or employee has acted in a manner warranting criminal or disciplinary proceedings, he shall refer the matter to the appropriate authorities.

§1180. <u>Immunities</u>. No proceeding, finding, recommendation, or report of the ombudsman conducted or made in accordance with the provisions of this law shall be reviewable in any court.

§1181. <u>Obstruction</u>. A person who willfully obstructs or hinders the proper exercise of the ombudsman's functions, or who willfully misleads or attempts to mislead the ombudsman in his inquiries, shall be guilty of a misdemeanor, punishable by imprisonment for not more than six months or a fine of $5,000, or both.

§1182. <u>Construction</u>. If any provision of this law or the application thereof is held invalid, the remainder of this law or other application of such provision shall not be affected. No legislation shall be held to supersede or modify the provisions of this law except to the extent that such legislation shall do so expressly.

Section 2. <u>Effective date</u>. This local law shall take effect immediately.

Section 3. Section 804 of the charter of the city of New York is hereby repealed.

Respectfully submitted,

Milton M. Carrow, Chairman

| Faith Colish | Stephen R. Kaye |
| Martin R. Gold | Kenneth J. Jones |

274

Bernard J. Ruggieri
Jerome E. Sharfman
Llewellyn P. Young
Joseph S. Borus
William Q. Keenan
Melvin D. Kraft
Stephen A. Lefkowitz
Seymour B. Quel
Bernard Schwartz
Thomas Thacher

*Ruth Toch
*Stanley Buchsbaum
*Victor F. Condello
Alexander Holtzman
Robert O. Lehrman
Malcolm S. Mason
Harold L. Richman
John E. H. Sherry
Norman Solovay

*Abstain

Dated: New York City,
        April, 1967

APPENDIX IX

Reports to the Governor
from the California Commission on
Judicial Qualifications

for the years 1961–1968

APPENDIX IX

Contents

    (Note: A letter of transmittal, signed by the
            the chairman, accompanied each year's
            report. Reports were submitted to
            the Governor, "pursuant to the pro-
            visions of Section 11091 of the
            Government Code.")

[1961] REPORT OF COMMISSION
ON JUDICIAL QUALIFICATIONS

This Commission came into existence November 8, 1960 when the voters of California approved Proposition 10 adding Sections 1b and 10b to Article VI of the Constitution. Thereafter the Supreme Court, the Governor, and the Board of Governors of the State Bar made appointments to the Commission and at the first meeting Justice A. F. Bray was elected chairman.

The 1961 session of the Legislature passed implementing legislation (Stats. 1961, chap. 564, Gov. Code §§ 68701-68755) and the Judicial Council adopted Rules for Removal or Retirement of Judges (56 A.C. 2d 307).

In August Jack E. Frankel, formerly assistant secretary of the State Bar, was appointed Executive Secretary, a stenographer was employed and an office opened in the State Building, San Francisco. An article about the Commission appeared in the November-December 1961 issue of the State Bar Journal.

It is the function of the Commission to conduct investigations and hear charges against any judge of a California court and to recommend to the Supreme Court the removal of a judge for wilful misconduct in office, wilful and persistent failure to perform his duties, habitual intemperance, or his retirement for permanent disability seriously interfering with the performance of his duties.

The Commission has held five meetings in 1961, in March, June, July, September and December. By December 31, 1961, 68 matters involving 75 judges were brought to the Commission's attention. (If a judge was involved in more than one case he was counted more than once. Some matters were against more than one judge.) Of the 75 judges, 16 were justice court judges, 35 municipal court judges, 20 superior court judges, one an appellate court justice and the names of three were not established.

The great majority of these cases were closed at an early stage as not warranting further action. The bulk of these were from dissatisfied litigants and others who for various reasons had taken a dislike to a judge. Several of a more serious nature have been actively investigated by the Commission. Two justice court judges, one municipal court judge, and one superior court judge resigned or retired while investigations concerning each were pending. No recommendation for removal or retirement has been filed with the Supreme Court as of December 31, 1961.

Some investigations which did not lead to formal proceedings by the Commission did result in a marked improvement in the particular judge's practice. In these matters examination by the Commission indicated that the action of the particular judge was unbecoming to a judicial office and without due regard to the dignity of his position. However, the grounds were insufficient to constitute cause for removal under the applicable constitutional language. The Commission investigation no doubt was a corrective influence and contributed to a higher standard of judicial conduct.

Where the services of an investigator were required the Attorney General has made available a special agent from the Bureau of Criminal Identification and Investigation. The Commission has received outstanding cooperation from such offices and agencies as the State Bar of California, the Judicial Council, and the State Department of Justice.

The merit of the Commission method has now been established. A state commission with authority to conduct inquiries and investigations and hold hearings on matters involving judges assures the public that any cases of misconduct, neglect of duties, habitual intemperance, and permanent disability will receive meaningful attention while encroachment on the proper independence of the judiciary is prevented.

[1962] REPORT OF COMMISSION
ON JUDICIAL QUALIFICATIONS

The Commission on Judicial Qualifications was formed and operates under Article VI, Sections 1b and 10b of the California Constitution.

It is the function of the Commission to conduct investigations and hear charges against any judge of a California court and to recommend to the Supreme Court the removal of a judge for wilful misconduct in office, wilful and persistent failure to perform his duties, habitual intemperance, or his retirement for permanent disability seriously interfering with the performance of his duties.

As of September 1, 1962 there were 904 judicial positions within the jurisdiction of this Commission as follows:

Supreme Court	7
District Court of Appeal	30
Superior Court	335
Municipal Court	237
Justice Court	295

The Commission has held five meetings in 1962, in March, April, August, September, November. Between January 1 and December 31, 1962, 95 matters involving 110 judges were brought to the Commission's attention. (If a judge was involved in more than one case he was counted more than once. Some matters were against more than one judge.) Of the 110 judges, 27 were justice court judges, 35 municipal court judges, 44 superior court judges and 4 appellate court judges.

The great majority of these were frivolous and unfounded and were in no way a reflection on the caliber or character of the judge. A number were investigated by the Commission. In six cases which warranted further

inquiry the judge chose to resign or retire after the
investigation was underway. Of these six, five were
municipal court judges and one a justice court judge.

The 1961 and 1962 figures on matters filed, those
receiving further inquiry and those resulting in the
resignation or retirement of a judge are shown by the
table below.

	Matters Filed	Further Inquiry	Resignations or Retirements
March 24, 1961 December 31, 1961	68	23	4
January 1, 1962 December 31, 1962	95	23	6

The Commission came into existence through the
enactment of a Constitutional Amendment November 8,
1960. March 24, 1961 the Commission members took office.
August 1, 1961 an Executive Secretary was selected and
an office opened. Those interested in the improvement
of the administration of justice nationally are taking
note of this pioneering development in California.

Judge Sterry R. Waterman of the United States
Court of Appeal for the Second Circuit, and President
of the American Judicature Society, in writing on Recent
Reforms in Judicial Administration described the establishment of the Commission as "model legislation."

The Commission is proud to be making a significant
contribution towards the effective administration of
justice in California.

STATE OF CALIFORNIA

1963 REPORT OF COMMISSION

ON JUDICIAL QUALIFICATIONS

Introduction

The Commission on Judicial Qualifications, established by Constitutional amendment in 1960, has the authority to investigate and conduct proceedings against any California judge when there may be willful misconduct in office, willful and persistent failure to perform his duties, habitual intemperance or disability of a permanent character seriously interfering with the performance of his duties.

The Commission consists of five judges appointed by the Supreme Court, two lawyers appointed by the State Bar and two public members appointed by the Governor. An office is maintained in the State Building, San Francisco, staffed by an Executive Secretary and a stenographer.

Information is received and examined and consideration given to determine if allegations are within the Commission's jurisdiction. A preliminary investigation may be conducted. If the Commission concludes that a formal proceeding should be instituted to inquire into the charges a hearing is held. The proceeding may then be dismissed or the Commission may recommend removal or retirement to the Supreme Court which acts after reviewing the record. Thus far, no recommendation has been filed with the Supreme Court.*

---

*Two articles by the Executive Secretary concerning the Commission were published early in 1963: 36 Southern California Law Review 72, Judicial Conduct and Removal of Judges for Cause in California; 49 American Bar Association Journal 166, Removal of Judges: California Tackles an Old Problem.

I

As of October 1, 1963, there were 927 judicial positions within the jurisdiction of this Commission as follows:

Supreme Court	7
District Court of Appeal	30
Superior Court	346
Municipal Court	253
Justice Court	291

Taking into account changes during 1963, there were about 1,000 judges within Commission jurisdiction.

The Commission has held six meetings in 1963, in January, March, May, June, September and November. Between January 1 and December 31, 1963, 114 matters against judges were brought to the Commission's attention. Most of these were clearly unfounded, in no way an adverse reflection on the judge, and were closed with no action other than to write the complainant that the Commission had no jurisdiction. In addition, the Commission staff received and attended to many letters and visits arising from claimed grievances against, and misconceptions toward, the judicial system.

In 40 cases out of the 114 complaints brought, some inquiry was made. Thirteen of these inquiries involved Superior Court judges, 11 Municipal Court judges, and 16 Justice Court judges. In ten cases the charges were sufficiently well founded to cause the particular judge to submit his resignation or retirement after being contacted by the Commission and notified of the reported information. Five of these judges were from Justice Courts, four from Municipal Courts and one from the Superior Court. A large share of Commission activities during the year involved the handling of these ten cases which culminated in the judges' retirement or resignation. The two most common difficulties in these ten cases were:

1. Disabling illness with incapacity to perform judicial duties and

2. A weakening of mental faculties connected with advanced age and reflected in unacceptable derelictions in court.

The function of the Commission is to enforce the standards of fitness as provided by law. This is done principally by taking the appropriate steps in those situations in which it has been demonstrated that a judge should not continue in office. The Commission has tried to exercise prudence and fairness yet with the knowledge that only a positive and resolute program would meet the Constitutional responsibilities with which the Commission has been charged.

Proceedings before the Commission are confidential and every precaution has been exercised to that end. On the occasions in which news media have asked whether there is an investigation regarding some judge, the reply has been that such can neither be confirmed nor denied. Commission correspondence to complainants bears the stamp "Confidential under California Constitution Article VI, Section 10b."

During 1963 various public agencies have given their cooperation. This has been essential for the proper performance of the Commission's task and is particularly true of the Administrative Office of the Courts and the Department of Justice.

II

There are certain secondary benefits which have resulted through the existence of this type of Commission.

1. It is useful for the public to have a place to register alleged grievances against judges even though

seldom is there a basis for further Commission action from such a complaint. An official state body to receive complaints against judicial officers furnishes as much protection to honest and dedicated judges as to the public.

2. Indirectly, the Commission's very existence as a standing tribunal empowered to investigate and act has effected standards of conduct and ethics. To a certain extent this is intangible and difficult to assess. Yet the Commission is a constant reminder that the public has a paramount interest in the integrity of the courts.

3. Some of the Commission's inquiries during the year, while revealing questionable practices, were deemed not to justify a removal proceeding. Sometimes transmitting reports of such shortcomings to the judge for his reply has had a beneficial effect. These are some of the reported failings warranting correction:

> a. Undue participation in a cause; appearing to take sides in a case and failing to observe the rule against ex parte communications;

> b. Insufficient industry; intrusion of private activities on court responsibilities;

> c. Faulty courtroom demeanor, unwarranted displays of temper and irascibility.

Although only a small minority of judges may properly be subject to this kind of criticism, there are persistent deviations from what may rightfully be expected of a judicial officer.*

---

*Articles by the Chairman and the Executive Secretary on this subject have appeared this year in the magazine of the Association to which Justice Court judges belong, and the newsletter of the Conference of California Judges, the organization of the Judges of courts of record.

III

The Commission is mindful that it is exercising a significant and sensitive attribute of state sovereignty. By operating carefully and unobtrusively a practical contribution to jurisprudence is being forged. It has now been demonstrated that an independent Commission, possessing the authority to investigate and hold hearings, can act for the maintenance of judicial fitness without infringing on the essential prerogatives of the judicial branch.

Conclusion

The operation of the Commission helps insure California's claim to an outstanding judiciary. California may be justly proud of the character and dedication of the great majority of its judges.

1964 REPORT OF COMMISSION
ON JUDICIAL QUALIFICATIONS

I

The nine members on the Commission on Judicial Qualifications consist of five judges (two from the District Court of Appeal, two from the Superior Court and one from the Municipal Court) appointed by the Supreme Court, two public members appointed by the Governor with the consent of the State Senate, and two lawyers appointed by the Board of Governors of the State Bar. Two of the judicial members, Justice A. F. Bray and Judge Ben V. Curler, who rendered dedicated service on the Commission since its inception, left in the latter part of the year due to their retirement from their judicial offices. Justice Bray was an outstanding chairman for three and a half years.

The Commission is charged by the Constitution with the responsibility of investigating, and taking further action with respect to any California judge if there appears to be willful misconduct in office or willful and persistent failure to perform his duties or habitual intemperance, or a disability seriously interfering with the performance of his duties, which is, or is likely to become, of a permanent character.

The Commission's procedure is to close complaints which are clearly unfounded; to evaluate and, if warranted, make inquiry and check on apparently actionable allegations; then, depending on the situation and what is appropriate, to contact the judge by letter or in person and, in the event it is justified, hold a preliminary investigation. The preliminary investigation is the first step under the prescribed rules of procedure for the removal or compulsory retirement of judges, and it includes a registered letter setting

forth the nature of the charges and requesting an answer.
It may also be accompanied by a field investigation.

After a formal proceeding the Commission may recommend to the Supreme Court a judge's removal or retirement. Only the Supreme Court may order the removal or
retirement.

During 1964 the Commission conducted a formal
hearing before seven of the nine members of the Commission in San Diego and then recommended the removal
of the judge. This recommendation was not sustained
by the Supreme Court.

II

As of November 1, 1964 there were 933 judicial
positions within the jurisdiction of this Commission as
follows:

Appellate Courts	37
Superior Court	353
Municipal Court	256
Justice Court	287

Due to changes in judicial personnel at some time
during the year there were probably over 1,000 individuals as judges in the state. Turnover at all levels
of the judiciary, mostly due to elevations and normal
retirements, is always taking place. It is, therefore,
obvious that only a very small number of such changes
have anything to do with the functioning of this Commission.

During 1964 67 complaints against judges were filed
with the Commission including those which were processed
as a "Commission Investigation." This does not reflect
the many communications which did not contain specific
charges against a judge but were in the nature of

displeasure with some phase of the legal system or a misunderstanding of the judicial process. Also not included are the complaints filed and worked on in 1963 but concluded in 1964.

Of the actual matters filed in the year 32 warranted inquiry and therefore there was some check made or additional information required. Of these 32 inquiries 18 included a written notice to, and in some cases a personal interview with, the judge to report the allegations and to request an explanation. In certain situations in which the judge replied to a written notice his account was completely satisfactory.

On several occasions there was substantial Commission investigation and evaluation. In six cases the judge chose to retire without a formal hearing taking place. As in other years, poor health was a leading factor. With some cases in which the charges would not warrant removal, although apparently valid, the Commission action may have had a remedial effect. Only a fraction of a percent of the state's judges were involved either in the matters which resulted in a termination from judicial office or in the matters in which any element of misconduct was discovered.

III

The Commission has received the support of judges, local bar associations, public officials and many others. The critical importance of this kind of cooperation was recognized by the Legislature when, as part of the enabling legislation, it enacted section 68725 of the Government Code.

> State and local public bodies and
> departments, officers and employees
> thereof, and officials and attaches
> of the courts of this State shall

> co-operate with and give reason-
> able assistance and information
> to the commission and any authorized
> representative thereof, in connection
> with any investigations or proceed-
> ings within the jurisdiction of the
> commission.

The ability of the Commission to fulfill its constitutional function is in large measure a reflection
of the extent to which it enjoys the support and assistance of presiding judges, bar association representatives, county officers and other key officials. As in
the past, the Commission has benefited immeasurably from
the helpfulness of the State Department of Justice and
the Administrative Office of the Courts. The Commission
has worked with the Constitutional Revision Commission
on some suggested changes in constitutional language.

IV

A gratifying by-product of the Commission's work
has been the interest shown outside the state. The
experience in California has had a national impact.
Glenn R. Winters, the executive director of the American
Judicature Society, described the Commission as "the
first effective system for discipline and removal of
judges," and reported, "This plan is now being studied
in more than a dozen states."*

---

*June 1964 Journal of the American Judicature Society,
The National Movement to Improve the Administration of
Justice, p. 17. A talk by the Commission's Executive
Secretary before the Annual Conference of Texas Judges
was printed in 27 Texas Bar Journal 791 (Oct. 1964),
Judicial Retirement, Discipline and Removal - The Cali-
fornia Plan. Also see 38 Florida Bar Journal 1033
(Nov. 1964), Discipline and Removal of Judges.

During 1964 members and former members of the Commission accepted invitations to speak before state judicial conferences in Louisiana, Texas, New Mexico, and Indiana, sponsored by the Joint Committee for the Effective Administration of Justice. The Executive Secretary consulted with officials in Maryland, Illinois and Texas concerning the development of programs in those states.

Conclusion

A revealing aspect of the Commission's development is in the area distinct from judicial removal. This point was well expressed in a letter dated January 14, 1964 from the Governor of California to the Dean of the University of Colorado School of Law in reply to a request for information, and it is worth repeating as a conclusion to this report.

> The law has been in effect for slightly over three years now, and I am convinced that it is a tremendous success. It is beyond argument that the operations of the Commission have had a marked effect in raising the already high level of our California judiciary, and I feel that as the Commission continues to operate this effect will be multiplied.
>
> In my opinion, the major thrust of the Commission's effect has been not simply in the fact that a small number of judges have resigned after the Commission has investigated their activities and found them wanting in quality. Rather, I note with pleasure the salutary effect which the Commission has had on the vast majority of our hardworking judges.

1965 REPORT OF COMMISSION
ON JUDICIAL QUALIFICATIONS

I

The Commission on Judicial Qualifications is charged with administering the law set forth in Article VI, Section 10b of the California Constitution the first sentence of which is, "A justice or judge of any court of this State, in accordance with the procedure prescribed in this section, may be removed for willful misconduct in office or willful and persistent failure to perform his duties or habitual intemperance, or he may be retired for disability seriously interfering with the performance of his duties, which is, or is likely to become, of a permanent character."

As of November 1, 1965 there were 935 judicial positions within the jurisdiction of this commission as follows:

Appellate Courts	37
Superior Court	359
Municipal Court	267
Justice Court	272

It is obvious that among the many changes normally taking place in the California judiciary only a few are related to the activity of this commission.

During 1965 85 complaints were filed with the commission against judges including those in the category of "Commission Investigation." Of the cases before the commission in the course of the year 38 warranted looking into to some extent by way of inquiry. Of these 38 inquiries, in 29 instances the judge was contacted about the complaint and an explanation requested. With respect to some of these, simple letter replies satisfactorily clarified, explained, or rectified the matter.

Several cases involved substantial investigation by the commission and written communications and discussions with the judge involved. Of the 29 times in which judges were contacted about the complaint eight included personal interviews with the judge and in six cases there was a full preliminary investigation as provided by Rule 901(b), California Rules of Court. In four of the 29 cases in which it was necessary to contact the judge he chose to resign or retire without a formal hearing. It should be clear that this constitutes a minuscule fraction of the judges in the state. The California judiciary richly merits its reputation of preeminence.

II

In other instances charges while apparently valid did not warrant holding formal hearings or further action by the commission. In some of these the commission has been satisfied that the problem was corrected after it was called to the attention of the judge. Wherever possible the commission has tried to exercise its influence towards effecting an improvement. This remedial scope was a more significant aspect in 1965 than heretofore as the number of serious problems present in earlier years has receded, and as it has become more generally realized that an avenue exists for the correction of lesser judicial transgressions not justifying removal from office.

Two critical points should be stressed in this connection. First, the success that the commission has had in this area would not have been possible without the constitutional requirement of confidentiality. The commission's rigorous adherence to this fundamental continues to receive the understanding of the media representatives and has been a substantial factor in carrying forward a constructive program of discipline.

Second, the remedial scope is a very narrow one and properly so. The limited purview is defined by the constitutional language (as set forth in the first paragraph of this report).

Some of the remarks of Chief Justice Roger J. Traynor as he addressed the citizens of Sacramento upon the occasion of the dedication of the new Sacramento courthouse October 16, 1965 concerning a judge's responsibilities are apropos.

> To be a judge you must also pass the ultimate test of honesty, to be honest with yourself. Ask yourself whether you have judicial temperament. Can you banish from your mind such predilections and prejudices as all people harbor in some measure, but which have no place in a judge's work? You are not to be under the influence of preconceived ideas while you are on the job....
>
> If you really have judicial temperament, you will not be dismayed by the limitations of your job. It is no mean incidental task to set a daily example of order and courtesy and fairness in the courtroom.

III

Five years of commission operation have revealed certain weaknesses and uncertainties in the language of Article VI, Section 10b. In 1964 this commission submitted its views on this to the Constitution Revision Commission for its consideration. While not completely accepting the views of the Judicial Qualifications Commission, the Revision Commission, after lengthy consideration, is preparing changes in Section 10b which in the opinion of the Judicial Qualifications Commission substantially resolve the difficulties. This commission believes it is in the public interest that these changes be made and therefore strongly favors the adoption of the Revision Commission's proposals on these questions.

These points specifically are as follows:

1. The misbehavior upon which the commission may take action is now expressed as "willful misconduct in office." One construction of this is that misconduct must be connected with the performance of judicial duties. Such an interpretation would be an unreasonable restriction. In order for the commission to take jurisdiction judicial misconduct should not necessarily be tied to the course of judicial duties, as arguably is the case now. The additional ground proposed by the Constitution Revision Commission, "conduct prejudicial to the administration of justice bringing the judicial office into disrepute," should solve the question without creating any undesirable consequences.

2. Under present language for misconduct the commission may only recommend to the Supreme Court the judge's removal. After reviewing the record the Supreme Court "shall order removal or retirement [for disability], as it finds just and proper, or wholly reject the recommendation." In the first case to reach the Supreme Court in which the commission had recommended a judge's removal the court without discussion rejected the recommendation and dismissed the proceeding leaving the impression there was no power of discipline short of removal.

There is mounting authority throughout the nation, supported by the experience of the commission, for the power to discipline by a means less than removal. The change being suggested by the Constitution Revision Commission would enable the commission to recommend to the Supreme Court the censure of a judge and after the review of the legal record the Supreme Court could discipline by censure.

3. The phrase "in office" is susceptible of the interpretation that action can not be taken if the alleged misconduct occurred in a preceding or different term of office. Thus, if the misconduct is not discovered until after a judge has started another term of office, or is re-elected or elevated before the conclusion of removal proceedings, the whole procedure may be frustrated. The proposal of the Revision Commission which removes this ambiguity permits discipline under the stated grounds for an offense "occurring not more than six years prior to the commencement of his current term."

4. A judge having once been removed should thereafter be ineligible for judicial office.

As the law now stands it is possible notwithstanding removal for a judge to return to judicial office and that possibility should be foreclosed.

5. It is thought that when a judge is facing serious criminal proceedings and when a removal recommendation is pending with the Supreme Court against him that he should not serve as a judge until he has been cleared. The Judicial Qualifications Commission therefore supports the proposal that under such circumstances the judge shall be disqualified from acting in a judicial capacity but without loss of salary.

The Commission on Judicial Qualifications favors the proposals pending before the Constitution Revision Commission on these points. The work of the Commission on Judicial Qualifications has shown the desirability of these changes and it is hoped that steps will be taken leading to their enactment.

1966 REPORT OF COMMISSION
ON JUDICIAL QUALIFICATIONS

I

The principal task of the Commission on Judicial Qualifications is to bring about the removal or retirement of unfit judges. The Commission may receive complaints, investigate, hold hearings, and recommend removal from office. An actual order for removal or involuntary retirement can only come from the State Supreme Court.

As a result of the work of the Constitution Revision Commission and the passage of Proposition 1-a, November 8, 1966, the constitutional language affecting this Commission has been simplified and improved. (See appendix to this report for the new language, Sections 8 and 18 of Article VI. For background, note part III of the Commission's 1965 report.)

Only a few of the dozens of changes taking place among the following 965 judicial positions to which the jurisdiction of the Commission extends have resulted from any activity of the Commission.

Appellate Courts	46
Superior Courts	367
Municipal Courts	288
Justice Courts	264

The presence of the Commission and its ability to take effective action encourages a realistic assessment by judges of personal capability for continued judicial service. This is one way in which the Commission contributes to a higher level of judicial performance.

II

Addressing the Pennsylvania Bar Association, Chief Justice Roger J. Traynor made these observations about the Commission:

> Until the Commission decides to recommend removal or retirement, it holds all proceedings in confidence. It operates under rules adopted by the Judicial Council to insure fairness. Once it decides to recommend removal or retirement of a judge, he is entitled to a full hearing before the Supreme Court.... About seven judges a year have voluntarily retired or resigned while under investigation.
>
> The California commission plan encourages voluntary and confidential solution of most problems of alleged judicial incapacity or misbehavior. It is particularly appropriate to the painful case where the judge must be given to understand that he has become physically or mentally incapacitated for the job.[1]

In nine cases coming before the Commission in 1966 in which an investigation disclosed convincing evidence of unfitness and incapacity for judicial office, the judge decided to resign or retire after proceedings started. This is a small fraction of the total number of judges in the state. The constitutional mandate of confidentiality safeguards the reputations of the individuals involved. (One of the nine cases was developed and principally investigated in 1965, but the actual separation from office did not occur until several months later in 1966. In two or three of these proceedings a resignation or retirement might have occurred during the year independently of the action by the Commission.)

III

There is another area in which the Commission has been able to help improve judicial performance. Some complaints have disclosed conduct, activities, or conditions which are outside the bounds of what is legitimate and acceptable. The first chairman of the Commission, Hon. A. F. Bray, has written about this aspect of the Commission's work.

> ...these situations, while they
> show questionable court activities,
> are not serious enough to warrant
> a removal proceeding or even neces-
> sarily a full preliminary investi-
> gation. By letter to the judge
> setting forth the reported practice
> or impropriety and requesting a
> reply the problem can be called to
> his attention for correction. The
> judge's explanation may absolve him,
> or there may be an unsatisfactory
> condition but outside Commission
> jurisdiction. While in this so-called
> corrective purview there are rela-
> tively few infractions overall,
> reliable studies emphasize the
> importance of this kind of an
> authority. Although infrequently
> needed, there is a salutary effect
> to an official confidential com-
> munication of alleged derelictions
> made to the judge.[2]

It should also be noted that the Commission performs a significant service in receiving and dealing with unfounded grievances and unsupported charges concerning judges which frequently are due to misconceptions and misunderstandings about the judicial process.

During 1966, of 75 complaints registered against judges, 33 required some investigation or inquiry. On 29 occasions, including the nine terminations, there was correspondence or personal interview with the judge.[3] Sometimes this exchange constituted a satisfactory accounting and showed nothing amiss. Normally the response from the judge has been marked and characterized by his good-faith explanation and cooperative attitude. In a few instances, after considering the judge's answer and completing its investigation, the Commission concluded there were derelictions and shortcomings that did not warrant removal proceedings but did justify criticism, and for which the judge was admonished by the Commission.

In recent years such infractions have included neglect and inattention to duties, disregard for rules and standards of practice, arrogance and aggravated discourtesy, and violations of canons of judicial ethics. Usually specific changes or improvements have resulted from the action of the Commission.

An efficient court structure must have effective machinery for the discipline and removal of the judge who, for any reason, fails in the fulfillment of his responsibilities. The California judicial system is highly regarded for several reasons, one of which is the effectiveness of the Judicial Qualifications Commission. Widely admired, it has come to be known as the California Plan in judicial reform circles and in its basic principles is being adopted elsewhere.

Appendix - New Constitutional Language

Article VI - Judicial

Section 8. The Commission on Judicial Qualifications consists of 2 judges of courts of appeal, 2 judges of superior courts, and one judge of a municipal court, each appointed by the Supreme Court; 2 members of the State Bar who have practiced law in this State for 10 years, appointed by its governing body; and 2 citizens who are not judges, retired judges, or members of the State Bar, appointed by the Governor and approved by the Senate, a majority of the membership concurring. All terms are 4 years.

Commission membership terminates if a member ceases to hold the position that qualified him for appointment. A vacancy shall be filled by the appointing power for the remainder of the term.

Section 18. (a) A judge is disqualified from acting as a judge, without loss of salary, while there is pending (1) an indictment or an information charging him in the United States with a crime punishable as a felony under California or federal law, or (2) a recommendation to the Supreme Court by the Commission on Judicial Qualifications for his removal or retirement.

(b) On recommendation of the Commission on Judicial Qualifications or on its own motion, the Supreme Court may suspend a judge from office without salary when in the United States he pleads guilty or no contest or is found guilty of a crime punishable as a felony under California or federal law or of any other crime that involves moral turpitude under that law. If his conviction is reversed suspension terminates, and he shall be paid his salary for the period of suspension. If he is suspended and his conviction becomes final the Supreme Court shall remove him from office.

(c) On recommendation of the Commission on Judicial Qualifications the Supreme Court may (1) retire a judge for disability that seriously interferes with the performance of his duties and is or is likely to become permanent, and (2) censure or remove a judge for action occurring not more than 6 years prior to the commencement of his current term that constitutes wilful misconduct in office, wilful and persistent failure to perform his duties, habitual intemperance, or conduct prejudicial to the administration of justice that brings the judicial office into disrepute.

(d) A judge retired by the Supreme Court shall be considered to have retired voluntarily. A judge removed by the Supreme Court is ineligible for judicial office and pending further order of the court he is suspended from practicing law in this State.

(e) The Judicial Council shall make rules implementing this section and providing for confidentiality of proceedings.

Footnotes

1. Traynor, <u>Rising Standards of Courts and Judges</u>, 40 California State Bar Journal (September-October 1965) 677 at 688.

2. Bray, <u>The Problem of Sanctions</u>, University of Chicago Conference on Judicial Ethics, Series 19 (1964), 42 at 47.

3. Three or more judges were involved on two occasions in such cases. However, these were each counted in the totals as single inquiries and contacts.

1967 REPORT OF COMMISSION
ON JUDICIAL QUALIFICATIONS

I

The Commission on Judicial Qualifications has now completed its seventh year of operation and its first year under the improved and strengthened language sponsored by the Constitution Revision Commission and enacted into the Constitution November 8, 1966. The current constitutional provisions with respect to the Commission are found in Article VI, Sections 8 and 18 (see appendix). To take into account the constitutional amendments the Judicial Council revised the Rules for Censure, Removal or Retirement of Judges which were the first changes since the original rules were adopted August 1, 1961.

The scope of Commission authority was broadened by the 1966 constitutional amendment particularly by the addition of "censure" as a disciplinary alternative and by expanding grounds for action to cover "conduct prejudicial to the administration of justice that brings the judicial office into disrepute."

Chief Justice Roger J. Traynor gave this apt resume of the Commission's function in a talk entitled, "Who Can Best Judge the Judges?" before the Virginia State Bar Association in February 1967.

> We reach finally the troublesome
> question of who can best judge the
> judges once they are in office....
>
> In determining who that someone
> should be, we can probably agree once
> again to rule out the usual venal
> or vociferous characters, who would
> bring the courthouse down with them
> in their wrath at this judge or that.

The problem of disqualification,
whether for incapacity or for
other reasons, is akin to the
problem of removing a defective
vessel from a china shop without
damaging the sound ones nearby.
I have noted elsewhere that in the
judiciary, as in every other walk
of life, a bad man is as hard to
lose as a good man is hard to find.

In 1960 California pioneered in
resolving the problem of the
defective vessel by establishing
an unsalaried Commission on Judicial Qualifications, through which
the judiciary can police its own
ranks. The china shop work can
be briefly summarized. Upon a
complaint to the executive secretary, the Commission investigates
the allegations. If it finds them
frivolous, it does no more than
inform the complainant accordingly.
If, however, it encounters a problem of judicial incapacity or
misbehavior, it seeks voluntary
solution, holding all proceedings
to that end in confidence. Such
an approach is particularly appropriate to the painful case where
a judge must be given to understand
that he has become physically or
mentally incapacitated for the job.
In this regard it bears noting
that voluntary retirement is rendered
less painful in California by a fair
pension system. Confidential preliminary proceedings are also appropriate in cases of errant behavior
not warranting removal.

The Commission consists of five judges
appointed by the Supreme Court from
specified lower courts, two lawyers
appointed by the Board of Governors
of the State Bar, and two laymen
appointed by the governor with the
consent of the state senate. This
combination gives the commission
a non-partisan public character
free of partisan or public pressures.

When the circumstances warrant
retirement or removal, and the judge
refuses to retire or resign voluntarily, the Commission arranges for
a hearing. Again, it bears noting
that there is a long-established
Judicial Council in California which
has formulated rules to ensure a
fair hearing. Once the Commission
decides to recommend retirement or
removal, the judge is entitled to
a hearing before the Supreme Court.

When a bench can quit itself of a
burdensome member through such a
commission, it gains as much as
the Bar and the public. It reaps
added benefits from each judge's
quickened awareness that he must
meet reasonable standards of competence and behavior in relation
to his office. [42 California
State Bar Journal (March-April
1967) 225 at 238]

II

The jurisdiction of the Commission extends to all
levels of the California judiciary. As of January 1,
1968 this totaled 999 judges as follows:

Appellate Courts	46
Superior Courts	393
Municipal Courts	303
Justice Courts	257

Naturally in a judicial branch of this size there are always changes taking place, very few of which are in any way related to the work of this Commission.

During the course of the year, out of 101 matters which came before the Commission for its consideration, 48 required some investigation. In 33 instances this included contacting the judge about the complaint either by way of letter or interview.

A number of times the judge's explanation was wholly satisfactory. In several other cases the judge, in effect, admitted to some transgression or poor practice and the Commission accepted his recognition of the fault and his apparent willingness to correct it.

There were other cases in which wrongdoing was denied, but the Commission, after studying the reply to the allegations and completing its investigation, concluded that the judge had been at fault and in effect admonished him. The Commission felt its confidential criticism and warning were the proper measure of discipline and that the circumstances did not justify a formal hearing.

Five judges resigned or retired during the course of an investigation. This is only one-half of one percent of the state's judges.

III

It can be seen from the preceding figures that during 1967 less than three percent of the judges of the state were asked to respond to an inquiry from the

Commission. Even with the relatively few valid complaints the exercise of a disciplinary function should not be equated with the presence of evil or incompetency. It is an entirely human trait for a shortcoming or questionable activity to develop in any large undertaking, which the judicial branch of government certainly is. While this is rather obvious in an abstract way, it is worth emphasizing in terms of the operation of the Commission since there are some who confuse the necessity for a judicial disciplinary body and its normal work product with weakness or inadequacy in the judicial branch. Virtually all qualified observers argue that a modern judicial system requires a continuing body to act effectively on claims of improper conduct or disability and that the existence of such an institution is basic to a strong and healthy judiciary. It is for that reason that other states are adopting comparable programs.

Professor Beverly Blair Cook of the California State College at Fullerton summarized the advantages of the Judicial Qualifications Commission concept in her recent book, The Judicial Process in California, page 55, "The commission fulfills several functions: it provides the public with a regular institution to listen to grievances against judges; it acts as a disciplinary force through its ability to issue warnings and to discuss personal problems with judges; and it provides a confidential arena removed from public political bodies to protect reputations until the verdict is reached."

310

Appendix

California Constitutional Provisions

Article VI - Judicial

Section 8. The Commission on Judicial Qualifications consists of 2 judges of courts of appeal, 2 judges of superior courts, and one judge of a municipal court, each appointed by the Supreme Court; 2 members of the State Bar who have practiced law in this State for 10 years, appointed by its governing body; and 2 citizens who are not judges, retired judges, or members of the State Bar, appointed by the Governor and approved by the Senate, a majority of the membership concurring. All terms are 4 years.

Commission membership terminates if a member ceases to hold the position that qualified him for appointment. A vacancy shall be filled by the appointing power for the remainder of the term.

Section 18. (a) A judge is disqualified from acting as a judge, without loss of salary, while there is pending (1) an indictment or an information charging him in the United States with a crime punishable as a felony under California or federal law, or (2) a recommendation to the Supreme Court by the Commission on Judicial Qualifications for his removal or retirement.

(b) On recommendation of the Commission on Judicial Qualifications or on its own motion, the Supreme Court may suspend a judge from office without salary when in the United States he pleads guilty or no contest or is found guilty of a crime punishable as a felony under California or federal law or of any other crime

[Editor's note: The Article VI provisions shown here and in the 1966 report (pp. 302-303) were also appended to the Commission's 1968 report.]

that involves moral turpitude under that law. If his conviction is reversed suspension terminates, and he shall be paid his salary for the period of suspension. If he is suspended and his conviction becomes final the Supreme Court shall remove him from office.

(c) On recommendation of the Commission on Judicial Qualifications the Supreme Court may (1) retire a judge for disability that seriously interferes with the performance of his duties and is or is likely to become permanent, and (2) censure or remove a judge for action occurring not more than 6 years prior to the commencement of his current term that constitutes wilful misconduct in office, wilful and persistent failure to perform his duties, habitual intemperance, or conduct prejudicial to the administration of justice that brings the judicial office into disrepute.

(d) A judge retired by the Supreme Court shall be considered to have retired voluntarily. A judge removed by the Supreme Court is ineligible for judicial office and pending further order of the court he is suspended from practicing law in this State.

(e) The Judicial Council shall make rules implementing this section and providing for confidentiality of proceedings.

1968 REPORT OF COMMISSION
ON JUDICIAL QUALIFICATIONS

I

The Commission has now completed seven and a half years of regular operation. The concept of a tribunal always available to receive and investigate charges against judges, which ten years ago was hotly debated, has long since received approval and support among all ranks of the judiciary. During 1968 Pennsylvania, Louisiana, Michigan, Alaska, Oregon and Idaho changed their state laws to put comparable programs into operation, all patterned after the successful experience in California. The relevant provisions from the California Constitution are on the last page. [Not shown here]

II

The statistical side of the year's work can be quickly stated. As of December 1, 1968, 1030 judges were within Commission jurisdiction as follows:

Appellate Courts	52
Superior Courts	406
Municipal Courts	324
Justice Courts	248

During 1968 132 complaints were filed with the Commission of which 48 warranted some inquiry or investigation. In 35 instances this included asking the judge for his explanation and reply. In two cases the judge resigned or retired from office thus terminating the investigation. This is but a fraction of the total retirements this year. The great majority of retirements and resignations are by judges who have never been brought to the attention of the Commission. There was no recommendation during the year to the Supreme Court for censure, removal or retirement. The number of valid complaints is small.

The great majority of the communications to judges for their comment were not major accusations but involved matters which the Commission concluded were of sufficient significance to deserve the particular attention of and, in some cases, correction by the judge. Often the judge's response absolved him of any fault. In several instances, after receiving their explanations, judges were admonished; in some cases the inquiry itself had the effect of a cautionary notice. In such matters the precise Commission action depends upon such factors as the nature and extent of the infraction and the attitude and cooperation of the judge. Some of these cases were terminated after an exchange of letters while others have required extensive investigation and review extending over many months. A substantial contribution to better judicial performance is being rendered by the ability of an impartial body comprised of representatives from the public, the legal profession, and the judiciary to act promptly, effectively and confidentially.

III

The word "Qualifications" in the Commission's title is to some extent a misnomer. Jurisdiction is limited to specific conduct, condition or activity which falls within one of the five grounds spelled out in the Constitution, i.e., wilful misconduct in office, wilful and persistent failure to perform duties, habitual intemperance, conduct prejudicial to the administration of justice that brings the judicial office into disrepute or disability that seriously interferes with the performance of duties and is or is likely to become permanent. Unless allegations come within one of these five areas a problem or situation is outside of the Commission's purview.

The power to act against a judge for misconduct or wrongdoing is totally different from the power to act for or against a prospect for judicial office during the selection process.

MEMBERS OF THE COMMISSION: YEARS OF SERVICE

(X) stands for Chairman
X stands for Member

MEMBERS	1961	1962	1963	1964	1965	1966	1967	1968
Hon. Louis H. Burke Presiding Judge, Superior Court Los Angeles	X^1							
Hon. Clarence L. Kincaid Judge, Superior Court Los Angeles	X	X						
Hon. Cecil E. Edgar, Judge Office No. 4, Municipal Court Fresno	X	X						
Hugh H. Evans, Sr. Public Member Los Angeles	X	X^2						
Hon. A. F. Bray Presiding Justice, Court of Appeal First Appellate District Division One San Francisco	(X)	(X)	(X)					

MEMBERS OF THE COMMISSION: YEARS OF SERVICE (cont.)

MEMBERS	1961	1962	1963	1964	1965	1966	1967	1968
Hon. Ben V. Curler Superior Judge, Lassen County Susanville		X	X					
Hon. Lloyd E. Griffin Presiding Justice, Court of Appeal Fourth Appellate District San Diego	X	X	X	(X)				
Edward W. Schramm Attorney Member Santa Barbara	X	X	X	X				
Irving M. Walker Attorney Member Los Angeles	X	X	X	X				
Benjamin H. Swig Public Member San Francisco	X	X	X	X	X	X	X	X
Theodore E. Cummings Public Member Los Angeles		X	X	X	X	X	X	X

Name / Title							
Hon. William Biddick, Jr. Judge, Superior Court Stockton					x	x	x
Hon. Martin J. Coughlin Justice, Court of Appeal Fourth Appellate District Division One San Diego			x	x	x	x	x
Ronald L. Tiday Attorney Member Garden Grove			x	x	x	x	x
John J. Goldberg Attorney Member San Francisco			x	x	x	x	x
Hon. William B. Neeley Judge, Superior Court Los Angeles	x	x	(X)	(X)			
Hon. Clarence M. Hanson Judge, Municipal Court Modesto	x	x	x	x			
Hon. Murray Draper Presiding Justice, Court of Appeal First Appellate District Division Three San Francisco	x	x	x		x	(X)	(X)

MEMBERS OF THE COMMISSION: YEARS OF SERVICE (cont.)

MEMBERS	1961	1962	1963	1964	1965	1966	1967	1968
Hon. Harold F. Collins Judge, Superior Court Los Angeles							X	X
Hon. Claude M. Owens Judge, Municipal Court Anaheim							X^3	
Hon. Gerald K. Davis Judge, Municipal Court Bakersfield								X

Jack E. Frankel
Executive Secretary
3041 State Building
350 McAllister Street
San Francisco

[1] March-October 1961
[2] March 1961-March 1962
[3] Former member; on Superior Court in 1967

APPENDIX X

The Ombudsman Office
at Michigan State University

A paper by Professor James D. Rust, University Ombudsman, Michigan State University, with sample form used by students.

THE OMBUDSMAN OFFICE AT
MICHIGAN STATE UNIVERSITY

Professor James D. Rust
University Ombudsman

This brochure has been prepared because I have received a considerable number of requests for information concerning the office of University Ombudsman which I hold at Michigan State University. I shall give, in what follows, a brief account of the office of the Ombudsman as it is found in several countries, but especially Denmark and Sweden, shall explain the appearance of this office on the campus of Michigan State University, tell something about the method and criteria of appointment, and describe the responsibilities and operations of the office.

First, some history of the institution in Scandinavia. It all started in Sweden during the reign of King Charles XII. As a result of the Russian victory over the Swedes at Poltava in 1709, the Swedish king was an unwilling guest of the Turkish Sultan until 1714. During the five years of his absence from Sweden, Charles ruled through a Council of Ministers and the bureaucracy of the Royal Court. In 1713 he wrote one of his trusted aides to keep an eye on the bureaucracy--especially the judges and the tax collectors. After his return from exile in 1714 he was so pleased with this arrangement that he made it permanent, giving the official the title of Chancellor of Justice.

Almost a century later, after Sweden had become a constitutional monarchy by the Constitution of 1809, the Parliament decided that it also needed a watchman. So came into existence the Ombudsman. The Ombudsman, however, has come to be the more active and important

of the two officials, and it is that title which has
come to be used in popular parlance in many countries,
regardless of what the official title actually is. Such
offices exist not only in Sweden, but in Norway, Denmark,
Finland, and New Zealand.

Most of these offices were established in response
to a feeling that government was getting so big and
impersonal that Joe Citizen needed someone in high position to look out for his interests because not always
do those who administer the law do it in the spirit in
which it was created. Human frailty being what it is,
sometimes bureaucrats become arrogant and need to be
checked, and even judges are not infallible so that it
does no harm to have someone looking over their shoulders
as they write their decisions.

What are the duties and the powers of Ombudsmen?
This question can be answered in part by saying what
they are not. The Ombudsmen do not take part in the
legislative process--they are not policy-makers. They
do not have the power to reverse decisions made by the
courts or governmental agencies. In Denmark the Ombudsman may order the public prosecutor to investigate the
conduct of a public servant or to commence criminal proceedings against him. It is interesting that in the
years since his appointment, the present (and only)
Danish Ombudsman has never ordered such action. The
Swedish Ombudsman has similar powers. In addition all
these officials in various countries have great powers
of investigation, with theoretically unlimited access
to official records. Finally, the Ombudsmen can often
explain actions by the courts or administrative agencies
which citizens do not understand. In this connection,
the Danish Ombudsman publishes frequent articles in
newspapers and magazines about problems that have come
to his attention. In this way, the Ombudsmen serve a
valuable educational function for the general public as
well as those immediately concerned.

However, the Ombudsman's principal power is
expressed in the Danish statute in this innocuous

sounding sentence: "In any case the Parliamentary Commissioner may always state his views on the matter to the person concerned." This simple statement contains the Ombudsman's real muscle. The fact that he has the power to voice his opinion enables him to exercise a guiding influence on public servants and provides him with a legal basis for negotiating with the agencies concerned. In those countries having an Ombudsman this power of criticism has been proved to be remarkably potent. Professor Hurwitz, the Danish Ombudsman, puts it this way, "Persuasion is more enduringly forceful than edict."

For the most part the Ombudsmen operate behind the scenes to correct conditions eliciting complaints. As a matter of fact, most of the time their reports simply announce conclusions that have been reached with various officials and reveal nothing of the negotiations involved. The process is aptly described as "discussion before pronouncement."*

As you have read this summary of the history and characteristics of the Office of the Ombudsman, I suspect that certain analogies have presented themselves to you. As government has grown so vast and complex that the individual citizen feels helpless and frustrated when he has to deal with a government agency, so have universities grown so large and complex that students often feel that they are no more than IBM cards. As citizens need help in dealing with government bureaucracy, so do students need help in coping with University faculty and functionaries.

The adaptation of the concept of the Ombudsman to an American "multiversity" began almost three years ago when the faculty and the administration at MSU became concerned about the so-called "alienation" of students. The President asked the Faculty Committee on Student

---

*This summary is based upon Walter Gellhorn, <u>Ombudsmen and Others</u>, Harvard University Press, 1966.

Affairs to study the whole problem and make recommendations that would hopefully give the students a larger share in the educational enterprise and help to alleviate the impersonality inherent in an institution with an enrollment of 39,000. One of the recommendations in the report of this committee was that an official should be appointed with the title of Ombudsman. The office is described in Article 8 of the report, as follows:

The Office of the Ombudsman

The President shall appoint from the senior faculty a high prestige official with the title of Ombudsman. The sensitive and confidential nature of the Ombudsman's work dictates that he conduct his operations with dignity and integrity. He shall respect the privacy of all persons who solicit his assistance and protect them against retribution. His functions shall include the following charges:

He shall establish simple, orderly procedures for receiving requests, complaints and grievances of students.

He shall assist students in accomplishing the expeditious settlement of their problems. He may advise a student that the student's request, complaint or grievance lacks merit, or that the student should seek his remedy before another duly constituted body or officer of the University; or the Ombudsman (if he deems it appropriate) may assist the student in obtaining an informal settlement of the student's problem.

In the performance of his duties the Ombudsman shall have broad investigatory powers and direct and ready

> access to all University officials
> from the President down.
>
> When the Ombudsman deems it neces-
> sary he shall report directly to the
> President valid complaints for which
> no remedy has been found. He shall
> also report any recommendations he
> wishes to make regarding such com-
> plaints.
>
> He shall make periodic reports to
> the President regarding the opera-
> tion of the Ombudsman's office.

Please observe the following about this article:
One, the charge to the Ombudsman is phrased in rather
general terms so that the person appointed would have
fairly wide latitude in creating the post to fit his
own conceptions of the role. Two, the Ombudsman should
be appointed from among the senior faculty and the position should be one of "high prestige." Three, he is
outside the regular table of organization, representing
the President of the University and reporting to him
(or to his deputy, the Provost). Four, the Ombudsman
has "broad investigatory powers" and "direct and ready
access to all University officials." Subsumed under
the phrase "broad investigatory powers" is the power of
access to all University student records except those
involving professional confidence, as in the Medical
Center or the Mental Hygiene Clinic.

You will also notice that the Ombudsman is to be
appointed by the President. The appointment process
was approximately this: The Provost solicited nomina-
tions from the Deans, from faculty members, and especially from student leaders. This process resulted in
a list of approximately 65 names. The Provost and a
selection committee from student government studied
this list, putting the names into three categories:
"recommended," "acceptable," and "not acceptable." At
length a first recommendation and alternates were
submitted to President Hannah, who then made his

recommendation to the Board of Trustees. Among the criteria for appointment seem to have been an ability to relate to students, experience as a classroom teacher and student adviser, the ability to say no as well as yes, a wide acquaintance among faculty and administration, and a good knowledge of the workings of the University. The funds for the operation of the office come from the general fund through the President's budget.

The office opened for "business" with the beginning of the Fall term 1967. The "simple, orderly procedures" prescribed in Article 8 have been established. The student who comes in to see the Ombudsman fills out a simple form, giving his name, student number, class, major, and college. Then he completes the following statement, "I wish to consult the Ombudsman about...."* Having filled out this form, he is given the opportunity to express his grievance privately, behind closed doors, to the Ombudsman.

In accord with the injunction of the Freedom Report, the Ombudsman tries "to assist the student in obtaining an informal settlement of the student's problems." The controlling word here is "informal." There is no formal hearing before a board or committee, only the student and the Ombudsman in a relatively quiet office. This is where the Ombudsman performs one of his most valuable services. He listens. He listens to the student's story, occasionally asking questions or making comments and taking notes. Many times has he been told, "You're the first person I have found who will listen to me!" Sometimes students have said that all they wanted was for someone to listen, especially when they had only generalized comments to make.

Following the conversation with the student, the Ombudsman investigates to determine whether the student's complaint is truly justified. If it involves an

---

*See attached sample.

instructor, he must be given the opportunity to state his view of the matter. If it involves an administrative official, he must be consulted to learn whether the student has fully and accurately reported the matter. Following the investigation, the Ombudsman reports, either orally or in writing, the results of his investigation to the complainant, together with a statement that his allegation has or does not have merit. If the former, a recommendation for further action is made or the matter is settled out of hand. Often this investigation involves merely a phone call; sometimes, however, it can consume hours and spread over several days.

The University Ombudsman, like his governmental counterparts, is concerned with complaints about arbitrary and capricious enforcement of regulations, with requests for help in a great variety of situations, with explanations of the meaning of regulations and the necessity for their existence. Students, being late adolescents or young adults, desire complete freedom of behavior, but they want also to be protected against possible results of their behavior. They are very quick to take offense against what they regard as infringements on their rights and, being human and relatively inexperienced, they sometimes misinterpret or misunderstand. As a result some of their complaints or grievances, when examined and investigated, are revealed to be without real foundation.

Let me quit speaking in generalities and discuss more precisely the various kinds of problems that students have brought to me. These fall into two large categories, which can in turn be further sub-divided. The first category consists of non-academic problems. These have been further classified as 1) Problems of fees and tuition 2) Problems of housing 3) Problems of vehicle registration and traffic regulations 4) Problems of student employment 5) Use of university facilities and services 6) University health center 7) University library 8) Personal problems 9) Miscellaneous.

The second category is academic problems. The sub-categories here are 1) Problems of admission and registration 2) Problems of instruction 3) Problems of academic requirements 4) Problems of academic status 5) Problems of academic advice 6) Miscellaneous.

I shall mention examples in each classification. Michigan State, like many other institutions, has been forced to raise tuition several times over the last few years. Consequently, students have come to me (in varying degrees of indignation) to protest the latest increase in tuition. The matter is further complicated by the fact that the student's tuition is based upon family income. Others come to the Ombudsman about fee refunds when they have reduced their academic loads, about late registration fees, and other charges, such as those for replacing a lost ID card or purchasing a bus pass. One of my most interesting cases involved a mistake made in the Course Schedule for Summer Term 1968. In error, a five credit course had been listed as a four credit course. The error was discovered before registration was completed and those who registered after this discovery were charged for five credits. Letters were sent to those who had paid for four instead of five, requesting an additional sum of money.

Several of these students came to the Ombudsman. After investigating, he recommended that since it was an error of the University, the students should not be required to pay the extra money. After some consultation with officials from the business office and the registrar's office, those students who had paid for five credits received refunds and those who had paid for four received notes cancelling the request for more fees.

One of the most frustrating duties the Ombudsman has is to explain why students from states other than Michigan must pay a considerably higher tuition than native students. They come for help when scholarship or loan funds are slow of arrival or when any one of an

almost infinite number of possible mistakes is made by
the Office of Financial Aids, the University Business
Office, or the Registrar's Office.

Housing problems arise when students living in the
University dormitory system (as they are required to do
until they reach the age of 21 or become seniors) wish
to move off campus into unsupervised housing. Problems
often arise between married students living in apartments built and maintained by the University and the
Married Housing Office. Students living off campus in
unsupervised apartments often come to me for advice
about leases, rents, and damage deposits. Not being a
lawyer, I advise them to seek legal help.

Many differences of opinion arise between students
and university officials, especially the campus police
force, about the registration of student automobiles
and about summonses given for violation of university
traffic and parking regulations. I have even been asked
whether I could fix a parking ticket!

Another source of difficulty and complaint is student employment. Hourly wage rates vary among different
departments of the university, leading to complaints
that students working in this or that kind of job are
being discriminated against. I have had several complaints from bearded and long-haired young men who have
been refused jobs in university kitchens or cafeteria
serving lines. An explanation of the sanitary hazards
involved usually cleared up the complaint. A few have
come to me because they felt they had been unfairly
fired from their jobs. One young woman had not received
a full two weeks termination pay; investigation proved
a mistake had been made and the error was corrected.

Students have complained about the service in the
University Health Center and some part-time students
have been helped to admission in the Center.

The University Library has been a source of fric-
tion, especially when students have been fined for not

returning books which they swear were returned before the due date. Most of these differences of opinion can be settled by referring the student to the proper official in the library.

There are always a few students who bring their personal problems to the Ombudsman. When it seems appropriate, they are referred to the Counseling Center for emotional or psychiatric counseling. Two or three unhappy pregnant coeds have asked advice and have been referred to social agencies or physicians. Most of them, however, simply wanted to talk to someone.

The other large category of complaints and grievances concerns academic matters. One of the principal reasons why the Faculty Committee on Student Affairs recommended the appointment of an Ombudsman was their concern over the number of students who had complained to them about bad teaching, about instructors who cut classes time after time, about rudeness and what can only be called arrogance on the part of some professors, and about various other forms of unprofessional conduct. Last year this category of grievances accounted for 52% of all the "business" the office of Ombudsman had.

The process of getting enrolled and registered in classes in a multiversity can be for many students a confusing and frustrating experience. Despite the fact that more than 90% of our students get the courses they want during the academic quarter they want or need them, there are always some who have trouble. The Ombudsman has helped, either by getting them into the courses they needed, by arranging a substitution, or simply by explaining why they could not have what they wanted. Problems arise also when a student wants to add a course after registration has ended or to drop out of a class in which he is enrolled. Errors sometimes crop up in a student's record which he has trouble getting corrected.

The largest single classification of academic problems is that which I have called Problems of Instruction.

This includes the inevitable disputes about grades, about which not very much can be done. No one can give a grade except the instructor who taught the course and he is the only person who can change it. The problem is that almost universally, professors believe they have given the correct grade and adamantly defend that position. According to the Academic Freedom Report (the name by which the faculty committee's report is commonly known) the student can have a hearing before a faculty committee on the department level and again on the college level. I have known of a few successful appeals on the departmental level but none have gone beyond that.

Other complaints are about professors not keeping appointments or office hours. Students complain about instructors who miss classes. They are confused because instructors do not give clear instructions about what they expect of students and because they do not give adequate criticism on written work. Some instructors change their minds about their courses half way through the term; they also revise their grading standards and systems, sometimes without telling the students. Of course, students complain about the professor who lectures from thirty-year old notes and gives the same exams year after year. They grumble also, and rightly, about the instructor in, let's say, English, who talks more about the Vietnam war and the political campaign than about Shakespeare. Students don't like sarcastic and sharp-spoken professors, or professors who mumble so they cannot be heard beyond the third row of the lecture hall.

Of course, the Ombudsman immediately gets in touch with the instructor concerned and hears his view of the situation. In the majority of instances the whole matter can be settled right then and there. Incidentally, the Ombudsman will not listen to a complaint of this kind unless the student has already discussed it with the instructor. Though many such complaints are really misunderstandings, there remains a hard core of legitimate grievances. The Ombudsman is often frustrated at his lack of power or the absence of a committee or judicial body with the authority to discipline rude, incompetent, careless, indifferent, or arrogant faculty members.

It might be well now to say something about how an academic Ombudsman operates.

What does he do when a student comes to him? What action does he take? What response does he make?

To repeat, he listens. A considerable number of students seem to want nothing more than a chance to talk to someone who will really listen. To be a courteous, even sympathetic listener is the first duty of a college or university Ombudsman. As a careful listener, not only can he reduce the student's head of steam, but he can also learn much that will be of value to him both in the current instance and also in future cases.

He advises. By no means all the students who come in are complaining about the arrogant, capricious, or unprofessional behavior of an administrator or a faculty member. A sizable percentage simply want advice about a wide variety of problems. These range all the way from legal questions, such as problems concerning leases in off-campus apartments, a divorce suit, a possible suit for false arrest, or many other situations. Of course, not being a lawyer, I make no effort to give legal advice on such matters; the only advice I give is for the student to get a lawyer and I help him do that if I can. Students also ask for advice concerning academic matters. I have had long conversations with students about their choice of majors and whether they should get a certain requirement completed early or postpone it.

He explains. It has been my observation over many years that students are sensible, reasonable people. Many of the complaints that they bring to me are the result of misunderstanding or insufficient information. When someone explains why it is that they must do this

or that or may not do the other, the great majority will
accept the situation with good grace. For example, when
a student learns why the faculty of the College of Arts
and Letters insists on second year foreign language competency for the B.A. degree, he may not be any more
enthusiastic about German, but he is more likely to work
for that competency without grumbling. So also the student from Ohio or New York who would like to pay in-state
tuition. "After all," he says, "I am married, I have
Michigan license plates on my car, I pay Michigan sales
taxes and income tax, and I am going to vote in Michigan
in the next election. Shouldn't I be permitted to pay
Michigan resident tuition?" When I have explained to
him the provisions of the Joint Resolution of the Legislature, which governs this matter, again he may not be
happy about it, but he understands why he must continue
to pay out-of-state tuition and feels less rebellious.

He refers. Many students come to me with questions,
complaints, or problems that can best be dealt with by
another faculty member or official of the University.
Thus a student who comes to me with a problem that is
properly the responsibility of the Dean of Students will
be referred to him, usually after a phone conversation
in which I explain the problem and perhaps recommend a
solution. Or the student will be referred to the Assistant Dean for Student Affairs of his college if he has
an academic problem. If it is a personal matter he will
be sent to the Counseling Center; to the Registrar's
office if it concerns his records, or to the Business
office, if money is involved.

This is the action taken in most of the cases that
come to me. It often seems to me that I function as a
kind of information center telling students where they
can find the answers to their questions and who can help
them. This information, however, is always accompanied
by a recommendation to the administrator or faculty member involved. I am sometimes surprised at how little
students know about the help available to them even
after four or more years on campus.

He reviews. Often a student comes to the Ombudsman because he is unhappy with a decision made by some University functionary. For example, perhaps he has asked permission to move from a dormitory room to a room or an apartment off campus. Of course, when a student enters a dormitory, he signs an agreement that he will stay there until the end of the school year. If he wishes to break what is in effect a lease, he must appeal to a committee. Sometimes the student whose appeal has been rejected will come to me for help. In such instances, I will review all the steps of the appeal, including all the evidence the student has presented to support his request. If I find that the student has been treated fairly, that he has received all the consideration that is his due, then I have to tell him that he has no grounds for complaint. However, I have been able several times to call the committee's attention to evidence which they had overlooked or to which they had not attached sufficient weight and they have changed their decision to favor the student.

In other instances I have reviewed the action of Assistant Deans in withdrawing students from school for academic shortcomings, have checked on the decisions of the Office of Fee Determination or the Registrar concerning refunds of fees.

In every instance, when I review decisions made by University officials or committees, it is with the purpose of determining whether the student has been treated fairly and justly.

As can be seen from this summary, the Ombudsman at Michigan State deals with problems and grievances of many different kinds. Many arise from misunderstanding or human fallibility. Some arise from the attempts by clerks and secretaries to deal with matters they are not really qualified to handle. Many, of course, turn out to be groundless when carefully investigated. Nevertheless, the fact that there was someone to whom the student could appeal is of considerable importance.

In the best of worlds, there would be no need for an Ombudsman, for all public servants and all faculty members and employees of universities would be doing their jobs perfectly. Until that world arrives, however, troubleshooters, whether called Ombudsmen or not, will be needed.

No. _____   [Sample]

OFFICE OF THE OMBUDSMAN

Date _____

Student Number _____

Name _____

College _____

Major _____   Class F S J S G
                            Spec. Program
                          (Circle One)

Local Address _____

_____

Telephone _____

I wish to consult the Ombudsman about

APPENDIX XI

The Ombudsmen: Comparative Analysis of Ten Civil Ombudsman Offices

Kent M. Weeks
The College of Wooster, Wooster, Ohio

June 1969

APPENDIX XI

Contents

A. JURISDICTIONS INCLUDED

Part One: The National Level (pages 341-360)

Denmark	Norway
Finland	Sweden
New Zealand	United Kingdom

Part Two: Provincial or State Level (pages 361-376)

Alberta, Canada	Quebec, Canada
New Brunswick, Canada	Hawaii, U.S.A.

B. CATEGORIES OF INFORMATION ANALYZED

APPENDIX XI (cont.)

CIVIL OMBUDSMAN OFFICES

PART ONE: THE NATIONAL LEVEL

Country	1. Size of population served (in millions)	2. Legal basis for the office	3. How the Ombudsman is named
Denmark	4.7	Constitution, June 5, 1953. First elected March 29, 1955; took office April 1, 1955. Influenced by Swedish model.	Appointed by Parliament after every general election.
Finland	4.6	Constitution Act of 1919. Influenced by Swedish model.	Elected by simple majority of Parliament; influenced by partisan considerations. Two or three candidates nominated.

Part One: The National Level (cont.)

Country	1. Size of population served (in millions)	2. Legal basis for the office	3. How the Ombudsman is named
New Zealand	2.7	Parliamentary Commissioner (Ombudsman) Act of 1962. Took office October 1, 1962. Influenced mainly by Danish model.	Appointed by the Governor General on the recommendation of the House of Representatives.
Norway	3.7	Act of June 22, 1962. Took office January 1, 1963. Influenced primarily by Danish model and also by Swedish.	Appointed by Parliament after every general election.
Sweden	7.6	Constitution of 1809.	Elected by Parliamentary Committee of 48 members: 24 Members from each chamber, based on the

342

Country				4. Term of office; removal procedures	5. Current incumbent
United Kingdom	55.0	proportional strength of the parties in the two chambers. Generally unanimous.	Appointed by the Crown on the advice of the Government.	Parliamentary Commissioner Act 1967. Took office April 1, 1967.	
Denmark				Term of Parliament. May be dismissed by Parliament.	Parliamentary Commissioner for Civil and Military Government Administration. Stephen Hurwitz, former Professor of Criminal Law, University of Copenhagen. The original and only incumbent.

Part One: The National Level (cont.)

Country	4. Term of office; removal procedures	5. Current incumbent
Finland	Four years, since 1957. Originally appointed for one year, then three years. Cannot be removed during term of office.	Parliamentary Commissioner. Risto Leskinen, lawyer, former judicial clerk and councillor of legislation.
New Zealand	Term of Parliament. May be removed or suspended by the Governor-General upon an address from the House of Representatives for disability, bankruptcy, neglect of duty, or misconduct.	Commissioner for Investigations to be called Ombudsman. Sir Guy Powles, lawyer and former diplomat.

344

Norway	Term of Parliament. May be removed by two-thirds vote of Parliament.	Parliamentary Ombudsman for Civil Administration. Andreas Schei, lawyer and former judge of the Supreme Court.
Sweden	Term of Parliament. Since 1941, four years' term. Prior to that, one year. May be removed by Parliament.	Parliamentary Ombudsman. Three serving in one office since 1968, with division of supervisory duties. Alfred Bexelius, lawyer, former judge (was Ombudsman for Civil Affairs before 1968 re-organization); Hugo Henkow, former judge (was Ombudsman for Military Affairs); Ulf Lundvik, former judge of the Supreme Court (was Deputy Ombudsman for Civil Affairs).

345

Part One: The National Level (cont.)

Country	4. Term of office; removal procedures	5. Current incumbent
United Kingdom	No set term. Must retire on attaining age of 65. May be released at his own request or removed on addresses by both Houses of Parliament.	Parliamentary Commissioner for Administration. Sir Edmund Compton, K.C.B., K.B.E., formerly Comptroller and Auditor General.

Country	6. Qualifications	7. Salary	8. Staff
Denmark	Required to have a legal education.	Same as a Supreme Court Judge.	Ten, six of whom are jurists.
Finland	Required to be a person distinguished in law.	Same as the Chancellor of Justice, the Presidents of	Three full-time and two part-time assistants. Deputy Ombudsman appointed

346

		the Supreme Court and Supreme Administrative Court.	by Parliament, serves when Ombudsman is on leave or incapacitated.
New Zealand	No special statutory qualifications.	Set by the Government; now less than Supreme Court Judges.	Three officers, one of whom is legally trained. Two secretary-typists.
Norway	Same as a judge of the Supreme Court.	Fixed by Parliament.	Five legally trained assistants and four clerical assistants.
Sweden	Must be persons of known legal ability.	Same as a Supreme Court Judge.	Fifteen jurists, mainly young judges who then return to their judicial positions. Deputy Ombudsman appointed by Parliament.
United Kingdom	No special statutory qualifications.	Fixed by Parliament.	About 60, all civil servants seconded from various Government departments; no lawyers.

Country	9. Principal duties	10. Average number of complaints received annually	11. Proportion of valid complaints	12. Fee for complaint filing
Denmark	To keep himself informed as to whether any person under his jurisdiction pursues unlawful ends, makes arbitrary or unreasonable decisions, or otherwise commits mistakes or acts of negligence in the discharge of his duties.	1,100	10% to 15% of those fully investigated.	None
Finland	To supervise the observance of the laws in the	1,000	8.6% of those disposed of.	None

proceedings of courts and other other author- ities.

| | | 700 | About 19% of those fully investigated. | $N.Z.2.2.00 ($2.25). Can be waived and sometimes is. |

New Zealand — To investigate any decision or recommendation made (including any recommendation made to a Minister of the Crown), or any act done or omitted, relating to a matter of administration and affecting any person or body of persons in his or its personal capacity.

349

Part One: The National Level (cont.)

Country	9. Principal duties	10. Average number of complaints received annually	11. Proportion of valid complaints	12. Fee for complaint filing
Norway	To endeavor to ensure that the public administration does not commit any injustice against any citizen.	1,000	From 10% to 20% of those investigated.	None
Sweden	To supervise the observance of laws and statutes as applied by the courts and by public officials and employees.	2,000	10% found to be valid upon investigation.	None

350

United Kingdom	To investigate complaints by the public submitted through a Member of Parliament, about injustice caused through maladministration in administrative action taken on behalf of the Crown.	1,000	Some element of maladministration found in about 10% of the cases fully investigated.	None

Country	13. Inspections	14. Access to documents
Denmark	Duty bound to keep himself informed. Inspects prisons, military units, and other institutions.	All documents except those pertaining to state secrets. No decision as to whether internal minutes must be submitted.

351

Part One: The National Level (cont.)

Country	13. Inspections	14. Access to documents
Finland	About 90 institutions visited annually, particularly those in which persons are confined. These inspections emphasized recently.	All documents, including internal papers of government agencies. Most documents in Finland are open to the public.
New Zealand	Authority to inspect governmental agencies; only a few inspections based on specific complaints.	May screen and examine papers unless Attorney General certifies that disclosure might in the circumstances prejudice the security of N.Z. or the investigation of offenses might involve the disclosure of confidential Cabinet matters.
Norway	No inspections generally, although bound to keep himself informed	Has same authority as any court to demand documents and records, as well as

	about conditions in the administrative branches in his jurisdiction.	secret documents. The internal working papers of departments are regularly available.
Sweden	Regular inspections of jails, government offices, courts, and military camps. Criminal and civil proceedings are reviewed to check on procedures.	All documents. Most are open to the public; however, secret files are not shown to the complainant, but civil service must relinquish them or be subject to prosecution.
United Kingdom	No authority to make independent inspections.	All documents of Departments under jurisdiction. Ministers of the Crown may restrict publication of documents which would be prejudicial to the state or public interest, but they may not restrict the Parliamentary Commissioner's access to such documents.

Part One: The National Level (cont.)

Country	15. Jurisdiction over local government	16. Jurisdiction over courts	17. Jurisdiction over the military
Denmark	Complaints involving local government councils acting as a body are excluded; however through own investigation can obtain a limited review of such councils' actions.	None	Ombudsman is responsible for both civil and military affairs.
Finland	Includes every level of local government.	Ombudsman has such jurisdiction.	Ombudsman is responsible for both civil and military affairs. Since 1933, Chancellor of Justice turns over complaints from military to Ombudsman.
New Zealand	In 1968, the Act was amended to provide for limited	None	Almost all military matters outside of jurisdiction.

354

	jurisdiction over local education and hospital boards.		
Norway	Originally no jurisdiction over local government. As of January 1, 1969, has jurisdiction over all municipal boards and officials, except decisions of town or county councils in matters which (pursuant to law) have to be decided by the council itself.	None	In 1952, the first Ombudsman in Norway was for military affairs. Today, there are two Ombudsman authorities, one for civil and one for military affairs.
Sweden	Originally no jurisdiction over local government. In 1957, jurisdiction was extended to all	Jurisdiction over members of the Supreme Court and members of the Supreme Administrative Court is limited, but no	From 1809 to 1915, the civil Ombudsman's authority extended to all military commanders and officers of lower rank. From 1915 to 1968 there was a separate

Part One: The National Level (cont.)

Country	15. Jurisdiction over local government	16. Jurisdiction over courts	17. Jurisdiction over the military
Sweden (cont.)	municipal boards and officials except elected members of municipal councils.	limitation in case of other judges.	Military Ombudsman. In 1968 the office of the Civil Ombudsman and the office of the Military Ombudsman were united to form one office with three Ombudsmen. One of the three Ombudsmen supervises the armed forces.
United Kingdom	None over municipal government.	None	Excluded from both civil and military personnel matters.

Country	18. Complaints initiated by Ombudsman	19. Legal action v. public officials	20. Annual reports
Denmark	Few; generally in response to articles in the press or complaints against local government.	Ombudsman cannot prosecute but may order the prosecuting authorities to institute preliminary proceedings or to bring a charge before the ordinary law courts for misconduct in public service or offices. Authority used infrequently.	Submitted to Parliament; considered by Parliament's Committee on the Parliamentary Commissioner's Office, then discussed and approved by Parliament.
Finland	Initiates complaints, many as a result of inspection tours.	Ombudsman can initiate prosecutions or more usually order prosecutor to bring action. Admonitions more common than official judicial action.	Submitted to Parliament; considered by Constitutional Law Committee of Parliament.

Part One: The National Level (cont.)

Country	18. Complaints initiated by Ombudsman	19. Legal action v. public officials	20. Annual reports
New Zealand	Few	No authority to prosecute officials but if evidence of any breach of duty or misconduct by a public official is discovered, the Ombudsman shall refer the matter to the appropriate authority.	Submitted to Parliament.
Norway	Initiated 14 in 1967, 35 in 1968.	No authority to order public officials prosecuted.	Submitted to Parliament; considered by the Justice Committee of Parliament.
Sweden	500 cases a year as a result of inspections and press reports.	Ombudsmen can act as prosecutors. Today many more "reminders" given out than in earlier times. Currently, about ten prosecutions a year.	Submitted to Parliament; considered by the First Law Committee of Parliament.

		21. Press coverage	22. Attitude of civil service when post created
United Kingdom	No authority to do so.	No authority to prosecute or have public officials prosecuted.	Submitted to Parliament; considered by Select Committee. Interim Reports can also be submitted.
Country			
Denmark		Press covers the office. Ombudsman responds to complaints in the press.	Originally opposed.
Finland		Not too much attention given to office. A few specialized journals, such as the police magazine, cover decisions.	Did not object.

359

Part One: The National Level (cont.)

Country	21. Press coverage	22. Attitude of civil service when post created
New Zealand	Focuses on the annual report and cases released to the press by the Ombudsman.	Originally opposed.
Norway	Little attention to the office.	Did not oppose.
Sweden	Considerable coverage to cases of public interest and to the annual report.	Not available.
United Kingdom	Now tends to focus on Reports to Parliament by the Commissioner and the Select Committee.	No opposition.

Part Two: Provincial or State Level

Province or state	1. Size of population served (in millions)	2. Legal basis for the office	3. How the Ombudsman is named
Alberta, Canada	1.5	An Act to provide for the appointment of a Commissioner to Investigate Administrative Decisions and Acts of Officials of the Government and its Agencies. May be cited as "The Ombudsman Act." Took effect July 1, 1967. Ombudsman officially took office September 1, 1967. Influenced mainly by New Zealand model.	Appointed by the Lieutenant-Governor in Council on the recommendation of the Legislative Assembly.

Part Two: Provincial or State Level (cont.)

Province or State	1. Size of population served (in millions)	2. Legal basis for the office	3. How the Ombudsman is named
New Brunswick, Canada	.6	Ombudsman Act, May 19, 1967. Took office October 11, 1967. Influenced mainly by New Zealand model.	Appointed by the Lieutenant-Governor in Council on the recommendation of the Legislative Assembly.
Quebec, Canada	6.0	Public Protector Act, November 14, 1968. Appointed and sworn in, May 1, 1969.	Appointed by 2/3 vote of the Legislative Assembly on motion of the Prime Minister.
Hawaii, U.S.A.	.8	Ombudsman Act of 1967 became law on June 24, 1967.	Appointed by both houses of the Legislature in joint session, with a majority

vote of each house.

Ombudsman was appointed April 17, 1969; effective July 1, 1969.

Influenced by model law proposed in Harvard Journal on Legislation.

Province or state	4. Term of office; removal procedures	5. Current incumbent
Alberta, Canada	Five years. May be removed or suspended by the Lieutenant-Governor in Council on the recommendation of the Legislative Assembly for disability,	Commissioner for investigations to be called the Ombudsman. Mr. George B. McClellan, who retired as Commissioner of the Royal Canadian Mounted Police August 15, 1967.

Part Two: Provincial or State Level (cont.)

Province or State	4. Term of office; removal procedures	5. Current incumbent
Alberta, Canada (cont.)	neglect of duty, misconduct, or bankruptcy.	
New Brunswick, Canada	Ten years. May be removed or suspended by the Lieutenant-Governor in Council upon the recommendation of the Legislative Assembly.	Ombudsman. Dr. W. T. Ross Flemington, former President of Mount Allison University and Director of Education for External Aid for Canada.
Quebec, Canada	Five years. May be removed by 2/3 vote of the Legislative Assembly.	Public Protector. Louis Marceau, lawyer and former Dean of Law at Laval University.

Province or State		6. Qualifications	7. Salary	8. Staff
Hawaii, U.S.A.	Six years, but limited to three such terms. May be removed or suspended by 2/3 vote of both houses of the Legislature for neglect of duty, misconduct, or disability.			Ombudsman. Mr. Herman S. Doi, lawyer, and former Director of the Legislative Reference Bureau.
Alberta, Canada		No special statutory qualifications.	Fixed by Legislative Assembly.	Four officers, one of whom is legally trained. Four clerical personnel.
New Brunswick, Canada		No special statutory qualifications.	Same as a Judge of the Supreme Court.	One bilingual secretary and a part-time legal advisor.

Part Two: Provincial or State Level (cont.)

Province or State	6. Qualifications	7. Salary	8. Staff
Quebec, Canada	No special statutory qualifications. Legal background implied, because statutes provide for possibility that Ombudsman may be a judge.	($30,000) Fixed by Legislative Assembly.	Eight, with a possibility of 16.
Hawaii, U.S.A.	No special statutory qualifications.	Same as a circuit court judge ($27,500). Fixed by the Legislature.	Three, one of whom will be an executive secretary.

366

Province or State	9. Principal duties	10. Average number of complaints received annually	11. Proportion of valid complaints
Alberta, Canada	To investigate any decision or recommendation made (including any recommendation made to a Minister) or any act done or omitted, relating to a matter of administration and affecting any person or body of persons in his or its personal capacity.	535 during 1968.	About one-third of those fully investigated.

367

Part Two: Provincial or State Level (cont.)

Province or State	9. Principal duties	10. Average number of complaints received annually	11. Proportion of valid complaints
New Brunswick, Canada	To investigate the administration by a department or agency or officer thereof of any law of New Brunswick, whereby any person is aggrieved.	270 during 1968.	About 43% of those fully investigated.
Quebec, Canada	To investigate an administrative function whereby any holder of any position, office, or employment	Not applicable.	Not applicable.

under the government or under any government department or body has wronged a person.

Province or State		12. Fee for complaint filing	13. Inspections	14. Access to documents
Hawaii, U.S.A.	To investigate the administrative act of a department or agency or officer whereby any person is aggrieved.		Not applicable.	Not applicable.
Alberta, Canada		None	Authority to inspect government	May review and examine all documents including

Province or State	12. Fee for complaint filing	13. Inspections	14. Access to documents
Alberta, Canada (cont.)		agencies; only a few inspections made based on specific complaints received.	internal minutes unless the Attorney General certifies that such documents might disclose the deliberations or proceedings of the Executive Council, or a committee thereof relating to matters of a secret or confidential nature which would be injurious to the public interest.
New Brunswick, Canada	None	Authority to inspect governmental agencies; only a few inspections based on specific complaints received.	May review and examine all documents and papers including internal minutes unless Attorney General certifies that such documents may disclose the deliberations or proceedings of the Executive Council, or any

Province or State	(continued)		15. Jurisdiction over local government	16. Jurisdiction over courts	17. Jurisdiction over the military
Quebec, Canada	committee thereof relating to matters of a secret or confidential nature which would be injurious to the public interest.	No authority to make independent inspections.	None		
Hawaii, U.S.A.	Receives all documents, including internal papers of government agencies.	Authority to inspect government agencies.	None		
Alberta, Canada	All documents including internal papers of government agencies.	None	None over municipal governments.	None	None. The military are under the control of the National Government.

371

Part Two: Provincial or State Level (cont.)

Province or State	15. Jurisdiction over local government	16. Jurisdiction over courts	17. Jurisdiction over the military
New Brunswick, Canada	None over municipal governments.	None	None. The military are under the control of the National Government.
Quebec, Canada	None over municipal or local governments.	None	None. The military are under the control of the National Government.
Hawaii, U.S.A.	All levels of local government.	None	The United States military are under the control of the federal government. But does have jurisdiction over State military officials.

Province or State	18. Complaints initiated by Ombudsmen	19. Legal action v. public officials	20. Annual reports
Alberta, Canada	Anticipates very few.	No authority to prosecute; but if evidence of any breach of duty or misconduct on the part of an officer or employee of any department or agency is discovered, Ombudsman shall refer the matter to the appropriate authority.	Submitted to the Legislative Assembly.
New Brunswick, Canada	None through December, 1968.	No authority to prosecute; but if evidence of a breach of duty or misconduct by a department, agency or officer	Submitted to the Legislative Assembly.

Part Two: Provincial or State Level (cont.)

Province or State	18. Complaints initiated by Ombudsmen	19. Legal action v. public officials	20. Annual reports
New Brunswick, Canada (cont.)		thereof is discovered, Ombudsman shall refer the matter to the appropriate authority.	
Quebec, Canada	Has authority to initiate complaints.	No authority to prosecute or to have a public official prosecuted.	Submitted to the Legislative Assembly.
Hawaii, U.S.A.	Has authority to do so.	No authority to prosecute; but if evidence of a breach of duty or misconduct by any agency, officer, or employee	Submitted to both houses of the Legislature, and to the Governor.

374

is discovered, Ombuds-man shall refer the matter to the appro-priate authorities.

Province or State	21. Press coverage	22. Attitude of civil service when post created
Alberta, Canada	Considerable coverage to cases of public interest and to the annual report.	Little opposition.
New Brunswick, Canada	Considerable coverage to cases of public interest and to the annual report.	No opposition.

Part Two: Provincial or State Level (cont.)

Province or State	21. Press coverage	22. Attitude of civil service when post created
Quebec, Canada	Considerable coverage during formative stages.	No opposition.
Hawaii, U.S.A.	Not applicable.	No resistance.

3

77

OMBUDSMEN'S MAILING ADDRESSES

Denmark

Folketingets Ombudsmand
Christiansborg Ridebane 10
Copenhagen K, DENMARK

Finland

Eduskunnan Oikeusasiamies
Eduskuntatalo
Helsinki, FINLAND

New Zealand

Office of the Ombudsman
The Terrace
Wellington, C. 1
NEW ZEALAND

Norway

Stortingets Ombudsmann for Forvaltningen
Oslo-Dep.
Oslo 1, NORWAY

Ombudsmannen for Forsvaret
Klingenberggt. 7
Oslo 1, NORWAY

Sweden

Riksdagens Justitieombudsman
Box 16327
Stockholm 16, SWEDEN

United Kingdom

Office of the Parliamentary Commissioner
Church House, Great Smith Street
London S.W. 1, ENGLAND

Alberta, Canada

Office of the Ombudsman
920 Centennial Building
Edmonton, Alberta, CANADA

New Brunswick, Canada

Office of the Ombudsman
Fredericton, New Brunswick, CANADA

Quebec, Canada

(Mr. Louis Marceau)
Protecteur du Citoyen
Hotel du Gouvernement
Quebec, CANADA

Hawaii, U.S.A.

Office of the Ombudsman
(Mr. Herman S. Doi)
Legislative Reference Bureau
University of Hawaii
2425 Campus Road
Honolulu, Hawaii 96822 U.S.A.

Selected Readings

Books and Pamphlets, Articles, Documents,
Unpublished Materials, and Bibliographies

SELECTED READINGS*

Books and Pamphlets

Aaron, Thomas J. The Control of Police Discretion:
the Danish Experience. Springfield, Illinois:
Charles C. Thomas, 1966. 107 pp.

Anderson, Stanley V. Canadian Ombudsman Proposals.
Berkeley: Institute of Governmental Studies, University of California, 1966. 168 pp.

Anderson, Stanley V., ed. Ombudsmen for American Government? Englewood Cliffs, N.J.: Prentice-Hall,
Inc., (for the American Assembly), 1968. 181 pp.

Angell, John E., et al. A National Survey of Police
and Community Relations. U.S. Government Printing
Office, January 1967. 386 pp.

Boim, Leon. The Ombudsman. Jerusalem: Academon,
1965. (Hebrew) 88 pp.; (English) introduction:
vi pp.

Gellhorn, Walter. Ombudsmen and Others: Citizens'
Protectors in Nine Countries. Harvard University
Press, 1966. 448 pp. [Gellhorn reference A]

_____. When Americans Complain: Governmental
Grievance Procedures. Harvard University Press,
1966. 239 pp. [Gellhorn reference B]

Gross, Zenith and Alan Reitman. Police Power and
Citizens' Rights: the Case for an Independent Police
Review Board. New York: American Civil Liberties
Union, n.d. 48 pp.

_____
*Based on Ombudsman: a Bibliography collated by
Charles L. Smith, cited below.

382

Hurwitz, Stephan. The Ombudsman. Copenhagen: Det danske Selskab, 1961. 63 pp. (Revised version of the article "Denmark's Ombudsmand..." in 1961 Wisconsin Law Review 2 (1961), also cited below.

Jagannadham, V. and H. R. Makhija. Machinery and Procedures for Redress of Citizens' Grievances. New Delhi: Indian Institute of Public Administration, October 1967. (mimeographed). 213 pp.

Kass, Benny L. Ombudsman: A Proposal for Demonstration in Washington, D.C. Washington, D.C.: Washington Center for Metropolitan Studies, 1968. 40 pp., plus appendices.

Mann, Dean. The Citizen and the Bureaucracy: Complaint-Handling Procedures of Three California Legislators. Berkeley: Institute of Governmental Studies, University of California, February 1968. 52 pp.

Mendelsohn, Harold. The Beautiful People of Denver: Myth or Reality? University of Denver Community Social Survey Project, Bulletin No. 2: February 1967. (mimeographed). 23 pp.

The Mexican "Amparo" as a Supplemental Remedy for the Redress of Citizen Grievances in California. Berkeley: Institute for Local Self Government, January 1967. 32 pp.

Michigan Assembly on the Ombudsman: Final Report. October 10-12, 1968. [Kenneth R. Callahan, Director.] McGregor Memorial Conference Center. [Detroit]: Wayne State University, n.d. n.p.

Morgan, Glenn G. Soviet Administrative Legality: the Role of the Attorney General's Office. Stanford University Press, 1962. 281 pp.

Murray, James N. The United Nations Trusteeship System. Urbana: University of Illinois Press, 1957. 40 Illinois Studies in the Social Sciences. 283 pp.

An Ombudsman for American Government? A Report of the
    Temple University American Assembly. February 26-28,
    1969. [Benjamin N. Schoenfeld and Jerome S. Sloan,
    Co-Directors.] [Philadelphia]: Temple University,
    n.d. 12 pp.

The Ombudsman. Pacific Northwest Assembly. Eugene:
    University of Oregon, 1968. 23 pp.

Rowat, Donald C., ed. The Ombudsman: Citizen's
    Defender. Toronto: University of Toronto Press,
    1965. 348 pp.

Sawer, Geoffrey. Ombudsmen. Melbourne University
    Press, 1964. 42 pp. Rev. ed., 1968.

Scott, Stanley, ed. Western American Assembly on the
    Ombudsman: Report. Berkeley: Institute of Govern-
    mental Studies, University of California, 1968.
    36 pp.

Southeastern Assembly on the Ombudsman: Final Report.
    March 13-15, 1969. [Leslie H. Levinson, Chairman.]
    Gainesville: University of Florida. n.d. (mimeo-
    graphed). 9 pp.

State Control in Israel. Jerusalem: State Comptroller's
    Office, 1965. 31 pp.

The State Comptroller of Israel and His Office at Work.
    Jerusalem: State Comptroller's Office, 1963. 92 pp.

System of Good Offices of Administrative Complaints by
    Administrative Management Agency. Government of
    Japan, Administrative Inspection Bureau, 1964. 27 pp.

Utley, T. E. Occasion for Ombudsman. London:
    Christopher Johnson, 1961. 160 pp.

Vieg, John A. Progress versus Utopia: The Use of Plans,
    Examples, Complaints and Standards of Improving Public
    Administration. New York: Asia Publishing House,
    1963. 84 pp.

Whyatt, Sir John, ed. <u>The Citizen and the Administration</u>. London: Stevens, 1961. 104 pp.

Articles

Aaron, Richard I. "Utah Ombudsman: The American Proposals." 1967 <u>Utah Law Review</u> 1: 32-93 (March).

Abel, Albert S. "The Franks Committee Study: A New Landmark." <u>Canadian Public Administration</u>, 2 (1): 7-18 (1959).

_____. "In Search of a Basic Policy." <u>Canadian Public Administration</u>, 5 (1): 65-75 (1962).

_____. Review of "The Citizen and the Administration," by Sir John Whyatt. <u>Canadian Public Administration</u>, 5 (4): 502-507 (1962).

Abraham, Henry A. "A People's Watchdog Against Abuse of Power." <u>Public Administration Review</u>, 20 (3): 152-157 (1960).

Abrahamson, Max W. "The Grievance Man: In Ireland?" <u>Administration</u>, 8 (3): 238-242 (Dublin) (1960). (Reprinted in part in Rowat, ed., <u>The Ombudsman</u>, 201-207.)

Aggarwal, J. P., ed. "Procuratorship." 3 <u>Journal of the Indian Law Institute</u> 71-86 (1961).

Aikman, C. C. "The New Zealand Ombudsman." 42 <u>Canadian Bar Review</u> 399-432 (September 1964).

_____ and R. S. Clark. "Some Developments in Administrative Law (1964)." <u>New Zealand Journal of Public Administration</u>, 27 (2); 45-55 (1965).

Anderman, Steven D. "The Swedish Justitieombudsman."
11 American Journal of Comparative Law 2: 225-238
(1962). Reprinted in Ombudsman Hearing, 96-106,
cited in Senate (document) reference B below.

Anderson, Stanley V. "Connecticut Ombudsman?" 70
Case and Comment 2: 1-8 (1965).

_____. "Ombudsman Proposals: Stimulus to Inquiry."
Public Affairs Report, 7 (6) (1966). Bulletin of the
Institute of Governmental Studies, University of
California, Berkeley. 4 pp. Reprinted in Congres-
sional Record, January 24, 1967, A238-A239.

_____. "The Ombudsman: Public Defender Against
Maladministration." Public Affairs Report, 6 (2)
(1965). Bulletin of the Institute of Governmental
Studies, University of California, Berkeley. 4 pp.

_____. "The Scandinavian Ombudsman." The
American-Scandinavian Review, 12 (4): 403-409 (1964).

_____ with Scott Buchanan, Hallock Hoffman and
Robert M. Hutchins. "An Ombudsman for the U.S.?"
Center Diary (14): 19-25 (September-October 1966).
Edited transcript of discussion, Center for the Study
of Democratic Institutions, Santa Barbara, California.

Andrén, Nils. "The Swedish Office of 'Ombudsman.'"
The Municipal Review, 33 (396): 820-821 (1962).

_____. "The Swedish Ombudsman." The Anglo-Swedish
Review, 97-103 (May 1962).

Arnold, Richard S. "An Ombudsman for Arkansas." 21
Arkansas Law Review 3: 327-335 (1967).

Ascher, Charles S. "The Grievance Man or Ombudsmania."
Public Administration Review, 27 (2): 174-178 (1967).

Bainbridge, John. "Our Far-Flung Correspondents: A Civilized Thing." The New Yorker, 136, 138, 140, 142, 144, 147-151. February 13, 1965. Reprinted in Ombudsman Hearing, 106-112, cited in Senate (document) reference B below.

Beral, H. and M. Sisk. "The Administration of Complaints by Civilians Against the Police." 77 Harvard Law Review 3: 499-519 (1964).

Berger, Raoul. "Administrative Arbitrariness and Judicial Review." 65 Columbia Law Review 1: 55-95 (1965).

Bexelius, Alfred and Sir Guy Powles. "The Ombudsman: Champion of the Citizen." 21 Record of the Association of the Bar of the City of New York 385-411 (June 1966).

_____. "The Swedish Institution of the Justitie-ombudsman." International Review of Administrative Sciences, 27 (3): 243-256 (1961). Reprinted in Administration, 9: 272-290 (1961-62); and in Ombudsman Hearing, 77-90, cited in Senate (document) reference B below.

_____. "The Swedish 'Ombudsman': Special Parliamentary Commissioner for the Judiciary and the Civil Administration." Reprinted in Ombudsman Hearing, 112-131, cited in Senate (document) reference B below. Reprinted from Royal Swedish Ministry for Foreign Affairs Press Department translation of "JO-Ämbetet 150 Aar" 45 Svensk Juristtidning 81-111 (1960). (mimeographed).

Blix, Hans. "A Pattern of Effective Protection: the Ombudsman." 11 Howard Law Journal 386-389 (Spring 1965). Reprinted in Ombudsman Hearing, 90-96, cited in Senate (document) reference B below.

Blom-Cooper, L. J. "An Ombudsman in Britian?" Public Law 145-151 (Summer 1960).

Bockman, Eugene J. "Ombudsman: Quis Custodiet Ipsos Custodes." Municipal Reference Library Notes, 40 (10): 165-171 (1966). New York Public Library.

Boim, Leon. "'Ombudsmanship': Redress of Grievances in the Polish People's Republic." Annuario di Diritto Comparato e di Studi Legislativi, 41 (2-3): 205-247 (1967).

_____. "The Parliamentary Control over the Administration, including the Ombudsman." Israeli Reports to the Seventh International Congress of Comparative Law 54-73 (1966). Jerusalem: Institute for Legislative Research and Comparative Law.

Bolang, Carl Olof. "But the Ombudsman Thought Otherwise." The American Swedish Monthly, 57 (7): 22-24 (1963).

Bradley, A. W. "The Redress of Grievances." Cambridge Law Journal 82-98 (1962).

Broderick, Albert. "An Ombudsman for Religious." America, 115 (16): 446-448, 455 (1966).

Buccieri, C. H. "Ombudsman: New Troubleshooter on Campus." College and University Business, 44 (3): 52-55 (1968).

_____. "Campus Troubleshooter Resetting His Sights." College and University Business, 45 (6): 51-53 (1968).

Caiden, Gerald E. and Nimrod Raphaeli. "The Ombudsman Debate in Israeli Politics." Parliamentary Affairs, 21 (3): 201-215 (1968).

Caiden, Naomi J. "The Ombudsman and the Rights of the Citizen." The Australian Quarterly, 36 (3): 69-77 (1964).

388

Caiden, Naomi J. "An Ombudsman for Australia?"
Public Administration, 23 (2): 97-116 (1964). Sydney.

_____. "Ombudsmen for Under-Developed Countries?"
Public Administration in Israel and Abroad 1967, 8:
100-115 (1968). Jerusalem.

Capozzola, John M. "An American Ombudsman: Problems
and Prospects." Western Political Quarterly, 21 (2):
289-301 (1968).

Carey, John. "Procedures for International Protection
of Human Rights." 53 Iowa Law Review 2: 291-324
(1967).

Chapman, Bruce. "The Ombudsman." Public Administration,
38 (4): 303-310 (1960). London.

Chitty, R. M. Willes. "Ombudsman??" Chitty's Law
Journal 172-174 (May 1966).

Christensen, Bent. "The Danish Ombudsman." 109
University of Pennsylvania Law Review 8: 1100-1126
(1961).

Cloward, Richard A. and Richard M. Elman. "Poverty,
Injustice, and the Welfare State--Part 1: An Ombudsman for the Poor?" The Nation, 230-235, February 28,
1966.

Coffield, James. "Ombudsman and Taxation." Freedom
First 54: 27-28 (Winter 1968).

Collins, Tom A. "An Ombudsman for Local Government."
1 Indiana Legal Forum 2: 376-397 (1968).

Compton, Sir Edmund. "The Parliamentary Commissioner."
Freedom First 53: 7-9 (Autumn 1967). Address to
the Society for Individual Freedom, July 10, 1967.

389

Cooper, Frank E. "The Need for an Ombudsman in State Government." Prospectus, 1: 27-44 (April 1968).

D'Alemberte, Talbot. "The Ombudsman: a Grievance Man for Citizens." 18 University of Florida Law Review 4: 545-552 (1966). Excerpted in National Civic Review, 55 (11): 625-630 (1966).

Davis, A. G. "The Ombudsman in New Zealand." 4 Journal of the International Commission on Jurists 1: 51-62 (1962); 2: 316-322 (1963).

Davis, Kenneth Culp. "Ombudsmen in America: Officers to Criticize Administrative Action." 109 University of Pennsylvania Law Review 8: 1057-1076 (1961). Reprinted in Ombudsman Hearing, 301-320, cited in Senate (document) reference B below; and excerpted in Public Law 34-42 (Spring 1962).

DeNardis, Lawrence. "'Little' Man's Watchdog: the Case for an Ombudsman in Connecticut." The Connecticut State Journal, 33 (7): 2-3, 17 (1966).

De Smith, S. A. "Anglo-Saxon Ombudsman?" Political Quarterly, 33 (1): 9-19 (1962).

Egan, James. "Ombudsman." Holiday 28-34. (November 1966).

Farley, Marta Pisetska and Andrew N. Farley. "An American Ombudsman: Due Process in the Administrative State." 16 Administrative Law Review 212-221 (Summer 1964).

Frank, Bernard. "The British Parliamentary Commissioner for Administration: the Ombudsman." 28 Federal Bar Journal 1: 1-24 (1964).

_____. "Proposals for Pennsylvania Ombudsman." 39 Pennsylvania Bar Association Quarterly 1: 84-95 (1967).

Frankel, Jack E. "Judicial Discipline and Removal."
44 Texas Law Review 6: 1117-1135 (1966).

_____. "Removal of Judges: California Tackles
an Old Problem." 49 American Bar Association Journal
2: 166-171 (1963).

Friedmann, Karl A. "Commons, Complaints, and the
Ombudsman." Parliamentary Affairs, 21 (1): 38-47
(1967-68).

Gellhorn, Walter. "Citizens' Grievances Against
Administrative Agencies--the Yugoslav Approach."
64 Michigan Law Review 3: 385-420 (1966). Included
in Ombudsmen and Others, cited in Gellhorn (book)
reference A above.

_____. "Finland's Official Watchmen." 114
University of Pennsylvania Law Review 3: 327-364
(1966). Included in Ombudsmen and Others cited in
Gellhorn (book) reference A above; and reprinted in
Ombudsman Hearing 221-243, Senate (document) refer-
ence B below.

_____. "The Norwegian Ombudsman." 18 Stanford
Law Review 293-321 (January 1966). Included in
Ombudsmen and Others cited in Gellhorn (book) reference A above; and reprinted in Ombudsman Hearing
243-264, Senate (document) reference B below.

_____. "Ombudsmen and All That." Harvard Alumni
Bulletin, 68(14): 584-589 (1966).

_____. "The Ombudsman in Denmark." 12 McGill Law
Journal 1: 1-40 (1966). Included in Ombudsmen and
Others cited in Gellhorn (book) reference A above.

_____. "The Ombudsman in New Zealand." 53
California Law Review 5: 1155-1211 (1965). Included
in Ombudsmen and Others cited in Gellhorn (book) reference A above; and reprinted in Ombudsman Hearing 150-
206, Senate (document) reference B below.

Gellhorn, Walter. "The Ombudsman's Relevance to American Municipal Affairs." 54 American Bar Association Journal 134-140 (February 1968).

_____. "Police Review Boards: Hoax or Hope?" Columbia University Forum, 9 (3): 5-10 (1966).

_____. "Protecting Citizens Against Administrators in Poland." 65 Columbia Law Review 7: 1133-1166 (1965). Included in Ombudsmen and Others cited in Gellhorn (book) reference A above.

_____. "Review of Administrative Acts in the Soviet Union." 66 Columbia Law Review 6: 1051-1079 (1966). Included in Ombudsmen and Others cited in Gellhorn (book) reference A above.

_____. "Settling Disagreements with Officials in Japan." 79 Harvard Law Review 4: 685-732 (1966). Included in Ombudsmen and Others cited in Gellhorn (book) reference A above.

_____. "The Swedish Justitieombudsman." 75 Yale Law Journal 1: 1-58 (1965). Included in Ombudsmen and Others cited in Gellhorn (book) reference A above; reprinted in Ombudsman Hearing 45-77, Senate (document) reference B below.

Gilbertson, Forbes. "Will the Ombudsman Come to Canada?" Canadian Business, 37: 29-39 (July 1964).

Gimble, Gilbert. "Panacea for the City's Ills: an Ombudsman." 33 D. C. Bar Journal 11: 616-620 (1966).

Gow, Neil. "An Ombudsman for Scotland? The First Report of the Council on Tribunals." Scots Law Times 119-120. June 25, 960.

Grossman, Howard J. "Do School Districts Need an Ombudsman?" American School Board Journal, 155 (6): 6-7 (1967).

392

Hambro, Edvard. "Sivilombudsman of the Norwegian Parliament." Recht in Dienste der Menschenwürde: Festschrift für Herbert Kraus, 111-122 (1964). Wurzburg: Der Göttinger Arbeitskreis.

Hamilton, Randy H. "Can you Fight City Hall and Win?" Public Management, 265-278 (October 1967).

_____. "Ombudsman or What?" National Civic Review, 57 (3): 132-137 (1968). Reprinted in Congressional Record, 114 (51): E2376-E2378. March 27, 1968.

Hansen, Povl. "The Ombudsman." Denmark, 129-131 (1961). Copenhagen: Royal Danish Ministry of Foreign Affairs.

Hart, Philip A. with Charles Remsberg. "Does America Need an Ombudsman?" Family Weekly, 4-5, March 10, 1968.

Hewitt, D. J. "The Origin of the Ombudsman in New Zealand and His Work." New Zealand Law Journal 14: 345-347 (1966).

Hill, Larry B. "The New Zealand Ombudsman's Authority System." Political Science, 20 (1): 40-51 (1968). Wellington, New Zealand.

Hogan, Mark A. "Experiences of an Amateur Ombudsman." Western American Assembly on the Ombudsman: Report, ed., Stanley Scott. (cited above) 3-13.

Holland, D. C. "A British Ombudsman." 1 Solicitor Quarterly 147-158 (1962).

Hunter, A. A. de C. "Ombudsman for Britain?" 4 Journal of the International Commission of Jurists 1: 150-159 (1962).

Hurwitz, Stephan. "The Danish Ombudsman and His Office." The Listener, 63 (1624): 835-838 (1960). Interview.

Hurwitz, Stephan. "The Danish Parliamentary Commissioner for Civil and Military Government Administration." 1 Journal of the International Commission of Jurists 2: 224-243 (1958) and Public Law 236-253 (1958). Includes Ombudsman Act and Regulations.

_____. "Denmark's Ombudsmand: the Parliamentary Commissioner for Civil and Military Government Administration" (with Ombudsman Act and Regulations). 1961 Wisconsin Law Review 2: 169-199 (1961). Reprinted in Ombudsman Hearing, 265-295, Senate (document) reference B below.

_____. "The Folketingets Ombudsmand." Parliamentary Affairs 12 (2): 199-208 (1959).

_____. "Public Trust in Government Services." Danish Foreign Office Journal (20): 11-15 (1956).

_____. "The Scandinavian Ombudsman." Political Science, 12 (2): 121-142 (1960). Wellington, New Zealand. Includes Danish Ombudsman Act and Regulations.

Jägerskiöld, Stig. "The Swedish Ombudsman." 109 University of Pennsylvania Law Review 8: 1077-1099 (1961).

Jolliffe, Edward B. "The Inevitability of the Ombudsman." 19 Administrative Law Review 1: 99-102 (1966).

K., J. de N. "Ombudsman for Canada?" 12 Chitty's Law Journal 89-91 (February 1964).

Kaplan, Milton. "Ombudsmen for Urban America: The Buffalo Experiment." 17 Local Government Law Service Letter Nos. 9-10 (November-December 1967). n.p.

Karve, D. G. "Parliamentary Supervision of Public Administration: A Danish Experiment." Indian Journal of Public Administration, 6 (2): 131-140 (1960).

Kass, Benny L. "We Can, Indeed, Fight City Hall: The Office and Concept of Ombudsman." 19 _Administrative Law Review_ 1: 75-92 (1966).

Kastari, Paavo. "The Parliamentary Ombudsman: his functions, position and relation to the Chancellor of Justice in Finland." _International Review of Administrative Sciences_, 28 (4): 391-398 (1962). Revised and extended in Rowat, ed., _The Ombudsman_ 58-74, cited in Rowat (book) reference above.

Kent, George. "Where You Can Fight 'City Hall.'" _Rotarian_, 38-40 (July 1963).

Kersell, John E. "Parliamentary Ventilation of Grievances Arising out of the Operation of Delegated Legislation." _Public Law_ 152-168 (Summer 1959).

King, David C. "What this country needs is a good Ombudsman." _Kiwanis Magazine_, 23-24, 53-54 (April 1967).

Lawson, F. H. "An Inspector-General of Administration." _Public Law_ 92-95 (Summer 1957).

Llambias, H. J. "Wanted: An Ombudsman for Canada." _Edge_, 2: 81-91 (Spring 1964). Edmonton.

MacLeod, Innis G. "The Ombudsman." 19 _Administrative Law Review_ 1: 93-98 (1966).

McWhinney, Edward. "An Ombudsman for Ontario: a New Base for Civil Liberties." 8 _Canadian Bar Journal_ 1: 28-36 (1965).

Madden, John D. "The Ombudsman: Protector of the Public." _St. John's University Alumni Magazine_, 13 (4): 2-9 (1967).

Marsh, N. S. "The Ombudsman in New Zealand and in the United Kingdom." 1 _New Zealand University Law Review_ 71-76 (1963).

Marshall, Geoffrey. "A Critique of the Ombudsman Report." 4 The Lawyer 3: 29-32 (Michaelmas 1961). London.

_____. "The New Zealand Parliamentary Commissioner (Ombudsman) Act, 1962." Public Law 20-22 (Spring 1963).

Mathur, Ramesh Narain. "Need for an Indian Ombudsman for Successful Planning." Indian Journal of Political Science, 24 (4): 347-354 (1963).

Middleton, K. W. B. "The Ombudsman." (N.S.) 5 Juridical Review 3: 298-306 (1960). Edinburgh.

Mitchell, J. D. B. "The Ombudsman Fallacy." Public Law 24-33 (Spring 1962).

Monteiro, J. B. "The Ombudsman and Its Relevance to India." The Modern Review, III (4): 326-328 (1962); (5): 406-411 (1962).

Mundell, D. W. "Ombudsman for Canada?" 7 Canadian Bar Journal 3: 179-209 (1964).

Murray, C. H. "The Grievance Man: In Scandinavia." Administration, 8 (3): 231-237 (Autumn 1960). Dublin.

Nader, Ralph. "An Answer to Administrative Abuse." Harvard Law Record 13, 15. December 20, 1962.

Newman, Frank C. "Natural Justice, Due Process and the New International Covenants on Human Rights." Public Law 274-313 (Winter 1967).

_____. "Ombudsman and Human Rights: the New U.N. Treaty Proposals." 34 University of Chicago Law Review 4: 951-962 (1967).

Northey, J. F. "A New Zealand Ombudsman?" Public Law 43-51 (Spring 1962).

396

Olson, Bruce T. "Ombudsman on the West Coast: An Analysis and Evaluation of the Watchdog Function of the California Grand Jury." Police, 12: 12-20 (November-December 1967).

Olson, Kenneth G. "The Service Function of the United States Congress" in A. de Grazia, ed., Congress: the First Branch of Government 337-374. Washington, D.C.: American Enterprise Institute for Public Policy Research, 1966. Excerpted in Ombudsman Hearing, 362-367 Senate (document) reference B below.

"Ombudsman: the Buffalo Experiment." Colleague, 3 (5): 1-3 (January 1967).

Orfield, Lester B. "The Scandinavian Ombudsman." 19 Administrative Law Review 1: 7-74 (1966).

"The Parliamentary Commissioner for Investigations." 37 New Zealand Law Journal 18: 273-274 (October 3, 1961); 19: 289-291 (October 24, 1961).

Patterson, A. N. "The Ombudsman." 1 U.B.C. [University of British Columbia] Law Review 6: 771-781 (1963).

Peck, P. W. "The Ombudsman in Slotsholmen." Public Administration, 44 (3): 333-346 (1966). London.

Pedersen, Inger Margrete. "The Danish Parliamentary Commissioner in Action." Public Law 115-127 (Summer 1959). Extracted in Utley, Occasion for Ombudsman, 145-60, book reference above.

_____. "The Parliamentary Commissioner: a Danish View." Public Law 15-23 (Spring 1962).

Peel, Roy V., ed. "The Ombudsman or Citizen's Defender: a Modern Institution." Annals of the American Academy of Political and Social Science, 377: 1-138 (May 1968).

Potthoff, E. H. "An 'Ombudsman,' U. S. Style." The American City, 83 (7): 152, 154-55 (1968).

Powers, Margrethe R. "An Ombudsman in New York?" 27 Albany Law Review 84-96 (1963).

Powles, Sir Guy. "The Citizen's Rights Against the Modern State, and its Responsibilities to Him." 13 International and Comparative Law Quarterly 4th series, part 3: 761-797 (July 1964); also found in Public Administration, 23: 42-68 (1964). Sydney.

_____. "The Office of Ombudsman in New Zealand." Journal of Administration Overseas, 7 (1): 287-292 (1968).

_____. "The Office of Ombudsman in New Zealand: its Origin and Operation." Ombudsman Hearing, 207-221, Senate (document) reference B below. Text of address to Canadian Bar Association, Montreal, September 1, 1964.

Purchase, C. E. "The Parliamentary Commissioner for Investigations." New Zealand Law Journal 38: 321-324, 374-377 (1962).

Quade, Quentin L. and Thomas J. Bennett. "Shield for the Citizen." Modern Age, 8 (4): 377-388 (1964). Reprinted in Current, 19-26, March 1965.

Reuss, Henry S. "An 'Ombudsman' for America." The New York Times Magazine, 30, 134-135. September 13, 1964. Reprinted in Congressional Record, September 23, 1964; 21839-21840.

_____. "A Trouble-Shooter for Congress." The Progressive, 30 (2): 23-26 (1966).

_____. "We Need an American Ombudsman." Christian Century, 82: 269-271. March 3, 1965. Reprinted in Congressional Record, March 15, 1965, A1165-A1166.

398

Reuss, Henry S. and Stanley V. Anderson. "The Ombudsman: Tribune of the People." Annals of the American Academy of Political and Social Science, 363: 44-51 (January 1966). Reprinted in Congressional Record, February 17, 1966, A835-A837.

Ridley, F. "The Parliamentary Commissioner for Military Affairs in the Federal Republic of Germany." Political Studies, 12 (1): 1-20 (1964).

Roberts, James S. "An 'Ombudsman' for Nevada." Governmental Research Newsletter, 4 (4): 1-4 (1966). Bureau of Governmental Research, University of Nevada.

Rosenblum, Victor G. "Controlling the Bureaucracy of the Antipoverty Program." 31 Law and Contemporary Problems 1: 187-210 (1966).

Rosenthal, Albert H. "The Ombudsman: Swedish 'Grievance Man.'" Public Administration Review, 24 (4): 226-230 (1964). Reprinted in Ombudsman Hearing, 321-325, Senate (document) reference B below.

Rowat, Donald C. "Finland's Defenders of the Law." Canadian Public Administration, 4 (3): 316-325 (1961); (4): 412-415 (1961).

_____. "An Ombudsman Scheme for Canada." Canadian Journal of Economics and Political Science, 28 (4): 543-556 (1962). Reprinted in Ontario Medical Review, 30: 213-217, 222 (1963). Extracted in Current, 34: 60-64 (February 1963). Shortened and revised as "The Parliamentary Ombudsman: Should the Scandinavian Scheme be Transplanted?" International Review of Administrative Sciences, 28 (4): 399-405 (1962). Revision reprinted in Macridis, Roy C. and Bernard E. Brown, eds., Comparative Politics. Homewood, Ill.: Dorsey, rev. ed., 1964, 470-479.

Rowat, Donald C. "Ombudsmen for North America." Public Administration Review, 24 (4): 230-233 (1964). Reprinted in Ombudsman Hearing, 325-328, cited as Senate (document) reference B below.

_____. "Recent Developments in Ombudsmanship." Canadian Public Administration, 10 (1): 35-46 (1967).

Saario, Voitto. "Control of the Constitutionality of Laws in Finland." 12 The American Journal of Comparative Law 2: 194-205 (1963).

Salier, W. A. "The New Zealand Ombudsman." 4 Sydney Law Review 3: 416-422 (1964).

Sanders, Marion K. "Sweden's Remedy for 'Police Brutality.'" Harper's Magazine, 132-136. November 1962.

Sandler, Ake. "The Ombudsman." Vital Issues, 17 (6): 1-4 (1968).

Sargant, Tom. "The Ombudsman and One-Party States in Africa." 8 Journal of African Law 3: 195-197 (1964).

Schei, Andreas. The First Year of the Norwegian Ombudsman. Translated by Joan Torykian for the Institute of Governmental Studies, University of California, Berkeley, 1965. (mimeographed). 10 pp.

Scher, Seymour. "Congressional Committee Members as Independent Agency Overseers." American Political Science Review, 54 (4): 911-920 (1960).

Secher, H. P. "Controlling the New German Military Elite: The Political Role of the Parliamentary Defense Commissioner in the Federal Republic." Proceedings of the American Philosophical Society, 109 (2): 63-84 (1965).

Sheppard, Claude-Armand. "An Ombudsman for Canada." 10 McGill Law Journal 4: 291-340 (1964).

Silver, Isidore. "The Corporate Ombudsman." Harvard Business Review, 77-87 (May-June 1967).

Sington, Anne. "Bureaucrats and Citizens: an Interview with Denmark's Ombudsmand." NATO Letter, 14 (2): 16-21 (1966).

Smith, Austin. "What This Country Needs Is an Ombudsman." Association Management, 15 (1): 40-44 (1963).

Stacey, Frank. "The Machinery for Complaints in the National Health Service." Public Administration, 43: 59-70 (Spring 1965). London.

"A State Statute to Create the Office of Ombudsman." 2 Harvard Journal on Legislation 2: 213-238 (1965). Reprinted in Ombudsman Hearing 336-361, cited in Senate (document) reference B below.

Stern, Henry J. "Duties of the Borough Presidents in the City of New York." Municipal Reference Library Notes, 37 (8): 245-248 (1963).

Storing, James A. "The Norwegian Ombudsman for Civil Affairs: The First Three Years." Western Political Quarterly, 21 (2): 302-324 (1968).

Thorson, Kim. "What About an Ombudsman?" 28 Saskatchewan Bar Review 169-179 (December 1963).

Unruh, Jesse M. "The California Ombudsman." 1 Journal of Constitutional and Parliamentary Studies 2: 13-19 (1967).

_____. "The Need for an Ombudsman in California." 53 California Law Review 5: 1212-1213 (1965). Reprinted in Ombudsman Hearing 334-335, cited in Senate (document) reference B below.

Vandyk, Neville D. "A Collective Ombudsman?" 104
The Solicitor's Journal 19: 357-359. May 6, 1960.
"Watchdog at Work." 105 (Part 2) 28: 601-604. July 14,
1961.

Vinyard, Dale. "Congressional Committees on Small
Business." Midwest Journal of Political Science,
10 (3): 364-377 (1966).

_____. "Congressmen as Washington Agents for
Constituents." Business and Government Review, 8
(5): 19-25 (1967).

Wade, H. W. R. "The British Ombudsman." 20 Administrative Law Review 3: 409-412 (1968).

_____. "The Council on Tribunals." Public Law
351-366 (Winter 1960).

Walls, Frank. "Savannah's New Problem Solver:
Georgia's First Ombudsman." Georgia Municipal Journal,
17-18 (February 1968).

Weeks, Kent M. "How the Ombudsman Works to Help Citizens." 38 Cleveland Bar Association Journal 6: 122-
123, 125-126 (1967).

Wheare, K. C. "The Redress of Grievances."
Public Administration 40: 125-128 (1962). London.

Willens, Sidney L. "An Ombudsman for Missouri?" 22
Journal of the Missouri Bar 6: 241-243 (1966).
Reprinted in Congressional Record, September 30,
1966, 23726.

Williams, Jerre. "The Administrative Conference of the
United States." Western American Assembly on the
Ombudsman: Report, ed. Stanley Scott. (cited above)
15-23.

Wold, Terje. "The Norwegian Parliament's Commissioner for Civil Administration." 2 Journal of the International Commission of Jurists 2: 21-29. (Winter 1959/Spring-Summer 1960).

Yamamoto, Shotaro. "Ombudsmen in Japan." Kwansei Gakuin University Annual Studies, 12: 75-91 (November 1963).

_____. "Operation of the Japanese Government's System of Administrative Inspection." Kwansei Gakuin University Annual Studies, 9: 59-78 (October 1960).

Zweig, Franklin M. "The Social Worker as Legislative Ombudsman." Social Work, 14 (1): 25-33 (1969).

Documents

State of California Legislature. Assembly. Interim Committee on Government Organization. Hearing. September 26, 1966. (mimeographed). 113 pp.

_____. _____. _____. ____. Testimony, Alfred Bexelius, Hearing. March 1, 1966. (mimeographed). 43 pp.

United Nations. Effective Realization of Civil and Political Rights at the National Level: Selected Studies. New York: Doc. ST/TAO/HR/33, 1968. 121 pp.

_____. Remedies Against the Abuse of Administrative Authority: Selected Studies. New York: Doc. ST/TAO/HR/19, 1964. 167 pp.

_____. Seminar on Judicial and Other Remedies Against the Abuse of Administrative Authority, with Special Emphasis on the Role of Parliamentary Institutions. Stockholm, June 12-25, 1962. New York: Doc. ST/TAO/HR/15. iii, 34 pp.

United Nations. Seminar on Judicial and Other Remedies Against the Illegal Exercise or Abuse of Administrative Authority. Kandy, Ceylon, May 4-15, 1959. New York: Doc. ST/TAO/HR/4. 99 pp.

United States Congress. Senate. Committee on the Judiciary. Subcomittee on Administrative Practice and Procedure. Administrative Ombudsman Hearing. Pursuant to S. Res. 25 on S. 1195. 90th Cong., 2d sess. January 16, 1968. Washington, D.C.: 1968. iii, 99 pp. (with appendices) [Senate reference A]

_____. ____. _____. _____. Ombudsman Hearing. Pursuant to S. Res. 190. 89th Cong., 2d sess. March 7, 1966. Washington, D.C.: 1966. iv, 383 pp. (with appendices) [Senate reference B]

_____. ____. _____. _____. Ombudsmen: 1967 (Compilation of State Proposals). 90th Cong., 1st sess. Washington, D.C.: November 1967. viii, 269 pp. [Senate reference C]

_____. _____. Joint Committee on the Organization of the Congress. Final Report, No. 1414, Pursuant to S. Con. Res. 2. 90th Cong., 2d sess. July 28, 1966. Washington, D.C.: 1966. v, 97 pp. [Senate reference D]

Unpublished Materials

Brown, William P. "The Review Board Proposals Do Not Go Far Enough." (typescript). Paper delivered to National Conference on Government, November 17, 1965. 13 pp.

Cahn, William. Ombudsman Report. Submitted to the Nassau County Board of Supervisors. Mineola, New York: 1966. (mimeographed). 28 pp.

404

The Chancellor of Justice in Finland. With governing
Rules of Procedure and Ordinance. Helsinki: Ministry
for Foreign Affairs, Finnish Features No. 13/64.
(mimeographed). 4+8 pp.

Goldberg, Arthur J. "Equality and Governmental Action."
James Madison Lecture, New York University School of
Law, February 11, 1964. 31 pp.

Hamilton, Randy H., ed. A Preliminary Inventory of
Selected Administrative Procedures for the Redress
of Grievances in California's Urban Areas. Working
papers for conference held in Los Angeles, September
15-16, 1966. (mimeographed). 100+ pp.

Hill, Larry Byron. "The Transference of the Institution of Ombudsman, with Special Reference to Britain."
M.A. thesis submitted at Tulane University, November 4,
1966. iv, 169 pp.

Klesment, Johannes. The Ombudsman and Related Systems
of Governmental Supervision in Scandinavian and
Other Countries. Library of Congress, European Law
Division, June 19, 1961. (mimeographed). 29 pp.

Kravitz, Walter. Case Work by Members of Congress:
Analysis Based on a Survey of Existing Literature.
Library of Congress, Legislative Reference Service
GGR-105, May 4, 1965. (mimeographed). 24 pp.

Llambias, H. J. "The Need for an Ombudsman System in
Canada." M.A. thesis submitted at Carleton University, Ottawa, 1964. 121 pp.

Marino, Joseph L. "A Detailed Study on the Need for
the Office of Public Protector (Ombudsman)." Report
submitted to the Special Advisory Committee appointed
by the Nassau County Board of Supervisors. 31 pp.
[1966]. [Subsequently published as a pamphlet.]

Mazuran, Michael J. The Ombudsman and City Governments. School of Public Administration, University of Southern California, Summer 1967. (mimeographed). 53 pp., plus appendices.

Memorandum on the Whyatt Report. Justice: British Section of the International Commission of Jurists, 1962. (mimeographed). 4 pp. Extracted in Rowat, ed., The Ombudsman, 183-185, cited in Rowat (book) reference above.

Olson, Bruce T. "The California Grand Jury: an Analysis and Evaluation of its Watchdog Function." M.A. thesis submitted at the University of California, Berkeley, 1966. 465 pp.

The Ombudsman. Honolulu: Legislative Reference Bureau, November 1965. (mimeographed). 25 pp., plus appendices.

Os, Audvar. The Ombudsmann in Norway. Royal Norwegian Ministry of Justice, No. 71, n.d. [1963]. (mimeographed) 21 pp. Revised in Rowat, ed., The Ombudsman, 95-110, cited in Rowat (book) reference above.

The Parliamentary Ombudsman of Finland. With Regulations of January 10, 1920. Helsinki: Ministry for Foreign Affairs, Finnish Features No. 6/64. (mimeographed). 4+5 pp.

Pazan, Dick. Ombudsman. State of Wisconsin, Legislative Reference Bureau Informational Bulletin 67-6, April 1967. (mimeographed). 12 pp.

Rowland, Howard Ray. "A Study of the Campus Ombudsman in American Higher Education with Emphasis on Michigan State University." Ph.D. dissertation submitted at Michigan State University, 1969. (Abstract 5 pp. mimeographed). 263 pp.

State of Washington. Legislative Council. Committee
on State Government. The Ombudsman in Scandinavia:
Advantages and Disadvantages...for State Government.
(mimeographed). n.d. 32 pp.

Bibliographies

Anderson, Stanley V. Ombudsman Bibliography (mimeographed by office of Congressman Henry S. Reuss)
April 1964. 8 pp. Includes Scandinavian language
items, with titles translated into English.

Hamilton, Randy H. Bibliography on the Ombudsman.
School of Public Administration, University of
Southern California, May 1968. 13 pp.

Kenyon, Carleton W., ed. The Ombudsman: a Bibliography.
California State Law Library, June 1966. (mimeographed). 7 pp.

"Ombudsman: A Bibliography of Literature in the
Municipal Reference Library." Municipal Reference
Library Notes, 40: 171-175. New York Public Library
(December 1966).

Orfield, Lester B. "Bibliography" in "The Scandinavian
Ombudsman." 19 Administrative Law Review 1: 69-74
(1966).

Rowat, Donald C. "Bibliography" in The Ombudsman.
University of Toronto Press, 1965. pp. 293-299.

Smith, Charles L., ed. Ombudsman: a Bibliography.
Northern California Friends Committee on Legislation,
rev. ed., March, 1966. (mimeographed). 10 pp.
Reprinted in Ombudsman Hearing 40-45, cited in Senate
(document) reference B above.

Smith, Charles L., ed. Police Review Boards. Berkeley: Institute of Governmental Studies, University of California, 1965, for the Northern California Friends Committee on Legislation. (mimeographed). 3 pp.

Sperry, Robert. "Ombudsman Bibliography." 155 New York Law Journal 33: 1, 3 (February 16, 1966).

Additional Books and Pamphlets
Late Arrivals

Carlson, Richard J., ed. University of Illinois Assembly on the Ombudsman: Final Report of Regional Assembly. March 13-15, 1969. The American Assembly of Columbia University and Institute of Government and Public Affairs, University of Illinois at Urbana-Champaign, May 1969. 39 pp.

A Report on the Findings of the Phelps-Stokes Intercollegiate Assembly on the Ombudsman for American Government. May 2-4, 1969. [Robert S. Browne, Chairman.] New York: the Phelps-Stokes Fund. n.d. 19 pp.